News on a knife-edge

Gemini journalism and a global agenda

Richard Bourne

John Libbey
JL
LONDON • PARIS • ROME

British Library Cataloguing in Publication Data

Bourne, Richard
    News on a knife-edge: Gemini journalism and a global agenda
    I. Title
    070.43

ISBN 0 86196 486 1

For my daughter Camilla

Published by

John Libbey & Company Ltd, 13 Smiths Yard, Summerley Street,
London SW18 4HR, England
Telephone: 0181-947 2777: Fax 0181-947 2664
John Libbey Eurotext Ltd, 127 avenue de la République, 92120 Montrouge, France.
John Libbey - C.I.C. s.r.l., via Lazzaro Spallanzani 11, 00161 Rome, Italy

Contents

Acknowledgements

I was asked to write a comprehensive history of the Gemini News Service by Derek Ingram, its principal founder and its editor from 1967 to 1993, who was acting on behalf of NewsConcern International Foundation, its governing trust. The foundation had earlier received a grant from the Commonwealth Relations Trust to commission such a history after Gemini had completed 25 years. The CRT rightly recognized that, although small, the agency has made a unique contribution to international journalism. My first thanks therefore go to the CRT and NewsConcern (particularly its successive chairs, James Porter and Trevor McDonald) and to Derek Ingram himself.

Governors, Ingram and the present staff of Gemini have been unstinting in their help, as have a large number of past and present Gemini contributors. They have not, however, sought to do more than advise and provide information. Any errors of fact or interpretation are therefore my responsibility alone.

Ingram, now a consulting editor and chairman of the News-Scan International holding company for Gemini, also kindly made available a mass of correspondence and records kept at his home (described for convenience in the footnotes as the 'Ingram Archive'). Present permanent staff who have generously aided me are: Daniel Nelson (editor), Bethel Njoku (managing director), Daya Kishan Thussu (associate editor), Lloyd Parker (artist) and Dupe Owodunni (production assistant). I should also like to thank Elaine Shein, a former Regina University awardee at Gemini who is now managing editor of the *Western Producer*, Saskatoon, Canada, for showing me preliminary work she did in 1993 for a Gemini history. Reproduction of articles and illustrations previously carried in the service are, of course, by permission of News-Scan and Gemini News Service, and each article is listed with its original service number.

In alphabetical order I should also like to thank, for their various types of help by interview and correspondence:

Paddy Allen, Chief Emeka Anyaoku, Kabral Blay-Amihere, Oliver Carruthers, Fred Chela, Andrew Clark, Nicola Cole, Djibril Diallo, Cameron Duodu, Tony Eggleton, Jill Forrester, John Gambanga, Daniel Girard, Barbara Hall, Richard Hall, Mohamed Hamaludin, Nicholas Harman, Bob Holmes, George Ivan Smith, D K Joshi, Mehr Khan, Christabel King, Gerald Knight, James Lemkin, Gerry Loughran, James Markwick, Kelly McParland, Sue Montgomery, John Mukela, Judith Mulenga, Chris Mullin, Alfred Nalube, Gamini Navaratne, Kuldip Nayar, Rex Nettleford, Elias Nyakutemba, John Ogen, Margaret Owens, Elizabeth Pritchard, Cedric Pulford, Brana Radovic, Alan Rake, Sir

Shridath Ramphal, Mark Richardson, Jenny Ridley, Patsy Robertson, David Robie, Aubrey Rose, Clyde Sanger, Prunella Scarlett, Philip Short, Peter Smith, David Spark, Hugh Stephenson, Jane Taber, Abby Tan, Allan Thompson, Jon Tinker, John Tusa, Mike Urlocker, John Williams, Gavin Wilson and Ian Wright.

If by chance I have omitted any other persons who have proffered information or guidance, I hope they will consider themselves included in my thanks.

Richard Bourne
May 1995

Preface

Rex Nettleford
University of the West Indies, Mona, Kingston, Jamaica

The two-thirds world, generally misnomered the 'Third World', is in the debt of all who opted three of so decades ago to be on the right side of history. The founders of Gemini News Service opted accordingly, reaching out to the developing world in ways that suggested that there was genuine understanding in the metropole that 'underdevelopment', viewed in narrow economic terms, did not deprive the millions of 'underdeveloped' peoples of their creative potential or their capacity for thought and action when needed in their own interest – in short of their *humanity* and their cultural authenticity.

No-one understood this better than Derek Ingram, whose by-line dominated many a news feature and news report that sought to encourage and reinforce the transformation of the old British Empire into a modern Commonwealth of independent states, all equals in the sight of humanity and with access to each other on the basis of mutual respect and an acknowledgement of the shared values of civil society forged, ironically under colonialism, in the struggles towards independence and a sense of true partnership.

That the obscenity of apartheid persisted with such virulence and energy and for so long all but threatened the logic of Gemini's own persistent resistance to the cancer. But the work of Gemini was too firmly rooted in a sense of decency and a full grasp of the futility of institutionalised racism, or of racism in whatever form, to fail to make an impact. The early struggles were indeed vindicated. The rest, as they say, is history.

This has not, however, meant a blind indulgence of the peoples of the developing world on the part of Gemini. For being human, Third World peoples do have their foibles too. So the opportunities given by Gemini for developing-country journalists to take the mickey out of themselves and the societies they inhabit was always a salutary reminder that life is best taken seriously rather than solemnly. 'Offbeat Gemini' gave such an opportunity to those who would have otherwise regarded themselves a *Planet* which at times can be the respecter of no person, what with the vagaries of natural disasters and the unpredictable paradoxes of everyday existence.

The message to the world that interdependence must be the guiding principle for the future is yet another gift of Gemini to a world long in preparation for economic globalization and the daunting challenges of the information technology revolution. Significantly, the message has been beamed without threat to the integrity of the specificity of peoples, nations, tribes and religions inhabiting the diverse geo-cultural zones of Planet Earth.

Sustaining the liberal tradition of metropolitan Europe which, in alliance with the progressive forces of the colonised world, has progressively rehumanized the globe from the time of plantation slavery through colonialism to the present debt crisis, was yet another contribution by the Ingram–Carruthers initiative of 1967.

The News Service is now well-poised for the changes that are steadily upon us down the decade into the third millennium. Experience and expertise are the key to its readiness. It is, after all, part and parcel of the discourse that has been apace since the 1960s targetting such issues as human-scale development, human rights, environmental integrity, an information order that includes North and South, East and West, cultural identity, ethnicity, sovereignty and the grounding of civil society in the cultural realities of the people responsible for the shaping of their own destinies.

Gemini has undoubtedly earned its keep. The world now needs to take notice in support of the secure future this seminal information agency so richly deserves.

Foreword

Hugh Stephenson,
Director, Graduate Centre for Journalism, City University, London

This is an unusual book. But then the Gemini News Service is an unusual organization. *News on a Knife-Edge* is at its first level a history of Gemini – its triumphs, its tribulations, its survival against most of the odds – from its beginnings in 1967 until today. Richard Bourne has produced a fair and most readable account. (Would that this were always the case with official histories of media organizations.) It is a fitting moment for such a history because Derek Ingram, Gemini's founding editor and the presiding inspiration for the first 27 years, has just given way to a successor, Daniel Nelson. The Gemini baton has been passed to a new generation.

At this first level the book is the story of a small London-based agency battling over the years to establish, hold and expand a niche in the international English-language news business, dominated as it has been and is by the big battalions: Reuters, AP/Dow Jones, and AFP on the spot news side and, increasingly, by the news and feature services of daily metropolitan newspapers, like *The Guardian*, *The Daily Telegraph*, the *Financial Times*, *The New York Times*, *The Washington Post* and the *Los Angeles Times*.

Given that Gemini's broad aim was to be a journalistic bridge between English-speaking industrial countries and the English-language media in the Third World, much of its history over the last quarter century has been entwined with that of the Commonwealth. So the book will be of particular interest to journalists and historians who have followed those events and crises: Southern Rhodesia's UDI, the dismantling of the Sterling Area, the Heath government's wish to resume arms sales to South Africa, the Thatcher government's initial inclination to do business with Bishop Muzorewa and not with Robert Mugabe.

This list of crisis points in the changing attitude of Britain to the Commonwealth and of the Commonwealth to Britain since the mid-1960s does not mean that Gemini was concerned with Africa and politics to the exclusion of all else. It has tried with success to provide material from an agenda that covered the whole world and emphasized many other topics – science, health and medicine, rural societies, the environment. Its special contribution has been week after week to send out from London to its subscribers packages of articles on these subjects seen always in the context of a North–South dialogue, and the interests and aspirations of the South.

News on a Knife-Edge, though, will be of interest not just to journalists and historians.

3

Particularly in these last post-Reagan–Thatcher years, where official concern for the problems of the developing world has been increasingly unfashionable, the Gemini story has involved facing and finding working answers to questions that are of central interest to those involved in development studies, and to communications or media students.

At this level that book is a living case study through which to explore all the political and cultural issues involved in the relationships between nations and the media; between commercial pressures and responsible journalism; between censorship and freedom of expression; between audiences in the Third World and news organizations based in the industrial world; between positive news and propaganda; between national interest and censorship.

Here the decision to include in the book a number of actual Gemini features gives it a whole extra dimension. Not only does it put flesh on the bones of the narrative, but it provides raw (or at least Gemini-edited) material for analysis of how in particular cases the conflicting pressures on the organization were resolved.

It is a pleasure to be reminded how Richard Hall and Gemini managed to scoop the rest of the world's media with its 1970 eyewitness account of the collapse of Biafra at the end of the Nigerian civil war. And it is warming to read after more than 20 years Trevor McDonald writing about Trinidadian politics, when he was still just a free-lance reporter on the beat.

Gemini's lifetime has spanned the period of the heated debate about the desirability or otherwise of a New International Information Order, aimed at doing something to redress the media imbalance from which the Third World so evidently suffers. During the 1980s the news service carefully picked its way through the battlefield, where the main protagonists were President Reagan and Mrs Thatcher on one side, and UNESCO and its director-general, Amadou-Mahtar M'Bow on the other.

All that Ingram and Gemini were doing lay at the heart of this argument. But they were not in fact in either of the two main camps. The whole *raison d'etre* of the news service from the beginning was the need to provide political, economic, social and cultural coverage of the world from the standpoint of the Third World, because this perspective was (and is) effectively ignored by the main international news organizations. To this extent the Gemini output, edited in London but much of it originated by its network of contributing Third World journalists, was in sympathy with UNESCO's thrust. The examples of Gemini pieces reprinted in this book show exactly how the news service provided English-language media round the world with positive images and friendly coverage to balance the doom, gloom, famine, coup and corruption agenda that dominates too much mainstream coverage of developing countries.

But Ingram and Gemini maintained from the beginning with equal fervour that journalists and journalism must never become part of a government machine, or an adjunct of government policy. On this basic point Gemini could never have supported the central proposals for the NIIO, motivated as they were by a desire to make the media serve the aspirations of developing countries.

4

In London the news service got an official reputation of being against (British) government policy in relation to the Commonwealth and the Third World, which must have helped its credibility abroad. But the Gemini starting point that government-owned media are not free media, and that censorship and abuse of human rights are to be deplored wherever they occur, clearly conditioned the whole of its output over the years.

The guiding light of Gemini has always been the beacon of good journalism, properly researched, intelligently written and, above all, tightly edited and re-edited. Ingram's earlier professional experience on the *Daily Mail* gave Gemini from the start a clear and simple writing style, with short sentences and reader-friendly presentation.

As it approaches its fourth decade under a new editor, Gemini will now have to find its way through new challenges. The NIIO debate ran into the sands, but two developments since the end of the 1980s re-pose many of the same questions and challenges in a new form. The eruption of CNN as a world news force at the time of the Gulf War and the other subsequent rapid developments in creating the global media village have given even greater influence over the world news agenda to a handful of international media corporations, where the driving ideology comes from the models of western capitalism and where the driving motive is the maximization of profit to shareholders. The need for an alternative voice (and a voice not speaking just in sound-bites) has never been greater for the English-language print media of the world. These media are no longer to be found only in Commonwealth or ex-Commonwealth countries, but are spread from Moscow and Tallinn to Buenos Aires, and from Riyadh to Bangkok and Beijing.

The second development and challenge for Gemini is the information super-highway. Sophisticated two-way communication via the Internet is upon us, available at a cost that is within reach even of small Third World publications, and of Third World journalists. No-one can predict what problems and possibilities this revolution will bring to an operation like Gemini. All that can confidently be predicted is that by the year 2000 Gemini's main service will not be proffered via the air mail.

I have a particular reason for being pleased to write this foreword. Over the years a number of those connected with Gemini have generously given of their time to lecture or teach our postgraduate journalism students at City University. The contributions over the years of Daniel Nelson and Richard Hall in particular have been substantial. In reverse, a number of City University journalism students have gone on to work for Gemini: to name a few, John Perlman on South Africa, Karen Dabrowska on the Middle East, Alhaji Tanko on the European Union, Mike Hall on Zambia, Lawrence Joffe on chess and computers, and Sirr Anai Kelueljang on Sudan.

It is, thus, from a position of double interest that I warmly commend this unconventional history of an unconventional organization to a wide variety of potential readers.

Introduction

The Gemini News Service is a triumph of hope and hard work over adversity. All media enterprises must expect competition and many new ones are short-lived. But the Gemini news feature agency based in London has had several additional handicaps: its service has always been seen as optional for newspaper subscribers, rather than essential, like a news agency supplying up-to-the-minute news; it has aimed to cover events in some of the poorest countries of the world, and from their viewpoint; it has always been under-capitalized; it remains very small, part of the price it pays for independence; and it has always lived on the edge of crisis.

What follows is an account of an unusual and influential enterprise. Its articles are read every day in scores of countries, and have been since 1967 when it began. Its core staff is tiny and, for most of its life, this has revolved round one talented and dedicated man, Derek Ingram. Yet this is not a biography of Ingram, it is a study of a service of a particular kind with a special connection to the Commonwealth, developing countries, and an evolving global agenda. This service occupies a unique niche in the English-speaking world and is playing a role in the education of journalists, and in broadening and deepening the concept of development journalism.

There is no better way to explain what Gemini is than to republish a selection of its articles. These are not necessarily the best ever, but they do represent its concerns down the years. In allocating substantial space to them it is hoped that schools of journalism and media studies will find aids to learning, while readers of all sorts may gain pleasure from pieces they had missed the first time round.

At heart Gemini comes down to a group of friends, and people who have acquired a kind of special bug which has justified enormous effort for modest reward. This network and this motivation have enabled the agency to survive perils which would have sunk a purely commercial concern. Not all these friends have been on the staff. One of the most significant, for example, has been Clyde Sanger, whom Ingram first got to know in the early 1950s on the *Daily Mail*, and then met again in the dying days of the Central African Federation when Sanger edited a radical journal, the *Central African Examiner*. As a young *Guardian* Africa correspondent he was based in Nairobi, and Ingram and Hastings Banda were both godfathers to his son Richard. Sanger was helpful to Gemini during the period when it was a *Guardian* subsidiary in the 1970s, and he was extremely active in garnering Canadian support for the NewsConcern International Foundation in 1982–83.

This capacity for friendship, and the journalistic impulse behind Gemini, have helped to set it apart and make it effective. Sterner critics, however, would say that the agency has often lacked a strong sense of business direction. Since the late 1980s, however, the budgeting has become tighter. In one year there was a complete pay freeze of the low salaries to enable the service to buy its first good Apple Macintosh computer – essential to maintain the standard of the graphics.

Gemini has been an agency living on a knife-edge which has specialized in serving countries and populations which are equally vulnerable. But it has not just survived, it has made progress. Aided by the rigorous cost control of Bethel Njoku, its managing director, it has achieved a surplus in the last year or two. It has increased its subscribers and persuaded them to pay more realistic rates.

Whereas in 1987 some 70 newspapers were taking the service, the number had risen to around 100 by 1994. In post-communist eastern Europe the takers had jumped from zero to 15. In Africa, historically one of Gemini's strongest markets as well as a source of some of its best reporting, the number had nearly trebled to 22.

It has put parts of the world in touch with each other on terms of understanding, which the big international agencies have only been able to see through Northern eyes. It has tried to emphasise the achievements of developing countries, not just their handicaps. It has challenged a global agenda which often merely reflects the hopes and fears of the richest quarter of the world's population. And it has managed to project a sense of humour. Its history is contemporary, and its business is unfinished.

1 History

In the first week of January, 1967, packets of material were posted from London to newspapers and news organizations around the world from a hitherto unheard-of agency called Gemini. Included in them was an interview with Mrs Gandhi, Prime Minister of India, by a well-known Indian journalist named Kuldip Nayar. Gemini's logo was a distinctive black and white pair of twins. Before long the different types of article were colour-coded: yellow for news, pink for economics, blue for general stories, white for specials, and green for a service titled 'What the Commonwealth Papers Say.'

The birth of the Gemini News Service was a dream come true for Derek Ingram who the year before had been Deputy Editor of the London *Daily Mail*. Although he has said that he got the idea for this service when he was lying on a beach in Morocco, and that he did not go ahead until he had checked its feasibility on a world tour in 1966, it is clear that his mind had been moving in this direction for at least eight years. And for his partner, Oliver Carruthers, who put up most of the money for the venture, it was also rather more than a commercial investment.

Writing 13 years later Ingram explained, 'The theory behind Gemini was simply this. By the mid-1960s the colonial age was dead, and in the new age of non-alignment and the desire to recreate separate national identities many newspapers no longer wanted the kind of material that had been flowing to them from the big agencies and from the syndicated services of the western, mainly British and American, newspapers. For one thing, most of this copy was written for western readers.'[1]

There were several ingredients: the framework of the Commonwealth (in whose future Ingram believed fiercely), where newspapers operated to similar patterns; more use of local journalists, indigenous to countries they wrote about; and a cross-fertilization of news around the globe, so that people would learn more about each other's countries, especially in the Commonwealth. In this last connection Kuldip Nayar, who was editor of *The Statesman* in New Delhi when Ingram visited him in 1966, recalls that he was interested then in getting non-political stories about development and culture.[2]

The 1960s were an exciting time in Britain for those concerned with news and international

1. *The Media Reporter*, 1980.
2. Interview, Kuldip Nayar, August 1993

affairs. The old British Empire was rapidly turning itself into a Commonwealth of sovereign states; South Africa had left the association in 1961 because no other member could accept the institutionalized racism of apartheid; and Ian Smith had declared UDI in Rhodesia in 1965. The Cold War was at its height, with the United States dragged unresistingly into a divisive war in Vietnam. Britain was debating whether to join the Common Market, as the community set up under the Treaty of Rome was still known. Television, so potent in reporting the Vietnam War, was beginning to dominate the instant coverage of events. *The Guardian* had changed from being a Manchester provincial paper into a nation-wide daily, as if in subliminal response to an appetite for more thoughtful commentary and analysis.

In short, this was a period – of the Beatles, of 'Swinging London', of the first Labour Government for 13 years – when people of all sorts were trying to do new things. The choice of the name Gemini, birthsign of Ingram and Carruthers which is supposed to favour the arts of communication, was a nod in a more hippy direction, and away from any stodgy or limiting description.

It was not as though there were no other features services. Agencies like Reuters were distributing 'backgrounders', often put together by bureau correspondents on days when there was no news. Forum World Features was indirectly funded by the US Central Intelligence Agency, but run out of London to supply editorial page commentaries in developing country papers. *The Observer* Foreign News Service had an established reputation. Editors in the South could get quite a lot of material for almost no cost.

The key elements in Gemini, however, lay in Ingram's own experience, his passion for the Commonwealth, and in a certain anti-apartheid flavour and Central African campaigning which he shared with Carruthers, Richard Hall and others who contributed to and supported Gemini in its early years.

Only child of a North London middle class family, Ingram had had a precocious career in wartime and post-war Fleet Street. He was sub-editor of the stories on the front page on the *Daily Sketch* at the age of 17, and was being paid the enormous sum of six guineas a week when he was called up at 18 in 1943. [3]When he went for his medical before entering the Navy, and the doctor asked him what he was earning, the doctor was so surprised that he stopped the queue and went across to tell a colleague.

In the last year of the war he served in the Mediterranean, and Ingram got to know journalists like Hugh Cudlipp and William Connor (the columnist 'Cassandra' on the *Daily Mirror*). Soon after the war ended he joined Lord Beaverbrook's *Daily Express*, before switching to Lord Rothermere's *Daily Mail* in 1949. There he climbed steadily from sub-editing to Chief Sub-Editor, Night Editor, Assistant Editor and Deputy Editor. Richard Hall, a friend from the late 1940s, recalls him then as very elegant, a fast and ruthless sub-editor, but not initially interested in international affairs. They wrote a Navy play together, *The Sun Was Hollow*, set in Naples, and their recollections vary as to whether it was ever performed.

3. Six guineas in decimal currency is £6.30.

The path that led to Gemini began with a late summer holiday in Cyprus in 1954. Ingram's journalistic antennae had been teased the year before when he had met Valentine Myer, the architect of the BBC's home at Broadcasting House. Myer told him that he had spent the summer of 1953 on the island and was extremely anxious about an impending catastrophe. He feared that the British colonial government there did not understand the pressures building up among Greek Cypriots for Enosis, union with Greece, or the risks of inter-communal conflict with Turkish Cypriots.

Ingram's own visit confirmed Myer's warnings, and on the last Saturday before Christmas 1954, British troops fired on unarmed Greek Cypriots at Limassol when a riot got out of hand. It was the start of five years of bloodshed. For Ingram it was a significant experience. It showed that the British colonial authorities were out of touch, and he would apply a measure of scepticism to British colonial and Commonwealth policies thereafter. It showed that decolonization could go violently wrong. And it was all, in a sense, unnecessary. Ingram felt that a more active information strategy would have brought home to Greek Cypriots that there were few advantages in Enosis compared with independence for the island on its own.

His taste for the emerging Commonwealth was strengthened by a visit to Northern Rhodesia in 1958, when he stayed with Hall and his wife at Mufulira, where Hall was now running a mining magazine. Britain was tussling with Sir Roy Welensky, the bluff leader of the short-lived and white-ruled Central Africa Federation, over the pace of African advance. Ingram wrote an open letter to Sir Roy in the *Daily Mail* the following year, telling him to have done with his tergiversations.[4] He followed this up with an idealistic book about the Commonwealth, *Partners in Adventure* for the paperback house Pan, in 1960.

> Two problems above all others torture our minds in this second half of the 20th century' he wrote, 'each a problem of social and political conscience. The first is the atomic threat to our civilization; the second the relationship between the black man and the white. The greatest single, significant factor about the Commonwealth idea is that it transcends all racial barriers ...'[5]

He went on to propose a Commonwealth Information Service to interchange news, views and ideas between Commonwealth countries, and to tell the world outside about developments in the Commonwealth.[6]

By this stage Ingram was Night Editor for the *Daily Mail*, a Conservative paper then going through a moderately liberal phase under two successive editors, William Hardcastle and Mike Randall. Many young Tories were sympathetic to the policies of decolonization pursued by Iain Macleod as Colonial Secretary, and Harold Macmillan – who had spoken of a 'wind of change' blowing through Africa – as Prime Minister. Nonetheless the elderly second Lord Rothermere, who owned the *Mail*, became suspicious of Ingram's radicalism.

---

4. *Daily Mail*, 3 April 1959.

5. *Partners in Adventure*, p. 43, Pan, London, 1960.

6. *Ibid*, p. 157.

Randall had protected Ingram from his proprietor's ire, but his star was waning. Ingram knew that if Randall went he would not become editor. Randall was forced to give way to pressures for Ingram's removal and a compromise was reached.

Ingram could certainly have taken other posts in Fleet Street. Instead, under a leave-taking deal at the end of 1965, he was paid to make a world tour writing reports for the *Mail* while at the same time establishing markets and contributors for Gemini. Soon after the start he had to break off and return from Cyprus to see his dying mother – he got back to London just an hour before she died – before resuming his trip. He, Carruthers and a young secretary, took an office in Paddington Street at the start of 1966.

Oliver Carruthers, the other twin at the start of Gemini, had been a former District Officer in the colonial administration of Northern Rhodesia. From that he had drifted into journalism there, but not before being summoned by Sir Evelyn Hone, the Governor, to be told, 'I want to say that this is a very special occasion. You are the last Carruthers in the Colonial Service.' An ancestor on his mother's side had fired the first shot against the British troops in the American revolution, and he had inherited a substantial fortune from the United States.

Carruthers, who edited a financial paper in Northern Rhodesia, was put in touch with Ingram by Hall. Carruthers and Hall were among a small group of expatriate journalists, strongly sympathetic to the anti-apartheid activists in South Africa. They were part of a 'freedom underground' which helped a number of persons to escape, some via the Caprivi Strip.[7] When Ingram told Hall of his idea for Gemini (a title Hall disliked), he said, 'I know just the man for you. Carruthers wants to come home and he has lots of money.'[8]

By comparison with Ingram, Carruthers seemed a dilettante journalist. He was a witty raconteur and willing to take a gamble. Essentially he was to be the business partner in Gemini, putting up the money and supplying the management. But it was to be an uneasy relationship, especially after the going got rougher financially. Ingram was a well-known London journalist who had been thinking about Commonwealth information issues for years. Carruthers wished to be recognized as an equal partner, and a journalist in his own right. He was less sanguine about the Commonwealth. His business acumen would also come into question.[9]

Launched with a party at the Royal Commonwealth Society the new service settled down quickly into a pattern, posting out two packets a week of six varied news features from London. Special arrangements for telexing stories were made on request, but the aim was to get as many regular subscribers as possible. On the whole it made a good impression, in the richer Commonwealth countries like Britain and Canada as well as in the developing nations. There were one or two early sceptics, however. Don Whitington of the Australian

---

7. Information supplied by Barbara Hall. Harold Wolpe and Arthur Goldreich were among the anti-apartheid activists whom they helped to escape.

8. Richard Hall recalls Carruthers turning to him in his office one day and saying 'I've just had it confirmed that I'm a millionaire in dollars'.

9. His management of *African Development*, after its separation from Gemini, was unsuccessful even though the magazine was filled with advertisements.

Press Service wrote to Ingram seven months after the start: 'Rupert Murdoch is prepared to have a look at Gemini material again, but is not enthusiastic or optimistic. He said from what he had seen of it it was too academic and remote from Australia, with far too much emphasis on Africa and India.'[10] Australia was always to be a tough market as, for foreign exchange and other reasons, was India.

After six months Gemini ran an advertisement proclaiming success. It had put out stories and features by more than 100 authors. It had run an exclusive interview with President Kaunda of Zambia, forecast a row between Malta and Britain, scored a first over Basil D'Oliveira, the South African-born Test cricketer. It had published a fortnightly London Line and Africa Column and a variety of off-beat stories: the mating of a celibate kiwi, where you can get a divorce for seven shillings and sixpence[11] and the Indian fashion for a mini-choli (the sub-continent's version of the mini-skirt).

In 1969, the year of a Commonwealth conference in London when Gemini provided virtually 24 hour a day coverage, it analysed the geographical origin of its reports: Africa – 86, Americas – 59, Asia – 85, Australasia – 66, Europe – 31, Britain – 195, and staff – 189. In fact a number of the contributors from Britain, like Fred Mpanga, a former Attorney-General of Buganda in Uganda who had had to go into exile, were not themselves British. However it was the case that many editors particularly appreciated Gemini staff copy, and the service clearly benefited from the sense of London as an international news centre, and of Britain itself as still having a special status in the Commonwealth.

The home of Gemini in its first years was Wheatsheaf House, between Fleet Street and the Thames, which had once been an office for the Harmsworth encyclopaedias. Alan Rake, a former editor of *Drum* in east Africa who joined at the end of 1968, recalls a haphazard atmosphere, weak on contractual arrangements, but nevertheless a refuge for old Africa hands, some of whom might not be too old. It was not clear who was working full-time, and who was just dropping by. One of the most gifted of these journalists who had been in Africa was Richard Hall, who witnessed the final collapse of Biafra at the start of 1970.

Half paid for by the magazine *Nova*, to write a story about the Holy Ghost Fathers in the breakaway Nigerian state, Hall flew in as Don McCullin, the famous *Sunday Times* photographer was leaving with Antony Terry. McCullin told West, 'You don't want to stay here, because you'll be part of the fucking autopsy.' Hall replied, 'Don, you're just trying to drive me off the story.' Hall, who was about to leave Gemini to edit *The Observer*'s colour magazine had lead stories in *The Sunday Times* and *The Observer* and, on his return, wrote his head off for other papers also under Ingram's urging.[12]

A critical contribution to the early identity of Gemini lay in its graphics. The illustrative

---

10. Letter dated 11 July 1967, Ingram Archive.

11. Seven shillings and sixpence in pre-decimal currency equals 37.5p after decimalization.

12. Interview, Richard Hall. It was, of course, unusual for a journalist to sell stories on the same event to rival Sunday papers, but Hall had posted a holding story to *The Observer*'s Foreign News Service in advance and, when he was able to dictate his fresh account to Gemini, Ingram sold it to the highest bidder which was *The Sunday Times*.

expression of factual material, in the British press and elsewhere, was still in its infancy. Yet visual awareness, with the increased sophistication of television and colour magazines, was growing. With the aid of three talented individuals, Cliff Hopkinson, Peter Clarke and Rade Radovic (a Serb refugee to Britain after the Second World War), Gemini began illustrating a high proportion of articles with rugged, black and white graphics and maps. These included charts and the superimposition of heads of political leaders onto maps or statistical graphs. (The trademark black and white twin motif was actually supplied by Richard Leadbetter, an artist Hopkinson had known on *The Observer*, and cost £10.)

For developing countries the graphics were a godsend. They could not have been provided locally, and they often required background research. Yet to run news features about faraway countries it was essential to give readers a map. The graphics that came in the post were almost as valuable as the stories, and could be run large to fill space.

From the word go there had never been any difficulty about getting enough copy for the service, even though it was then only paying a rock-bottom flat rate of £15 per article. But what papers were actually taking it? In June 1970, out of a total income of £26,559 for the year, UK newspapers contributed £4,285, Africa £5,592, Europe £3,943 and Canada £2,690. However Pakistan, India and Ceylon (Sri Lanka) together only paid £730, not much more than the £720 from the Caribbean. In spite of many trial offers and a visit from Carruthers to drum up business, Australia only paid £1,090, less than the £1,524 from New Zealand.

Amongst the individual papers there were, however, some good names. In Britain they included *The Sunday Times* and *Evening Standard*, *The Sun*, the *Bradford Telegraph & Bradford Argus*, the *Wolverhampton Express & Wolverhampton Star*; in Africa the *East Africa Standard*, *The Times of Zambia* (a particularly good customer, which often ran several Gemini articles in the same issue) and the South African Associated Newspapers; in Europe, *Politiken*, *Dagens Nyheter* and Deutsche Welle radio; and in North America papers in San Francisco, Ottawa and Hamilton.

The collapse in commodity prices and the oil shock of the Yom Kippur war still lay in the future, but it was already clear that Gemini was having problems in getting users to pay for the service. This was not just in developing countries with foreign exchange restrictions, but one Australian paper was eight months behind on payments, and there was a suspicion that some editors were treating Gemini as free copy. Although the revenue had risen from well under £10,000 in the first year to nearly £30,000 in the fourth the company had actually spent £200,000–£250,000 over this period to get started.

The difficulty of making an unsubsidized service break even financially – which was to be an enduring problem for Gemini – along with the vitality of its early staff, helped to explain an extraordinary transformation of a tiny news feature service into a mini-conglomerate. By 1972, when the firm had moved into new premises in John Carpenter House, it was employing 29 persons: eleven in Gemini News Service, five on a magazine called *African Development* which it had bought at the end of 1968, seven in GeminiScan, a

Fig. 1. Gemini's first birthday, 1968; left to right, Arnold Smith, first Commonwealth Secretary-General, his wife Eve, Derek Ingram.

Fig. 2. Gemini's first birthday, 1968; left to right, Gamini Seneviratne, the Zambian High Commissioner, Derek Ingram.

Fig. 3. The team in 1969; third from left, front, Rade Radovic with Oliver Carruthers behind him; Alan Rake, four left from Carruthers; far back right, Fred Mpanga; far right, Derek Ingram.

design firm where Cliff Hopkinson and Peter Clarke held half the shares, and six on group administration and accounts.

GeminiScan was the most spectacular of these satellites, though *African Development* was to have the longer life and greater commercial success. GeminiScan started in 1968, making use of the considerable talents of Hopkinson and Clarke. Among many activities its chief ones were the production of educational kits, but it was also responsible for the design of *Orbit* (a Zambian educational magazine, published for the government, which featured a Zambian in space and the adventures of a Zambian air hostess), and *What*, a short-lived enterprise of Michael Young (later Lord Young of Dartington) who had pioneered *Which* and *Where*.

The educational kits involved tie-ups with IPC, BPC and the *Daily Express* and topics such as 'Make your own Book', the World Cup, 'Who are you?', London, the Human Body, Pope John, Monsters of the Past, Wild Life and Winning the West. They were aimed at seven to 12 year olds. The most exciting was the Apollo moonshot kit, launched with an enormous party at the London Planetarium. Detailed information from NASA was incorporated. 'Touchdown on the Moon – Spacecraft Commander's Briefing Kit puts you inside Apollo to share every hour of flight and lunar exploration', ran the advertising. The clarity of the presentation was a gift to London newspapers also.

GeminiScan faced distribution and marketing problems and never earned what its protagonists hoped. The kits were mass market items and the royalty paid was small. But this did not stop GeminiScan from boosting its own products. Announcing an astrology kit it said, 'A team of experts hired by the GeminiScan Company has spent a full year working on the ancient mysteries of Astrology ... They have taken these methods and simplified them – but have preserved the authentic values of Astrology. Thus mystery is swept away ... You need no skill. As soon as you open this GeminiScan kit you can begin compiling personal horoscopes which can be kept in personal form..'

At the same time as all this, of course, GeminiScan was providing graphics for the news service. A similar symbiosis was possible with *African Development*, an almost defunct magazine bought at the end of 1968 which, after the end of its Gemini ownership turned into two – *New African* and *African Business*. Richard Hall was put in as editor but very rapidly Alan Rake – still editing *New African* in 1994 – was doing most of the work. Instead of items about British exports in a giveaway publication, *African Development* quickly became a genuinely journalistic product, but Rake would sometimes 'camp out' in particular African states until enough ads had been sold to justify printing an issue.[13] It was a useful source of free air tickets to Africa as well.

On the surface, therefore, all was hectic activity in John Carpenter House – a little like the efforts of the Harmsworth brothers at the end of the nineteenth century, with energy fired in every direction in hopes that one or more sally would strike gold. Gemini was circulating fiction, crosswords, astrology columns, knitting patterns and football pool material. One of Carruthers' idiosyncratic ideas was 'The Last Penny' – pennies sold as collector's items in a holder with a history of the coin, to coincide with decimalization in Britain in 1971.

But almost from the start there had been financial difficulties, and Carruthers' pocket was not deep enough to sustain the losses for ever. In a note of mid 1969 the lawyer to Gemini, James Lemkin, reported that Carruthers had said he would give Gemini five years from 1 January 1967 to see that it 'makes a go', but 'I will not be surprised if he put some limit on his ultimate liability.'[14] By 1972 the news service at Gemini was far from being viable, with an annual expenditure of around £57,000 but an income of only £30,000. The other enterprises were not doing well enough to rescue it. For instance GeminiScan had made a loss of £11,244 on a turnover of £51,754 in 1971-72, and a profit of only £2,699 on a turnover of £77,760 the following year.

Ingram did not pretend to be a businessman, saw the news service as central and everything else as peripheral, and was working flat out, editing copy and writing a thousand words a week himself: he had taken no salary for the first year of Gemini, and had had little in the way of holiday for the first three years. Increasingly he felt that his partner was incapable of supplying the management that was needed, and that the marketing was inadequate. Relations became poor, with shouting-matches at the office and in board meetings.

In a private letter to Carruthers in May 1971 Ingram complained that office wrangling had

---

13. Interview, Alan Rake.

14. Ingram Archive.

worn down Richard Hall, and led to his departure. 'When you go around wasting everyone's time and tempers making preposterous and juvenile proposals you make me despair...'.[15] May must have been a bad month because there was also a notable row between Peter Clarke, who had only taken nine days of holiday in three years, and Carruthers.

Clarke asked for three months' holiday money in advance. Carruthers retaliated by charging £17 interest. Clarke then charged £17 for an article he had written and illustrated for Gemini. Carruthers wrote gravely, 'All three companies are in dire financial straits. The accumulated loss on GNS is about £120,000, on *African Buyer & Trader* (*African Development*) about £35,000 and on Scan about £15,000. Of the three only *AB&T* can predict a period of profit and that for a restricted period. In such a situation, and it has been the same since we started, particular care and sacrifices must be expected from the directors and shareholders...'.[16] With the renewal of Carruthers' personal guarantees to the bank a regular boardroom saga, and Ingram threatening to resign as a director in April 1972,[17] crisis was unavoidable. Gemini must either close or be sold.

The first approach was to see whether another wealthy individual might take it on. Greville Howard, a Conservative MP and long-time personal friend of Ingram, appointed the Royal Bank of Canada at the end of 1971 to investigate the situation with a view to a possible investment of £100,000. Nothing came of this. In 1972 approaches were made to a consortium of papers around the Commonwealth, with a June prospectus designed to raise the same sum.

One of these papers was *The Sunday Times*, now edited by Harold Evans, a friend and admirer of Ingram's. Another friend, Mike Randall, was in a senior executive position there. Gemini had been providing *The Sunday Times* with regular stories and graphics, and Evans' former paper, the *Northern Echo* in Darlington, was also taking Gemini. In the second half of 1972 it looked for a while as if Times Newspapers, owners of *The Sunday Times* during the Thomson era, would buy Gemini, setting up a joint company with its own syndication service.

However, after various delays, the Gemini board was informed in December that *The Sunday Times* had decided not to go ahead. The reasons given by Derek Jewell on behalf of *The Sunday Times* were three: that it would be difficult to sell Gemini/*Sunday Times* material into rival papers to those with which Times Newspapers already had syndication contracts; the areas where Gemini was strong and Times Newspapers were weak 'are not particularly good markets and from which, based on bitter experience, it is sometimes difficult to extract money even when agreements have been made'; and that *The Sunday Times* would have to put in a lot of risk capital and a lot of organization and energy for something which was not a high enough priority.[18]

---

15. Letter 10 May 1971, Ingram Archive.

16. Ingram Archive.

17. He wrote: 'I do not believe that the way in which we are carrying on (and have been carrying on for some time now) is any longer practicable, sensible or desirable. Nor is it a way in which I am personally prepared to carry on any longer.' Letter of 18 April 1972, Ingram Archive.

For Carruthers, continuing to lose money, it was past the eleventh hour and he proposed immediate closure of Gemini.

However this was staved off for six months more and, in an act largely of altruism, *The Guardian* newspaper – that is The Manchester Guardian and Evening News Ltd, its holding company – bought Gemini in June 1973.

Why did *The Guardian*, which was to own Gemini for almost nine years, want a struggling news feature service? It made clear at once that it did not want the other companies in the Gemini group, and it ran the news feature service with minimum staffing.

To a considerable extent the decision to take Gemini was made by James Markwick, then rising the managerial ladder, and he helped protect it thereafter.[19] He had a nod of approval from Alastair Hetherington, then editor of *The Guardian*, but it was never to command interest on the editorial floor. He also took advice from Lord Barnetson, head of United Newspapers and a power in the Commonwealth Press Union. Barnetson told him, 'If you put in the right infrastructure you won't lose much, and people will think well of you.'[20]

Markwick's move was largely inspired by admiration for Ingram, whom he regarded as someone who could have got to the top in Fleet Street, but who had preferred to set up a small outfit to do a job he believed in. They had a common friend in Clyde Sanger, one-time editor of the *Central African Examiner* in Salisbury, Rhodesia. Sanger went on to be a *Guardian* correspondent in Africa, and later Director of Information for the Commonwealth Secretariat.

But there were also tax losses that came with Gemini, usable in reducing taxation on the *Guardian* group for as long as it kept Gemini running. And there was, it would appear, some interest at this period in *The Guardian* management in taking on and developing small businesses.[21] *The Guardian* did what *The Sunday Times* had intended to do. It merged the finances of its own syndication service with Gemini in a separate division, subsequently adding customer offers and other pieces of revenue.

From some viewpoints *The Guardian*, as a liberal paper of the left which had staunchly fought apartheid and argued for decolonization, was an entirely appropriate home for Gemini. Prior to owning it, it had already used Gemini features. On one celebrated occasion, for example, Cameron Duodu in Accra had written a strong Gemini article challenging Nigeria's military rulers to produce the playwright Wole Soyinka, when rumours were circulating in Ghana that he had been tortured to death. He was being

18. Letter from Derek Jewell, Ingram Archive.

19. James Markwick, who once ran as a Conservative parliamentary candidate in Salford, was to become Managing Director of *The Guardian*. A forebear in his family, Edward Markwick, had been a partner of Alfred Harmsworth at the start of the meteoric publishing career of the founder of the *Daily Mail*. In April 1995 it was announced that he would become Chief Executive of the Guardian Media Group in January 1996.

20. Interview, James Markwick.

21. The Guardian Media Group by 1994 was a diversified company with both large and small enterprises. In the early 1970s it had, for instance, developed Guardian Business Services with some success and bought a chain of newsagents.

accused of aiding the Biafrans in the civil war. Soyinka was indeed produced alive and released soon after, and the fact that *The Guardian* had printed Duodu's piece had certainly been helpful.[22]

However *The Guardian*, although it was straightforward in its dealings with Gemini, was always a slight disappointment to Ingram who felt that the paper should have made more use of Gemini material and the management (other than Markwick) should have done more to promote it. Prevailing sentiment among senior editorial people there was not sympathetic to the Commonwealth concept. With Britain signing up to the Treaty of Rome the Commonwealth, still significant to Gemini, seemed to represent the past in contrast to a European future; for the more leftist *Guardian* journalists it seemed like a colonial hangover. For *The Guardian* management – apart from Markwick and Gerald Knight, who was responsible at a hands-on level – Gemini was too small to waste time on when it was still a struggle to make the flagship viable.

Ian Wright, who was Foreign Editor at *The Guardian* during this period, was interested in many of the regions where Gemini had a presence. *The Times* had been influenced by 'Trilateralism', and had reduced its coverage outside Europe, Japan and North America. It thus left competitive scope for *The Guardian* elsewhere and Wright, who had himself reported from Africa and Vietnam, was alive to the opportunities.

However Wright was anxious to exercise the power of choice in foreign editing, and was in no mood to delegate this to a news feature service whose contributors he could not assess personally. Instead he relied on a small number of experts he knew well, most of them already on the paper, who could advise him on stringers and stories from different regions. Essentially he saw a difference of purpose between a newspaper and a news agency, and radical differences of culture and resources between *The Guardian* and papers which had little money and were only too glad to take Gemini.[23] It was also the case that *The Guardian* was serving a British audience, whereas this was not the prime Gemini objective.

In any event, whereas the *Daily Mail* tradition from which Ingram had sprung was centralist, where managers and editors had great power, *The Guardian* was more anarchic. Specialists and the controllers of sections tended to be the power brokers there. Management did not dictate to editorial. It was perfectly possible, as had been the case for years, for *The Guardian* and the *Manchester Evening News* to belong to the same group without ever cooperating editorially on anything.

After the excitements of life in the days of the Ingram-Carruthers partnership the Gemini News Service settled down, as a *Guardian* subsidiary, to just doing its job as a news feature service. Initially it was in John Carpenter House, off Fleet Street, then in John Street, Holborn. It then moved to the old *Manchester Guardian* office in Fleet Street, which had

---

22. Interview, Cameron Duodu. Soyinka's autobiography, *All that Fall*, confirmed that he had been tortured.

23. Interview, Ian Wright. For Africa, he relied on James McManus, in Asia on Martin Woollacott, both on the staff. For Latin America he was advised by Christopher Roper, who edited *Latin American Newsletters*.

been a southern outpost in the days before *The Guardian* printed in London. Gerald Knight, the general manager, recalls a hand-cranked Roneo machine, operated by Ingram, and trails of ink on the two days the service went out. It was a big drag to print and collate the pages. An attempt to operate a Gemini schools service, which might have taken advantage of *The Guardian*'s strong educational reputation and work which the early Gemini had done with the Commonwealth Institute, never took off.

Brana Radovic, who was a graphic artist with Gemini from 1975 to 1979, recalls a small but highly motivated team of no more than five. When he was twelve, his father Rade had paid Brana £1 an hour to help him with Letraset in the early days of Gemini, and he joined himself on leaving college. 'I, Derek Ingram and Dickie Walters, who was Derek's deputy and did much of the sub-editing, all felt we were doing something important,' he said. Visitors such as Donald Woods, the escaped editor from South Africa and Peter Snow, the TV presenter, would drop in. The challenge of producing illustrations was never-ending.

However when after four years the young Radovic went for a job that had been advertised by the *Financial Times* he was offered more than twice the money he had earned at Gemini. Indeed, because of the disparities in salary, Ingram found himself constantly training graphic artists for other Fleet Street employers.[25]

The Guardian did not interfere editorially with Gemini but Knight was worried. He feared that it could never be viable financially as it stood, even with its low overheads, for its customers were amongst the poorest people in the world. He was worried that it was becoming marginalized, because it did not have resources for technological improvement and still depended on the twice weekly package deliveries by mail. During the period of *Guardian* ownership it lost the ground it had held in the British and Canadian press as these papers adopted the new technologies.[26]

Above all he was concerned that it was too dependent on the support of one person in the management, James Markwick, who might leave the company. (In fact Markwick was to become managing director of *The Guardian* later, but no-one could have forecast this.) Although *The Guardian* was benefiting from artwork which did not have to go through expensive union hoops, and was using up Gemini tax losses, questions were asked as to why the paper was running it at all. Was Gemini's policy *Guardian* policy? Why was *The Guardian* itself using so little when all the contributors were being paid with cheques drawn on The Manchester Guardian and Evening News Ltd?

At a time of high inflation in Britain financial figures were deceptive. Although it looked

---

25. Interview, Brana Radovic. Over the years Gemini illustrators would also go to the Press Association, to Reuters and to *The Guardian* itself.

26. Australia was still difficult. Although the *Melbourne Age* was taking the service when Gemini suspended in April 1982, Margaret Jones, *Sydney Morning Herald* Foreign Editor had written to Ingram in September 1978, 'The *Sydney Morning Herald* is not likely to become a regular customer, I'm afraid. We have saturation coverage from our own correspondents and stringers, the wire services, and the special services to which we subscribe. Our problem is shortage of space, not shortage of features and foreign news. We are already over-supplied from existing sources.' Ingram Archive.

as though income and expenditure on Gemini had trebled between 1975 and 1981 the business had not really grown. In four weeks to 23 August 1975 it earned £2,115 and spent £2,902; in the same four weeks six years later it had earned £7,433 and spent £7,261. Interestingly the comparable figures for *The Guardian*'s own lossmaking syndication service were substantially below Gemini's, and had grown much more slowly. [27]All of these figures, including reader offers, *The Guardian* Diary income and other odds and ends were lumped together under the Gemini News Service heading which was then just in profit.

In the late 1970s the commercial management at *The Guardian* became more aggressive. From September 1977 *The Guardian Weekly,* Guardian Business Services and Gemini News Service were brought together in a separate division named Guardian Publications: it aimed to produce profits of £100,000 a year. Markwick reported to the board on this as a profit centre.

However the sharp recession in Britain, which occurred shortly after the Thatcher Government was elected in 1979, brought on a crisis. 'I remember saying to Derek, "We've been blown out of the water here",' is how Markwick put it.[28] *The Guardian* in 1981 was unable to pay the standard 10 per cent wage increase agreed for the newspaper industry by the Newspaper Publishers Association, giving its printers and journalists only 7.5 per cent instead. Real losses on *The Guardian* were rising, the benefit of the tax losses on Gemini had run out, and the building in Fleet Street where Gemini was hiding on the top floor was the subject of two good offers which *The Guardian* wanted to realize.

The position was put frankly to Ingram by Gerald Knight in a letter of 24 September, 1981:

> It has always been my fear that one day events in the Company as a whole would focus attention on Gemini and the true position be revealed. This has happened. The group will lose over a million this year, and every area of activity has been examined as a consequence. Gemini loses money, Gemini can never be made profitable, therefore Gemini must go. It is the end of the road for Gemini as far as *The Guardian* connection is concerned.[29]

Knight added there would be no sudden death or formal announcement, and *The Guardian* would help if it could. He wrote that in his view there were four options: that Gemini became a trust (not unlike the Scott Trust which controlled *The Guardian*, but with the advantage that it could raise additional monies for the service); that it became an official Commonwealth News Service (presumably by agreement with the Commonwealth Secretariat); that it merged with a commercial partner; and only if these ideas failed would it have to close.

This was the second potentially terminal crisis to hit Gemini, and it devastated Ingram. His friend Markwick could do little, because of the scale of *The Guardian*'s own problems,

---

27. The Guardian syndication service for the same four weeks to 23 August 1975 showed a revenue of £1,199 and an expenditure of £1,235. In the same four weeks in 1981, its income was £2,750 and its expenditure was £3,083.

28. Interview, James Markwick.

29. Ingram Archive.

except to say that Ingram could have Gemini back if he wanted it.[30] Ingram could not put together a package quickly enough and, in spite of a plea to *The Guardian* by Shridath Ramphal, Commonwealth Secretary-General, Gemini suspended its service on 30 April 1982.[31]

What happened next was unexpected. It showed the value attached to Gemini by its friends in the Commonwealth and by newspapers which had been taking its service. The reaction too was buttressed by the admiration and affection which its editor had acquired over the years. For, almost as soon as the twice-weekly packages ceased going out, plans advanced for a resurrection.

The first critical decision was to announce the cessation as a 'suspension', not a closure. This was the eleventh hour product of late night phone calls to Canada between Ingram and Clyde Sanger and Arnold Smith, the retired but still active former Secretary-General of the Commonwealth. They were already thinking that it might be possible to mobilize Canadian and other international funds to support Gemini's work, and argued that there was no need to let people think the service was finished.

The second decision that mattered came from *The Guardian*, which permitted Ingram to go on using his old office at no cost while he negotiated with potential funders. (In fact, as the British recession worsened, demand for the Fleet Street property diminished and *The Guardian* recognized that it might have to refurbish to make it saleable.)

Ingram's own enormous determination, which had seen him through so much work and previous anxiety, was now underpinned by the worldwide response of customers. There was an almost universal shriek of horror that the service was suspended; 150 papers in over 60 countries had been taking it. In the eyes of users Gemini was irreplaceable, both in its commitment to development coverage and its Anglophone and Commonwealth interests. The passage of time had made this uniqueness more obvious: Forum World Features had disappeared, the Rome-based Inter Press Service, with its Christian Democrat and Latin American orientations, was offering something different, while the big international news agencies were biased to spot news and an Anglo-American agenda still driven by the Cold War.

It was this genuine demand, albeit from newspapers which could not pay high subscriptions, which gave a fillip to efforts to relaunch Gemini. A number of people helped; indeed Chief Emeka Anyaoku, the Commonwealth's Deputy Secretary-General who subsequently succeeded Ramphal, was at one point exploring sources of support in Hong Kong.[32] But the key figures were perhaps James Porter, Director of the Commonwealth Institute in London, and Sanger and Smith in Canada. Luckily, Sanger and Smith managed

---

30. Interview, James Markwick. In fact, *The Guardian* had paid nothing for Gemini when it bought it and there was only a small and belated payment to Carruthers and Ingram, made in proportion to their shares and the reduction in Corporation Tax for The Guardian and Manchester Evening News company. In July 1984, Ingram was told that Carruthers would obtain £856.40p and he, Ingram, would get £68.60p.

31. Interview, Sir Shridath Ramphal.

32. Interview, Chief Emeka Anyaoku.

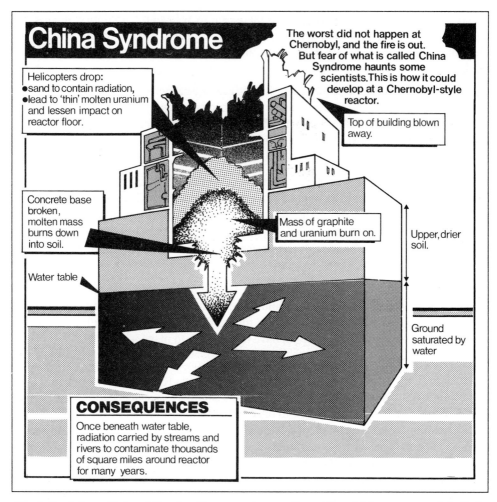

China Syndrome

The worst did not happen at Chernobyl, and the fire is out. But fear of what is called China Syndrome haunts some scientists. This is how it could develop at a Chernobyl-style reactor.

Helicopters drop:
●sand to contain radiation,
●lead to 'thin' molten uranium and lessen impact on reactor floor.

Top of building blown away.

Concrete base broken, molten mass burns down into soil.

Mass of graphite and uranium burn on.

Upper, drier soil.

Water table

Ground saturated by water

CONSEQUENCES

Once beneath water table, radiation carried by streams and rivers to contaminate thousands of square miles around reactor for many years.

Fig. 4. Gemini supplied, and its subscribers came to expect, graphics which were accurate in their information, easy to understand, and simple to reproduce as in the following three examples. China Syndrome (September 1986).

to recruit the support of Lewis Perinbam, a senior official at the Canadian International Development Agency. Their efforts focused on supporting Gemini by means of a non-profit trust, governed by reputable international names, which could collect funds. These funds would indirectly subsidize the news feature service for purposes of education or development.

From Ingram's viewpoint this was a more attractive option than any of the others raised by Knight. A commercial partnership, which had been attempted with *The Guardian*, could not last because it would still be difficult to make the service commercially viable; sooner or later it would be closed or, which could amount to the same thing, merged into something else. The idea of the Commonwealth Secretariat taking it over was not really a starter: the Secretariat was always short of money and there would be inevitable and unacceptable risks of editorial interference in such a solution.

But the trust idea was not entirely simple. In deference to Canadian opinion the word 'foundation' was substituted for 'trust.' The two main difficulties lay in the size of the ongoing financial requirement, and the need to square the purposes of the donors with Ingram's adamant determination to protect the editorial independence of the service.

Ingram did not hide the financial need. The budget circulated to would-be donors suggested that with revenue of £57,000 and costs of £119,600, there would be an annual shortfall, stretching into the future, of £62,600 a year in present money. This did not presuppose any more lavish arrangements than had applied with *The Guardian*, where a senior journalist had described Gemini staff as being 'as poor as church mice.' Less than half of

Fig. 5. Edgy neighbours (October 1994).

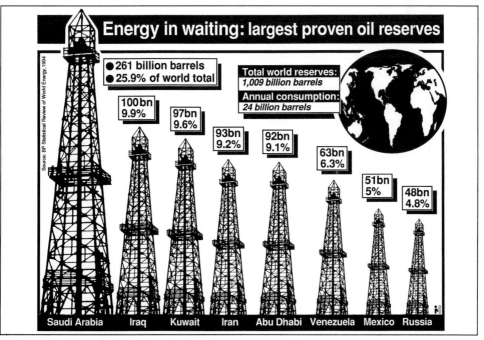

Fig. 6. Energy in waiting (September 1994).

the proposed budget after restart would have to pay for six people – an editor and assistant editor, a graphic artist, a general manager and two secretaries.

The need to protect editorial independence was a sensitive point, and not only for Gemini. In Canada, when the Canadian International Development Agency, CIDA, decided to give CAN $100,000 as a restart grant to Gemini, the *Toronto Star* ran a headline 'Canada gives $100,000 to a Fleet Street Agency'. Perrin Beatty, a Progressive Conservative MP in the Federal Opposition in Ottawa, campaigned vigorously against the grant. (A few years later much of CIDA's support came in the form of the purchase of subscriptions for papers in developing countries.) However the way in which the international foundation was structured was designed not only to assure donors, but to safeguard Gemini from inter-ference.

James Porter of the Commonwealth Institute had got to know Ingram as one of his governors there. He and Trevor McDonald, then diplomatic correspondent for Inde-pendent Television News and a former Gemini contributor, signed an appeal letter on behalf of an impressive range of trustees-designate: Chinua Achebe the Nigerian novelist, the poet and writer Andreas Christofides from Cyprus, the journalist Willie Musururwa from Zimbabwe, Rex Nettleford, professor of media studies and founder of the Jamaica National Dance Theatre Company, and Clyde Sanger and Arnold Smith from Canada. *The Guardian* agreed to be a governor, of what was to be called NewsConcern International Foundation, in a corporate capacity. The foundation had some funds before the appeal was launched: UNICEF, which had already been assisting the Inter Press Service, sponta-neously offered £10,000 on learning of the suspension. *The Guardian*, in a roundabout deal which also involved a rental for the Fleet Street office and a subscription from *Guardian Weekly*, also contributed £5,000.

Approaches were made to bodies including CIDA, the Swedish International Develop-ment Agency (SIDA), the Netherlands Development Agency, UNDP, Southam News-papers in Canada, the *Melbourne Age*, and a wealthy Indian-born industrialist in Britain, Swraj Paul. It was hoped to raise £100,000 before a relaunch, enough to guarantee two years' losses, but this was not achieved. In fact Gemini restarted after a 10 month suspension in March 1983, and by 1 March the total collected was only £57,287.21p; much the most significant contributor was Canadian CIDA, although over the next couple of years other bodies such as UNICEF, UNDP and UNFPA were also useful donors.

Gemini was back in business. Subscribers were asked to pay more. Jolted by the realization that they had come to depend on the service, they agreed. But the operation was still a very hand-to-mouth affair. The income forecast in Ingram's circular before the restart did not materialize and costs had to be curtailed. In the first year of resumption, from January 1983 to March 1984, the total expenditure was only £91,195 but there was still a deficit of £44,806: this was covered by the grant income raised by NewsConcern.

From 1983, therefore, Gemini entered its third phase. Its new structure defined it as a news feature service with a special mission. It was recognized as something more than a supplier of articles. It was in its own right a kind of development tool, circulating stories about the achievements and problems of the Third World or South, assisting their newspapers, and

26

offering a means of international expression to their journalists. Whereas the private fortune of Carruthers had subsidized Gemini in its first phase, and a heterogeneous mixture of reader offers and other *Guardian* byproducts had made up for the losses in its second, its news service was now being overtly funded by international agencies because of what it was. (Ingram always argued that he and the other journalists had provided the most steady subsidy of all, by working for well below the usual rates.)

While Ingram himself may have been slow to see that Gemini was being perceived differently, its new status had interesting consequences. One of the first occurred within a few months of the relaunch, when a young Canadian journalist named Jane Taber arrived in London with a CAN$20,000 grant for 12 months from the International Development Research Centre in Ottawa.

She had been working on the *Ottawa Citizen* and had wanted to study Nigeria during the elections of that year. However although IDRC was happy with her proposal the Nigerian government was not. IDRC said she could go anywhere else and, in a lucky fluke, she got in touch with Sanger who told her about Gemini. A deal was arranged by which she would come to London for editing experience, go to a developing country for field reporting experience (in the end this was Zimbabwe) and then return for a further stint in the London office. She still recalls the excitement she felt:

> I would be working on Fleet Street – every newspaper person's dream – and living abroad. Though I spoke the same language I went through culture shock in England. London was beautiful. But, in many respects, it was still back in the dark ages as far as technology. For instance, I left a fully computerized newspaper to come to an international news service that still relied on typewriters, photocopiers and physically stuffed the stories into envelopes twice a week. I couldn't believe it. But somehow in that rabbit warren of offices it all worked. And, in the end, that's what counted.[33]

In this haphazard way an annual IDRC Gemini Fellowship was born. From Gemini's viewpoint it provided an able young journalist at no financial cost, an extra pair of hands it could not have afforded. For the journalist it offered a spell abroad and a career opportunity. For IDRC it suggested a new way to permeate the Canadian media with people awake to ideas of North-South cooperation and the needs of development.

The coverage in the Gemini service did not obviously change. It still sought a geographical and topical balance. The graphics remained important – indeed one of Gemini's most gifted graphic designers, Paddy Allen, worked there for over three years in the 1980s. Paragraphs were still kept short, possibly a legacy from Ingram's experience at the Mail in the 1950s and 1960s.

But there were subtle alterations in the London office which impacted on the service. They can be summed up in the contribution of three different personalities, Daniel Nelson, Kelly

---

33. Jane Taber, letter to author, 8 February 1994.

McParland and Elizabeth Pritchard, and in the way that Ingram came to be seen increasingly as tutor and mentor.

Nelson had, as a young man, been editor of *The People* newspaper in Uganda in 1965 and, as a result of a visit by Ingram to Kampala, had taken the Gemini service when it began two years later. He had contributed himself and encouraged some Ugandan journalists to do likewise. He had become increasingly interested in development and ecological issues while pursuing a roving career as a journalist. When he returned to Britain in 1981, after a stint with the *Financial Times*, he had one of his periodic lunches with Ingram. Ingram told him that *The Guardian* was pulling out and that he was giving himself a year to get the service restarted. He invited Nelson to join him as assistant editor.

'I said I'd stay for three months on a freelance basis. I actually stayed for six years,' Nelson recalls.[34] He brought with him a great professional competence and commitment – a colleague at the time remembers how passionate he could be on the iniquities of Third World debt – as well as a sense of *joie de vivre*. IDRC fellows, and those who came later from the Regina School of Journalism in Saskatchewan, found him a helpful adviser. During Gemini's periodic cash-flow difficulties he would ease the strain by holding back on his entitlement to pay. Whereas for Ingram a formative experience had been the modernizing of the Commonwealth in the 1960s, for Nelson, who had an air of perpetual youthfulness, the development and environmental campaigns of the 1970s and 1980s were of lasting importance.

'Danny was such a brilliant geezer. It was not just that he had this grasp of issues. He had a brilliant sense of humour. It was a riot when he and Kelly McParland were there. I laughed so much sometimes it made me cry. And when disaster struck, he could turn it into a joke,' Paddy Allen says now.[35] There was a Post Office in the Fleet Street building which housed Gemini. On days when the service was running late one of them would run downstairs and put a foot in the door to prevent it closing. Up at the top, where it was possible to see St Paul's Cathedral, you fried in the summer and an artist worked with gloves on in winter; in spring, tiny plane seeds blew in through the windows.

Allen looks back on his time at Gemini as 'great days.' One product of this vitality was a strip cartoon for the service, *Didi*. It was jointly created by Nelson, Allen and McParland and featured a worldly-wise woman in a developing country, cynical and ironic about the ways of men, her government and the international community. It deserved greater success than it had, but Deutsche Presse Agentur marketed it expensively for Gemini, so that it was cheaper to take the American *Peanuts* strip than *Didi*, which petered out.

McParland was an example of the added value provided by the IDRC connection. He followed Jane Taber, with a project to visit Kenya and Zimbabwe. 'Gemini's effect as far as I was concerned was to vastly expand my horizons and my awareness (if not understanding) of the world's complexities. When the year of my fellowship was up the last thing I wanted to do was return to the self-absorbed world of the *Toronto Star* newsroom.

---

34. Interview, Daniel Nelson.

35. Interview, Paddy Allen.

When Derek and Daniel offered the opportunity to stay I didn't hesitate, and ultimately stayed for four years'.[36]

His presence in London was helpful to other young Canadians who were passing through, and he also threw himself into the training and educational projects which were supported by international funders. One of the most interesting was the Village Reporting project, first backed by CIDA, and later by Swedish SIDA and Britain's ODA. This was an attempt to recognise the reality that so many people in the South live in rural communities, with needs, stories and interests of their own which are often ignored by media based in their capitals, let alone international opinion.

Gemini obtained finance for a scheme under which local journalists were paid for up to three months to live in one village. More than 15 reporters in almost a dozen countries, ranging from India and Sri Lanka to Fiji and Lesotho, took part. Shyamala Nataraj, an Indian who spent two months in a village in Tamil Nadu, found it, 'one of the most rewarding experiences I've ever had. I've enjoyed myself tremendously, learned so much about my country and my people that I would have been totally blind to otherwise, and came away feeling so emotional about the whole thing that I waited to just let that first wave subside before I did any writing'.[37]

McParland edited their copy and a training manual, *Views from the Village*, which was filled with practical advice on making stories more interesting, treating statistics with discretion, and putting the focus on the human and the village rather than the national or international agencies.

Elizabeth Pritchard was general manager from 1981 until 1988, when she was succeeded by a highly experienced Nigerian newspaper manager, Bethel Njoku. Pritchard, who was Swedish, also epitomized the subtle change of direction of the 1980s. She had been involved in the international campaign for breastfeeding and against the heavy promotion of proprietary baby foods in developing countries. She had met Nelson over that. She was therefore more of an activist than a publisher when she was recruited. She was put in touch with Gemini by James Porter, for she had worked at UNICEF with Julia Spry-Leverton, who had gone on to become head of public relations at the Commonwealth Institute.

She was responsible for switching from Gestetner to photocopying, for helping move Gemini from Fleet Street to the basement of *The Guardian* offices in Farringdon Road, and for the introduction of computers in the office. (She had a good sense of humour, too – sending messages from herself 'and Fred the computer'.) She, like Nelson, was positive about the educational work required by Gemini's new regime and, with Ingram, provided an interface with the trustees of the NewsConcern foundation.

But she said later that she had never lost so much sleep as when she was at Gemini, even when her baby was a two-year-old. (She left when she was pregnant, coming back for a while on a part-time basis.) There were months when she was not sure whether the income would be enough to pay the staff or correspondents, and when she and Ingram had to make

---

36. Kelly McParland, letter to author, 25 February 1994.

37. *Views from the Village*, edited by McParland, published by Gemini News Service, p. 31.

difficult calls on the bank. Worry over money caused a temporary rift with her own sister-in-law, Jenny Ridley, a trained nurse who became a graphic artist at Gemini. There were anxieties over new competition – Compass, a news feature agency backed by the Aga Khan, which sought to poach Gemini correspondents but which fizzled out during the 1990 Gulf crisis. Compass caused a lot of bitterness, because Gemini felt that its approach and methods had been devised with the benefit of a Gemini funding application to the Aga Khan Foundation.

Pritchard paid tribute to Ingram's coolness during every crisis, and concluded that Gemini was the kind of bootstrap operation which would survive a recession, but which could come to look outdated in a boom.[38] One of the difficulties during the 1980s was that while Africa was in economic decline, Britain and Canada were enjoying a boom.

Following the restart in 1983 Gemini came to seem more international in two ways, both in its London office and in its governance by NewsConcern. In the mid-80s in London there were always at least two Canadians (McParland and the IDRC fellow) and for three months a third, a young journalism graduate from Regina; there was the Swedish Pritchard and the Nigerian Njoku (who had held senior posts with Shell and the *Nigerian Daily Times*, but fallen foul of politics in Lagos); and there was a an Indian typist, Ajaib Singh, who was cheered when he arrived one morning having put his Sikh turban on again in a gesture of return to his roots.

The NewsConcern governors, who had meetings in Cyprus and Vancouver as well as in London, brought a new factor into Gemini's affairs. Ingram tended to see them as chiefly a source of funding, reporting to them on the latest financial need. They, however, were positively attracted to the project side of education and training while still keen to support the basic news service, and to prevent it from being distorted into providing copy for UN agencies or other funders. In part their interest in project work – and by the late 80s Gemini was running at least two training seminars a year in the developing world as well as a science writing initiative – arose because of their talks with funders. As Trevor McDonald of ITN commented, 'We found that Gemini was not exactly the package they wanted'.[39]

There was a lack of clarity about the role of the governors, who felt that their creative ideas were not always followed up by the overstretched Gemini office. Porter, the first chairman, handed over to McDonald, who handed the chair back to Porter again in 1993 when his ITN duties became too onerous. The staff, however, felt it was unfortunate that the governing body did not contain more businessmen, or persons with relevant newspaper management experience. Porter, who found that chairing could be wearing, considered that the most productive meeting was the one in Vancouver in 1987 which did, incidentally, result in an increase in funding from Canadian sources.[40]

The drumbeat of financial anxiety never ceased. In a letter to Pritchard of 25 September 1987, concerning the accounts for 1986–87, the accountants warned that grant income was

---

38. Interview, Elizabeth Pritchard.

39. Interview, Trevor McDonald.

40. Interview, James Porter.

Fig. 7. Derek Ingram's annual year end reviews were widely used and usually embellished with a montage illustration. This, from December 1986, was by Paddy Allen.

still £20,000 short of expenditure and the company was technically insolvent to the tune of £36,000. It was only able to continue trading thanks to the generosity of creditors who were witholding demands for payment, and the directors were personally liable.[41]

But what became clear during 1988, when News-Scan International (Gemini's name for accounting purposes) recorded a surplus of £11,147, was that the strategy of project grants and support for distribution of the service could work. In that year, when there was a steep rise in grant income because of the rural reporting initiative, income from grants at £77,316 outstripped income from the sale of news features. This continued to be the case until 1992, when income from news features (£95,469) was narrowly greater than grants (£95,076) following the end of the Cold War, and a jump in the use of Gemini in east European countries.

Viability was won thanks also to the most rigorous cost control. For instance, when Pritchard left Gemini, Njoku took on her job as well. His own was never replaced, and he came into the office seven days a week for several months. The saving on the post was about equal to News-Scan's first surplus. By 1993 a standard contributor's payment for an article was £60 which, though it might be a month's salary for a professor in Nigeria, was about half the going rate for a piece of 800 to 1200 words in a developed country.

The governors of NewsConcern were, nonetheless, worried about the long-term future of Gemini. They had not succeeded in their aim of winning core funding for the foundation.

---

41. Letter, Alan Walker & Co. to Elizabeth Pritchard, 25 September 1987.

The team of Nelson, Pritchard and McParland, built up around Ingram, was dispersing. As early as 1985–86, with the service running regularly again, Ingram had been hinting that he would like to move on and do other things. It had seemed so very much his baby that there was a fear that it might not be possible to run it on the same basis without him.

It was against this background that the governors – particularly McDonald as chairman – became heavily involved in a proposal to link Gemini with the Panos Institute, an environmental research and information body based in London. This occupied much time for both parties in 1989 and, though it finally veered away from any formal connection, had the useful result for Gemini of providing new office space with Panos in Islington, and a profitable deal to run the Panos Features service under contract. Yet this was still a crisis for Gemini, even if it was less serious than those of 1971–72 or 1982–83; for there is no doubt that Ingram saw the deal as potentially fatal to the news service.

Panos had a staff of 35, and offices in New York, Paris and Budapest as well as London. It had been built up by Jon Tinker, an energetic former *New Scientist* journalist, who had a flair for designing large-scale projects and raising substantial donor funds to pay for them. He was younger than Ingram, had better personal contacts in the world of international donor agencies, and was riding hard the fashionable interest in environment and development. In personal terms he was regarded by McDonald as tigerish, and rather different from the gentlemanly Ingram for whom the news values of independence, objectivity and accuracy remained all-important.

The idea for the link came from Nelson, who had moved to Panos to run a new east European operation there, but had ended up getting drawn back into editorial work. As Tinker put it, 'His concept was simple: Panos was good at raising money, Gemini wasn't. Derek wanted to retire, but didn't want to let go of Gemini. Gemini was as usual on the verge of bankruptcy for a few tens of thousands a year. Panos and Gemini both ran features services. Why not put them together, and make the whole more than the sum of the parts? Danny persuaded me that the concept had merit, and asked me to discuss it with Derek'.[42]

From the Panos side it was a frustrating period, for the short-term pressures on Gemini made it difficult for it to prepare the papers and budgets that the larger organization was used to. Gradually, however, the discussion moved from a merger to a joint venture: Panos and Gemini were to form a joint subsidiary to operate both feature services, with a common staff, controlled by a joint board which Ingram would chair. However that too fell through and the features contract and tenancy in Islington were all that survived. A key stumbling-block was that, in spite of all the hopes, no new money had ever been guaranteed.

What did Ingram have against the Panos deal? In a memo to directors and UK governors of NewsConcern he wrote, 'The central question for Gemini is whether the tie-up is going to impede the independence and integrity of the news service that is so respected and without which it would not long survive (and without which I would certainly not want to be associated with it)'.[43]

42. Jon Tinker letter to author, 26 April 1994.

43. Ingram Archive.

Fig. 8. Christmas party, 1991, right to let: John Ogen, Dupe Owodunni, Bethel Njoku, Derek Ingram, Tom Aston, Jim Peet, a friend, Alan Thompson.

Ingram's unhappiness was fundamental, and gradually communicated itself to the governors and funding agencies. It was both institutional and personal. He was worried that a Gemini link with a body which he saw as campaigning rather than journalistic could impugn the news service's reputation. He was worried too that acceptance of funds from some governments would be harmful (even though by then Gemini itself had been indirectly funded by the Canadian and Swedish governments). He feared that, because of the differences in size, almost any deal would amount in time to a takeover by Panos. And, although he blew hot and cold over his personal plans, he felt that the outlines prepared by Panos at one point ignored his own need for a salary.

In the end Tinker concluded that he had wasted 18 months, and that he had misread Ingram's intentions:

> Looking back on it all, it's one of those tantalizing might-have-beens. The joint venture was a good scheme that could have put Gemini on a sound financial footing once and for all, and enabled it to expand considerably. But Derek only pretended to be interested, and sabotaged any fundraising by studied indifference to donors ... I should have sussed this out far sooner than I did. And, on the Panos side, almost all my colleagues came to regard the Gemini link as a personal enthusiasm of mine in which I gave one concession after another to Gemini, and which diverted me from my proper task of running Panos and raising money for our own activities.[44]

Fig. 9. Gemini Fellows at the 1992 Regina conference on Reporting the Developing World after the Cold War. Back row, Jill Forrester, Elaine Shein (*Western Producer*, Saskatoon), Brenda Kossowan (*Red Deer Advocate*), Allan Thompson (*Toronto Star*), Teresa Mazzitelli (*Family Physician*, Toronto), Tina Spencer (*Ottawa Citizen*), Scott Simmie (CBC), Marcus Schwabe (CBC), Darren Foster, Rick Boychuk. Front row: Stefani Langenegger (Canadian Press), Gavin Wilson. Others in the picture include extreme left, Bethel Njoku and extreme right, Derek Ingram and front left Louise Behan of the International Development Research Centre, Ottawa.

It was a strange episode. It reflected a period of low morale at Gemini (which had just celebrated its 20th birthday with appropriate fanfare in 1987), as well as the altered image of the agency. If in the late 1960s it had been seen as a Commonwealth news features agency, by the late 1980s it was regarded more as a journalistic service about development. Even some of the NewsConcern governors, including McDonald, saw no obvious incompatibility in Gemini linking with an environment and development body. There was also a feeling that Ingram, who had always hoped that Nelson would be his successor, was still exploring that option even though Nelson had joined Panos.

The slightly sour upshot of all the talking was that Gemini provided Panos with features in a grudging manner, seeking to maximize a financial return rather than to lay the basis for a new partnership. However the new offices were an improvement on *The Guardian*'s basement and, under Njoku's careful stewardship, the finances of the agency began to

---

44. John Tinker, letter, *ibid.*

look a little healthier. There was a regular upward adjustment in subscriptions and an important growth in users in eastern Europe.

The end of the Cold War freed up media in the former Soviet bloc, and papers from Bulgaria to the Baltic republics started subscribing to Gemini via DPA. In spite of the former propaganda of international solidarity, and the real economic similarities between east European and developing countries, the east European publics wished to identify with western Europe and reacted to the South with disdain. At the same time, however, their editors were attracted to a low-cost, low-technology service.

In fact Gemini also experimented with Presslink, a computerized service for distributing its feature packages. Unfortunately Presslink tended to deliver to art editors rather than news or features editors – this was the way Presslink was organized. It therefore did not solve the problem of restoring the service's competitive edge in developed markets which looked askance at mail delivery as old-fashioned. In the United Arab Emirates, nevertheless, it led to the loss of one account when a rival paper started downloading from Presslink. Other electronic distribution systems could be uneconomic for a service which usually distributed only twelve articles a week. (By 1994 Gemini was using GreenNet for receiving and sending messages.)

Although Gemini was unique in content and approach its penetration in developed countries in the 1980s, which could easily afford subscriptions on a commercial basis, was not high. This was partly because newspaper owners were keen to squeeze more profit and saw foreign news as expensive and not interesting to the bulk of readers; development issues and a Southern perspective were often unpopular in the North, and the Gemini output was relatively small. The service also had its share of bad luck. In Britain, for instance, it had terminated agreements with several provincial papers in order to give an exclusive and lucrative contract to the new paper, *Today*, which was launched in March 1986. But *Today* changed direction, and never made much use of Gemini.

In the 1990s the Gemini operation, so long on a knife-edge, could still not be described as secure. Elizabeth Pritchard commented that although she was surprised that it had completed 20 years, she was not quite so surprised that it had reached 25. But its basic approach of using resident journalists in developing countries had not changed. As one of the commemorative articles put it in 1987:[45]

> It is a fundamental precept at Gemini and one that has allowed it to avoid the pitfalls associated with sending flying squads of reporters into distant and unfamiliar surroundings. Rather than reporting Third World disasters and coups solely from a Western viewpoint, most Gemini correspondents are from the region they are writing about, providing a continuing and topical perspective of the countries they know best.

In December 1993 Ingram, so much the architect, finally stepped down as editor though he remained company chairman and agreed to carry on contributing. He had just been to his 13th Commonwealth summit conference and produced his usual stream of copy. His

---

45. From Gemini folder, *Celebrating 20 Years.*

trip to Limassol in October 1993 was actually his third visit to Cyprus, his original inspiration on Commonwealth matters, in one year: he had also attended the Commonwealth Parliamentary Association conference and a meeting of the Advisory Commission of the Commonwealth Human Rights Initiative, which was followed immediately by a meeting of Commonwealth Ministers responsible for Women's Affairs. But even with his stamina, time was marching on: he was in sight of his 69th birthday.

With his encouragement the NewsConcern governors appointed Nelson as his successor. Although Nelson had been bitter at the way in which the Panos deal had broken down – at one point at Panos he cancelled the features supply arrangement because he felt Gemini was not taking it seriously – the two former colleagues had made up their differences. For several years Nelson had been heir apparent, if only Ingram was satisfied that he himself could let go. The timing was now right for Nelson, one of nature's wanderers, to put down anchor. After leaving Panos he had freelanced around the world – he had helped run an unofficial newspaper at the Rio Earth Summit in 1992 – and had latterly had a stint in New Delhi. But for him too an awesome birthday was coming up, in his case a 50th. The offer of the editorship of Gemini, with all the risks entailed, was something he wanted to take.

It was clear that Nelson brought great gifts and experience of the developing world to the post. He would be more comfortable with the project funding and educational work than Ingram, and less interested in the Commonwealth as such. But otherwise it was hard to imagine a journalist more imbued with the spirit of Gemini. He typified the loyalty engendered by this small organization. As Ingram had written in his memo about the abortive Panos link-up, 'The paradox is that Gemini is tiny in staff (maximum 8) and big in spread and influence and reputation'.[46] Its story deserves to be told.

---

46. Ingram Archive, *ibid*.

2 Exclusives

E very newspaper and broadcasting station likes to have stories ahead of its rivals –
stories that others feel obliged to follow up, and which give readers or listeners the
privileged feeling that they learned it first. For a few of Gemini's customers,
working as a monopoly, this attraction was not so important. However for most, particularly as journalistic competition intensified around the world, a Gemini report which could
genuinely be described as exclusive, on a topic of widespread interest, was almost
guaranteed publication.

Over the years Gemini has published a number of 'hot' exclusives. For an agency which
depends so heavily on postal delivery, such stories are not easy to find. Retaining such
exclusivity can be even more difficult. Competing international news agencies, CNN and
World Service TV, have electronic immediacy on their side. Indeed Gemini has, in general,
established its niche by writing to a different agenda, and by taking a more considered or
lateral approach to news.

Nonetheless, in the first of a representative selection of reports put out by Gemini over the
years, it is worth quoting from those which were exclusive at the time. What is noticeable
is that many of them have a 'first person' quality: that is to say they are exclusive because
the Gemini correspondent was an integral part of the story. The italic introduction is
provided for the present book, although every report originally included its own 'stand-
first'. Each article is unabridged here, and appears as it was originally sent out.

Millions are on the run as Federals break through

by Richard Hall
São Tomé

*Described as 'a scoop for Gemini News Service' in the UK Press Gazette of 19 January
1970 this report was the agency's best-known exclusive in the early years. Hall's by-lined
reports appeared in* The Sunday Times, The Observer, The Guardian, The Sun *and*
Evening Standard *in Britain, as well as in papers around the world. The catastrophic
starvation he foresaw was limited by Federal and international action and, after a period
in exile, General Ojukwu returned to Nigeria. (11 January 1971 – GN 327)*

Biafra is dying bloodily and terror stricken. The triumphant Nigerian Army
is advancing into the chaotic heart of Ojukwu's breakaway country. The

demoralized Biafran Army has been stunned by the *blitzkrieg* onslaught mounted by the Federal forces and is now offering little resistance and fleeing.

Five million civilians are running rabbit-like from the remaining crowded areas. Several Nigerian MiG fighters added to the confusion by rocketing and machine-gunning lines of refugees.

Amid the crowds were wounded and shell-shocked Biafran soldiers. Artillery is thundering around the collapsing Biafran perimeter.

On Saturday night I was the last journalist out of Biafra. Uli airport had twice been bombed.

Relief workers of many nationalities are being urgently evacuated to São Tomé and Libreville.

Many more are coming tonight, but some, including Irish priests and nuns, have decided to stay to attend the overflowing hospitals and starving refugees.

During the inevitable overrun of Biafra their lives lie in the balance. Relief planes are still going in and pilots have been asking me how far the Biafrans are now from Uli. They fear being hit by Nigerian bullets on landing.

As I left, Owerri was being shelled and rocketed. It is now a ghost town, yet on Thursday night it contained some quarter of a million people.

As I went north – the only foreign correspondent left inside Biafra – I saw appalling sights of Biafra's death throes. They are burned in my memory: men, women and children carrying pathetic belongings, some collapsing weeping at the roadside. There is nowhere for them to go.

The Nigerian breakthrough came on Thursday with amazing speed ten miles south east to Owerri. Till then Biafra's fragile defences were standing firm and a brave normality continued in Owerri.

But the Saladin and Ferret armoured vehicles raced through a gap punched by heavy artillery, along with several battalions of crack Nigerian troops.

Biafrans have mostly not eaten for three days and took flight leaving their officers.

As I left, the town was being bombarded and MiGs, like deadly paper darts, were swooping overhead. Owerri fell last night. Federal troops will race up the main road towards Uli airport.

On Friday Ojukwu visited a hospital where 700 badly wounded soldiers were lying. He looked haggard and dazed.

It is likely that Biafran leaders and senior army officers will kill themselves with pistols or poison before Federals get to them. But the five million ordinary people inside the closing Federal net wait bewildered. They ask you constantly: 'how can we survive?'

Devout Christians, they speak repeatedly of God. 'God will help us,' they say.

Educated Biafrans feel they have little hope at the hands of the enemy. They have seen too much pain already.

Among simple villagers they sense doom in the humid air. All normal human behaviour is collapsing. Women are abandoning their babies. Soldiers are going berserk. Before I escaped I saw scenes I shall never forget.

In the coming catastrophe hundreds of thousands will die of mass starvation. This must be faced by the world.

A skeleton staff of relief workers are staying inside Biafra at great risk, but their organization cannot help. Whole districts are now isolated.

Almost everybody in Biafra is in some stage of starvation and it is likely that unless the speediest help is organized the country will be littered with the dead by the month's end. The Nigerians will certainly not cope with the consequences of their own military success. It may take two months to restart relief.

But then it may be too late for millions of men, women and children. From what I have seen this is hard reality and fully confirmed by doctors flying out.

It is also imperative that a military observer force be placed in the Biafra heart land. Otherwise there is a prospect that the trigger-happy victors will reap a terrible harvest.

The way events are moving to a last climax must mean that Biafra will cease to exist within a week, except in the hearts of the survivors.

The time is one for weeping in Biafra, yet Ojukwu is still revered in the country, which has learnt at a dreadful price that courage cannot beat unlimited guns, planes and armoured cars.

Also the Biafran soldiers have collapsed through sheer hunger. Their discipline has gone at last, but the world powers, especially Britain, must act urgently to save the terrified millions from death by hunger or bullets.

The next week will be the ultimate test of Britain's influence in Lagos.

The day I had a knife at my back: hijacked hostess tells her story

by Liz Wrigley
Port-of-Spain

Liz Wrigley had been an air hostess for BWIA for two years when her flight was hijacked to Cuba. The naïve immediacy of the account, from someone who was not a professional journalist, makes this incident – one in a world-wide explosion of air piracy – come alive to readers. Certain attitudes and expressions (such as the description of one of the hijackers as 'a Negro') now seem dated. The article was supplied with an alternative heading: 'So This Is What It's Like To Be Hijacked'. (11 December 1970 – GG 2010/5)

It's an odd feeling, to put it mildly, when you suddenly realize that somebody behind you has stuck a knife in your neck.

I got this feeling when I was looking after the first class cabin of the Boeing 727 on British West Indian Airways Flight 400 from Kingston, Jamaica, to Miami via the Cayman Islands.

Or, rather, I should say when you suddenly realize that the prickly feeling in the back of your neck is caused by the point of a knife held there by somebody who has no friendly motive.

I had turned round expecting to see a familiar face – one of the other girls maybe, or a passenger I knew – but, no. There was a total stranger, about five feet nine, light brown skin and an odd eye which stuck out and had a film over it.

He must, I thought, have come from the second class; otherwise I must have seen him. I thought he looked drugged and this scared me because I was afraid he might do something crazy.

And then also I thought about the recent Black Power troubles, violence and riots, which we had been having in Trinidad where I live. But I knew, whoever it was, that he meant business, and I suppose I was frightened.

'If you don't want trouble,' said the man, 'take me into the cockpit'. We were actually standing not far from the cockpit door and, as I opened it, another fellow, a Negro, came up with a gun in his hand.

This one stayed outside as we went into the cockpit with his gun covering the passengers who knew by now – that is the first class, not the economy, that this was a hijack.

The captain, an Australian, Keith Melville, also knew that there was something wrong because the chief hostess, Jennie Selman, had given the pre-arranged alarm signal, three short buzzes on the galley buzzer.

'Change course for Paris,' the man said; just like that. The captain turned to him and said this was impossible in a 727 and, besides, they only had enough fuel for four hours flight.

'Okay, go to Cuba to refuel. Don't talk to Jamaica'. The man seemed as nervous as I was; and the other man standing just outside the open cockpit door looked terribly tense.

So we made a wide sweep around to the north and headed for Cuba. Incidentally, I discovered afterwards that an Air Jamaica 707 saw us go down to Havana and told the BWIA people in Miami that it looked as though one of their planes had been hijacked.

The man with the knife led me out of the cockpit and made me sit in a passenger seat while he and his pal alternated between the first class and the cockpit. Even now I don't think the economy class passengers knew what was going on though they must have been surprised that it took so long to get to Grand Cayman.

About an hour after that knife was stuck in my neck the seat lights came on and I could see we were over Havana but apparently, we were no longer in flight BW400. 'This flight', said the number one hijacker over the intercom, 'is now known as AAF1 for Afro-American Freedom Fighters Flight One to Havana'.

I think the captain had some difficulty in finding the airport because we seemed to be turning and banking quite a bit. The Cuban landscape looked beautifully green.

The other four hostesses had been ordered, after the hijackers' announcement, to sit in the back of the economy compartment and I had no contact with them.

We made a perfect landing and taxied to the terminal. Steps were brought up to the front door and some armed Cubans started to come up. The hijackers told them to go away or the aircraft would be blown up and they told the captain to tell the tower to order the soldiers to stay away.

So the armed Cubans went and stood about round the plane. I was told afterwards that they wanted to take a pot at the hijackers from the ground, but the captain said No.

Refuelling started and the engineer was allowed to leave the aircraft to supervise this. Meanwhile the hijackers went on arguing with the captain. They said they wanted to go to Algiers and the captain, I think it was, suggested flying via Surinam or French Guyana and Senegal. And the funny thing was that Trinidad, where BWIA has its headquarters, must have been told about this because I was told afterwards that arrangements had been made to send a new crew and the necessary charts to Guyana.

All this discussion seemed to take hours. Eventually, after about four hours on the ground, two of the hostesses were allowed to serve soft drinks to the passengers and some food to the children on board.

On the whole everybody was very calm. I heard one man say: 'Trust in God and everything will be all right'. Quite a lot of passengers slept and even I dozed a bit. Smoking was eventually allowed.

Then, some time between 10.30 and 11.00 the endless talk in the cockpit came to an end. Apparently the captain had suddenly – and conveniently – discovered an oil gauge which showed that one of the fuel tanks was leaking. He said there was no hope of getting to Algiers, even with refuelling stops. (Actually the gauge was faulty, not the tank).

The hijackers, convinced at last that there was no chance of getting to Algiers, agreed to accept asylum in Cuba. They opened the rear door and lowered the stairs and two Cubans in khaki uniforms, bristling with guns, came on board and led the hijackers off. What amazed me was the Cubans' obvious lack of sympathy for the two men.

Then the captain came out of the cockpit and walked down the centre. 'We've been through a bit of trouble', he said, 'but it's all over now. We've been invited to have a meal and spend the night in Havana and we'll take off for Miami early in the morning'.

You could almost *feel* the relief of the passengers as they began disembarking from the aircraft. Then the security people came and talked to the crew and we all talked to the press. Our passports were examined (mine is British and so is the captain's) and I was terrified they would stamp it and so make it difficult for me to enter the USA again; but all was well.

Then we joined the passengers in the restaurant and, as he walked in, the captain was applauded. Good for him, I felt.

We had soup, steak and chips, and a sort of cake for dessert. It was well prepared and the waiters, considering it was now past midnight, were incredibly amiable; they literally beamed as they brought drinks to the passengers; and afterwards cigars and cigarettes were distributed free.

A drive of about thirty minutes in a bus took us to the Hotel Riviera in Havana. It looked enormous and I believe it was formerly the Hilton; chandeliers, marble, creeping plants – that sort of thing, all beautifully kept.

At the reception desk they couldn't have been nicer and made every effort to put the married couples together in the same room. We saw no other guests in the hotel that night.

I shared a room with three of the other girls and I suppose we got to bed about one thirty, having been up since about six that morning. I remember the bellboy was very proud to show us that we could not only get hot water from the tap, but also ice-cold water. I have never seen this in any other hotel in the world.

In contrast to the downstairs the bedroom was shabby: carpets thin and worn, the lining of the curtains torn, dim lighting, a TV set which didn't work and an air-conditioner which didn't work either. The room smelt as though it hadn't been used for ages and it wasn't any too clean.

We were woken up about eight o'clock with a message from the captain to come down in our uniforms. We were conducted to a small restaurant on, I suppose, about the tenth floor and together with the passengers, were given ham and eggs and excellent coffee. The service was first class and the waiters were smartly dressed in white coats. Once again, free cigars, cigarettes and matches were handed out.

The captain then told me that, instead of going back to the airport immediately after breakfast, we had been invited to a special lunch. The girls asked if they could take a stroll around the town, but they were told No.

A couple of us did, however, leave the building and stroll along and sit on the sea wall across the road opposite the hotel. Fellows started whistling and things like that, so we went back inside.

One passenger couple told me that their camera had been taken away from them, the film removed and then returned.

Before lunch I noticed that some of the immigration, or security, people who had met us at the airport in uniform had now come to the hotel in civilian clothes and one of them took Jennie and me to the bar for a drink – needless to say Cuba Libres.

He was a charming fellow and started telling us about the fine things in Castro's Cuba. There was, he said, no prostitution; transport was virtually free and you could go from one end of Cuba to the other for about ten cents; birth control was not necessary because more people were needed to work.

His wife, he said, taught French at the University and he said he had been married three times. Why didn't we stay another night? There was a special cabaret show that evening at the hotel.

It was all very pleasant and Jennie and I both enjoyed the hour or so we spent at the bar.

Then it was time for lunch and we went back up to the same room where we had breakfast. All the passengers and several of the security-cum-immigration people were there. It was an excellent meal – a fish dish to begin with and a savoury meat dish to follow, plus all the wine you wanted (not for the crew because we were flying soon), coffee, and more cigars and cigarettes.

We had become quite friendly with the waiters and when we left to get into the bus it was all 'Goodbye, come again, hope you enjoyed it, nice having you', and so on; and all seemed absolutely genuine.

The drive back to the airport gave me my first proper impression of Havana and it seemed to me to be rather drab-looking. Most of the buildings seemed to need a coat of paint; there didn't seem to be much in the way of decorative and colourful flowers, which surprised me – just bits of grass here and there. The people in the streets looked dull; there was nothing exciting; a few ancient American cars, and the bus, which had hard seats, rattled a lot.

When we got to the airport there was a delay of about two hours before the passengers came on board. The aircraft, however, had been cleaned and some smiling and friendly airport employees brought crates of soft drinks on board.

Not long after we were airborne we started dumping most of the fuel which we had acquired – and presumably paid for in Cuba, because the flight was less than an hour and it is better not to land with all the unnecessary weight.

The Federal Aviation people and the FBI were waiting for us at Miami and the crew were questioned about the whole episode for about two hours, particularly the captain. They let the passengers go.

Then to our hotel and back the following evening to Trinidad as super-crew.

On thinking the whole thing over, two things in particular come to mind. The first is that we were treated well and liked because we were not American – mostly West Indians, Canadians, British and a couple of people from SAS – Scandinavian Airlines System. I think everybody spoke English. I hate to think what might have happened if we had had any Americans on board.

The other thing was that I gathered BWIA had to pay quite a tidy sum – US$25,000, it was said, though I have no confirmation of this, before the Cubans would release the aircraft. This amount, apparently, was about a third of what an American airline would have to pay to get a hijacked aircraft out of Cuba.

In other words the Castro government must be earning quite a tidy sum each year from hijackings.

How Goering cheated the hangman – the inside story

by Desmond Zwar

Only 26 years after the end of the Second World War the question of how Goering committed suicide after his Nuremberg trial for war crimes was still of widespread interest. Desmond Zwar, an Australian, had been a colleague of Ingram's on the Daily Mail. *This report illustrates how Gemini could get desirable material through the journalistic sleuthing of its contributors. (19 October 1971 – GG 3089)*

Just 25 years ago, Nazi leader Hermann Goering swallowed cyanide in his Nuremberg cell and died. He cheated the hangman he was due to face in 60 minutes.

How could a prisoner – perhaps the most notorious of all at the War Crimes trial – get access to poison and take it when he was being scrutinized by guards 24 hours a day? Dismayed by the scandal in the most massively-guarded prison in the world, the Quadripartite Commission, representing the four Great Powers, set to work to find out.

Goering had been searched with the others before every court session, and after it when he changed again into prison clothes. While he was in court his cell had been minutely gone over. How was it possible for the man to hide a vial of cyanide? Whatever the inquiry found they revealed little to the outside world – except to say that Goering certainly had hidden the poison at times on himself, and at times in his cell toilet.

After the trial, and for the next 20 years, men associated with the prison wrote books and articles claiming they knew how he had obtained the means of cheating the hangman's noose. Even Frau Emmy Goering, his wife, wrote her theories. Some said he had had the cyanide smuggled in, hidden inside the massive Meerschaum pipe he had sent out for repair. Others alleged that Frau Emmy had passed it to him when she kissed him goodbye.

But nobody offered proof of what they were saying.

Twenty years after Goering's suicide I found the one man who should have known: Colonel Burton C. Andrus, former Commandant of Nuremberg Prison during the International Military Tribunal that tried the Nazis.

'How did Goering keep the poison hidden'? I asked him. Col. Andrus, then 74, and with a tough, leathery face looked at me sternly: 'I have no idea'.

Colonel Andrus admitted he had run to Goering's cell and arrived two minutes after the warden had given the alarm. But by then Goering was dead. He said: 'The blankets had been dragged from him exposing black, silk pyjama trousers; his toes were curling down towards the soles of his feet. One arm, in a pale-coloured pyjama jacket, with blue spots, hung down. His eyes were shut. One of the guards – or Chaplain Gerecke, who had arrived at about the same time – handed me a single folded piece of paper which had been on Goering's bunk. It was addressed to me. I did not read it. I took it straight to the office of the Quadripartite Commission and they began the suicide investigation. I never read that letter. I was never told what was in it'.

His military honesty and his desire for impartiality in an affair that directly concerned his running of the prison prevented him reading what Hitler's henchman had scrawled. The world was left wondering about the most fantastic suicide of the century.

Col. Andrus had brought with him from Nuremberg, to his home in Tacoma, Wash., USA, several crates of papers and documents. They included letters from Goering and Keitel to Eisenhower, and the replies. There were complaints about the food, suicide notes from two of the prisoners, discussions on guarding the prison: but no clue to Goering's suicide. Together we began a search which took us through wartime records, military museums and national archives.

'The Quadripartite Commission would have the letter', said Col. Andrus, 'but it no longer exists'. He would have been interested now to read it, but he was ready to give up.

At the Imperial War Museum in London I made an astonishing discovery. Masses of fascinating war documents lay gathering dust, still stamped with the word *Classified*, when in fact what they revealed was of no further possible use to an enemy. Why were they not released to the world? 'Because that requires a declassification board', a curator told me. 'And there isn't one. It was disbanded'.

Finally, when I was ready also to give up, a letter arrived from the General Services Administration, National Archives and Records Service, in Washington. It enclosed a photo-copy of 'exhibit AM', from the Report of the Board's Proceedings in the Case of Hermann Goering (Suicide). It was the missing link.

Goering had written: 'To the Commandant: I have always had the capsule of poison with me from the time that I became a prisoner. When taken to Mondorf (the interrogation centre) I had *three* capsules. The *first* I left in my clothes so that it would be found when a search was made. The *second* I placed under the clothes-rack on undressing and took it to me again on dressing. I hid this in Mondorf and here in the cell so well that despite the frequent and thorough searches it could not be found.

'During the court sessions I hid it on my person and in my high riding boots. The *third* capsule is still in my small suitcase in the round box of skin cream, hidden in the cream. I could have taken this to me twice in Mondorf if I had needed it. None of those charged with searching is to be blamed, for it was practically impossible to find the capsule. It would have been *pure accident*.

'Dr Gilbert informed me that the control board has refused the petition to change the method of execution to shooting'. (Signed) Hermann Goering.

Goering, said the Report of the Proceedings, admitted in other notes to his wife, and to the German people – none of which were released – that he had secreted the vial of cyanide at times in his anus, at times under the rim of his cell toilet bowl, and at times in his navel. He had switched it from one hiding-place to the other – and into his boot during the court proceedings – without ever being seen. After the inquiry the War Department said no blame could be attached to any prison official.

Herman Goering, right to the end, had been too cunning for them all ...

Questions still unanswered in the curious case of 'Super' Khan

by John Beasant
Hong Kong

There have been periodic scandals in the Hong Kong police. Here, because of the direct involvement of a trusted and regular Gemini correspondent, the agency was able to put out a detailed 'special report' on a mysterious case of official harassment. Gemini's role in publicizing stories which are not made known in their countries of origin is emphasized by Beasant's concluding paragraphs, where he states that the climbdown by the authorities was never reported locally. (31 March 1987 – GS 4306)

For the reputation of the Hong Kong press, the sequence of events could not have been more unfortunate. On 11th March the colony's Legislative Council passed into law the Public Order (Amendment) Bill, which makes it an offence to publish 'false news' that in the opinion of the authorities is 'likely to cause alarm to the public'. The legislation carries a fine of $13000 and two years imprisonment.

Just two days later Hong Kong's most influential English-language paper, the South China Morning Post, destroyed 120,000 copies of its Saturday Review, which contained as its lead story my account of a seven-year legal battle by a former Superintendent of Police in the Hong Kong Auxiliaries to clear his name, following his summary dismissal from the force in 1978.

The eleventh-hour decision to destroy the copies was taken on the advice of lawyers, who had earlier approved the article. The lawyers say they changed their minds after seeing the headline, Rough Justice, and the introduction, which read in part: 'It is a story that poses disturbing questions about the conduct of many in positions of authority'.

Coming so soon after the 'Press gag bill' there are few who believe the explanation.

Suspicions were fuelled when the article later appeared under the anodyne headline, The Yacub Khan Case, minus the introduction and with pivotal references to the role played by the present Deputy Commissioner of Police, Eric Blackburn, pointedly removed.

Such suspicions were compounded by the few copies of the original article which reached the streets, enabling comparisons. Copies of the original, it is reliably reported, now change hands for up to $100.

Yacub Khan, a Pakistani born in Hong Kong in 1930, joined the colony's Auxiliary Police Force in 1952 and served with particular distinction during the long hot summer of 1967 when the turmoil generated by China's Cultural Revolution swept across the border into the colony.

The following year he was awarded the prestigious Colonial Special Constabulary Medal and shortly after that became a gazetted officer with the rank of assistant superintendent.

Yet within two years he was officially in disgrace and his career in the Auxiliaries, to which he attached much importance, was on the verge of ruin.

His long ordeal began in August 1970 when he was put into reserve. No reason was given although Khan wrote some 65 letters to Police Headquarters asking for a valid explanation; they were not even acknowledged.

In April 1971 however, he was reinstated following the action of a senior colleague, Chief Superintendent John Grieve (now retired in Scotland). Grieve dismissed as without substance three disciplinary charges that the police wanted to bring against Khan, an opinion that was endorsed by the government's Legal Department.

However, within two months he was again returned to the reserve, again with no explanation. The officer who took the action was never made known to him. Soon after, he was requested to return his uniform and equipment, on the grounds that he had been in reserve too long to keep them. Within days his mother's house was raided and his uniform and equipment removed, although the raid was carried out without the necessary warrant.

Again Chief Superintendent Grieve intervened, ordering that Khan's uniform be returned to him. But there was more to come, particularly after Grieve was suddenly transferred from Auxiliary Headquarters. One day in 1974 Khan's warrant card was taken from him. No receipt was issued, and no explanation offered.

Khan fought back, threatening legal action. The warrant card was returned, but in April 1975, a new round of bizarre events commenced.

He was assigned to various two-month temporary postings throughout the colony, an unprecedented course of action and one that went against established policy. Khan remained a superintendent but had no men under his command and was lectured by station sergeants, whose permission he had to ask before going off duty.

He also claims that, on occasions, the register was purposely concealed to make it difficult for him to sign 'on' and 'off'. This was later to be given as a reason for his eventual dismissal, that his pay claims had been 'irregular'.

Throughout the two-year period Khan wrote repeatedly to Police Headquarters asking for a 'proper permanent posting', but as on previous occasions, his requests went unheeded.

In October 1976 Khan was told that he was to be investigated for an alleged 26 cases of fraud, later known in court as the 'irregular pay claims', involving a total sum of $7. Yet within one month he was appointed commandant of a police training camp, which placed 150 men under his command and made him responsible for approving their pay claims in addition to his own.

Five months later he was posted to the Wong Tai Sin District of Hong Kong as divisional superintendent of Auxiliary Police. It was a posting that charged him with maintaining law and order among some 700,000 citizens in the largest land area of any police formation in the colony. He was so effective that the local Residents Welfare Association wrote to the then Commissioner of Police commending Khan for the service he was rendering to the community.

Then, without prior warning, Khan was summoned to Police Headquarters on 10th May 1978 and handed a letter of instant dismissal. The following year he petitioned the then Governor, now Lord Maclehose, who instructed that Khan be given the reasons for his dismissal. In due course Khan received a letter which gave two reasons – the irregular pay claims and his 'personal investigation into alleged money-lending without prior approval'.

This second reason, which had never before been raised with Khan, concerned his 1975 involvement in the entrapment of a 'loan shark', who was subsequently released. The same man is now in custody, awaiting charges of massive fraud.

Yacub Khan began his long and lonely legal battle against the Police for wrongful dismissal in January 1980, but it was not until November the following year that the Crown admitted in an affidavit that 'we have made allegations which are factually inaccurate, which could not be sustained by proof, nor indeed would one try to prove'.

It continued, 'It is no longer contended that the plaintiff was given something in the nature of a hearing satisfying the requirements of natural justice prior to his dismissal'. Curiously, this admission by the Crown was not reported in Hong Kong newspapers.

The Crown's admission was compounded in a letter written to Khan's solicitors on March 11 1982 by the Government's Legal Department which read, in part 'Neither the contents of the Secretary of Security's minute effecting Mr. Khan's dismissal, nor the contents of Mr Blackburn's letter of January the 18th, 1978 are in issue any longer'. This was a reference to a recommendation by Eric Blackburn to the Secretary for Security in which he made several allegations against Khan and recommended his dismissal.

This confirms that the man who is now deputy commissioner of police made allegations against Khan which led to his dismissal, but which the Crown was subsequently unable to justify.

On December 2 of last year the Court of Appeal awarded Yacub Khan almost nine years of legal costs against the Crown, and which will have to be borne by the colony's taxpayers.

At the same time, the Court of Appeal judges ordered that the two remaining issues in Khan's case – a declaration that his dismissal was illegal, null and void and the matter of damages – be returned to the High Court. After his 16 year search for justice Yacub Khan is a bitter and angry man. He was deserted by his wife and disinherited by his late father who believed that his son had disgraced the family name.

He says he is still subjected to police harassment. As recently as Christmas Eve 1986 documents from his solicitors, which he was copying at a commercial stationers, were seized by the police. While the shop's proprietors were issued with a receipt for the seized documents and they were later returned to Khan in circumstances which he describes as 'odd', he cites as 'proof' of police harassment that they knew of his visit to the premises concerned.

The curious case of former Superintendent Khan has yet to reach a conclusion and for many the story poses more questions than it can possibly answer.

The net tightens on tigers of Tamil Eelam

by Gamini Navaratne
Jaffna

Gamini Navaratne, a Sinhalese, continued editing the Saturday Review *in Jaffna, in the Tamil area of northern Sri Lanka, despite threats to his person and the shelling of his printing plant. He simultaneously ran a press agency in Colombo. His reputation for independence and objectivity made him an appropriate go-between for a government which wished to see whether talks were possible with the Tamil militants. (30 June 1987 – GS 4312)*

Despite his public support for a military solution to the rebellion of Tamil militants, Sri Lanka's President Junius Jayewardene made repeated efforts to lure Tamil leaders to the negotiating table before sending armed forces into the region in May.

The *Saturday Review* of Jaffna, which I edit, has been closely involved in a number of these attempts. In September 1984, the paper said: 'Just as the Palestinian question cannot be resolved without the participation of the Palestine Liberation Organization, no lasting settlement of Sri Lanka's ethnic problem is possible without the participation and agreement of the militant groups'.

In December 1984 Jayewardene sent me as an unofficial emissary to sound out the then Madras-based militant leaders of the Liberation Tigers of Tamil Eelam (LTTE) who are spearheading the Tamil fight for independence. It

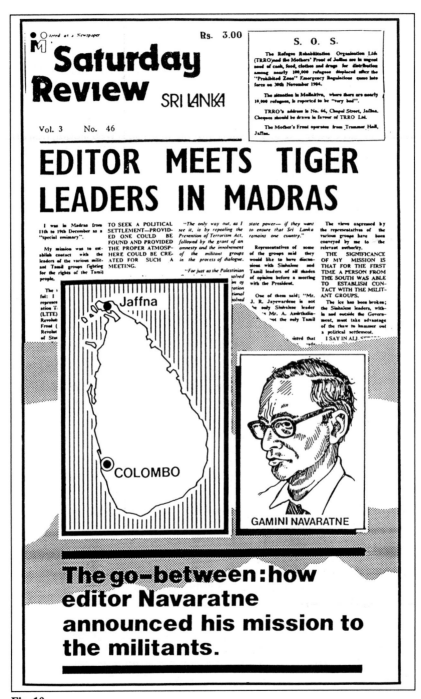

Fig. 10.

was the first time anybody from the majority Sinhalese community had established such contact with the militant leaders.

They were agreeable to talks provided the government showed its sincerity by, among other things, withdrawing its security forces from the north and east, releasing all youths held under the Prevention of Terrorism Act and revoking the emergency regulations which had converted the north into a virtual prison. These conditions were not acceptable to the government and the war intensified.

Efforts by India to restore peace through talks first at a neutral site in Bhutan in mid-1985 and later in New Delhi and Colombo, made little headway initially. Though the militant leaders were consulted, the talks were mostly on a government-to-government level.

Then in November 1986, just before the South Asian Association for Regional Co-operation (SAARC) met in Bangalore, Jayewardene again attempted to establish direct contact with the Tigers. He asked me to find out whether Tiger leader Velupillai Prabhakaran was willing to meet him there.

I met the Tiger leadership in Jaffna, the northern capital, and they contacted Prabhakaran in Madras by wireless. The answer was Yes. But the meeting never took place. At the last moment, Prabhakaran issued a press statement that he was 'not going to do anything behind India's back', despite the fact that Indian Prime Minister Rajiv Gandhi would also be present at the SAARC meeting.

On December 19, 1986, Sri Lanka and India finally agreed on a set of proposals designed to satisfy most of the demands of the Tamils for a degree of regional autonomy through councils in each of the island's nine provinces.

However Jayewardene refused to budge on the militants' demand to unite the Tamil-dominated northern and eastern provinces into a single unit. Sinhalese Sri Lankans fear a formal link would lead to stronger ties with Tamils in the South Indian state of Tamil Nadu, creating a potent threat.

Although government critics said the proposals 'went too far', Jayewardene announced he was willing to implement them. The Tigers refused, despite prodding by India.

Before launching 'Operation Liberation' – code name of the government's recent military effort to 'flush out' the peninsula in early May, Jayewardene made a last-minute effort to arrange talks. Again he asked me to see if Prabhakaran, who had returned to Jaffna, could be drawn to the negotiating table. I went to Jaffna on April 26 as the President's special emissary and made contact with the Tigers.

The mandate was to obtain a clear Yes or No within ten days to new talks with the December 19 proposals as the starting point. There were to be no pre-conditions from either side. But Prabhakaran was 'not available' to discuss it.

Soon after, Operation Liberation was launched, with combined attacks by the army, air force and navy. Accurate statistics are not available but unofficial estimates put the death toll at more than 1,000, most of them civilians. Property damage was heavy.

Jaffna has been reduced to a ghost town as people fled, closing down offices, schools and shops. Serious shortages of food, fuel and other essential commodities were created and thousands had been made homeless.

Despite protests from New Delhi, Sri Lanka says it had no alternative to the exercise 'in the face of the intransigence of the LTTE to come to the negotiating table despite all efforts, including by India and other concerned parties'.

New Delhi's subsequent air-drop of supplies to the beleaguered peninsula were barely enough for one meal for each of Jaffna's 100,000 inhabitants.

The Tigers have suffered severe reverses in the Trincomalee, Batticaloa and Ampara districts in the eastern province, and Mannar, Mullaitivu and Kilinochchi districts in the northern province, and have been put on the defensive in Jaffna district as well. Unless India intervenes, the militants appear to be doomed.

Colombo's current position is summed up by National Security Minister Lalith Athulathmudali, who says that 'any talks with the LTTE will be held only after the government has established a clear military advantage'.

In Burma today – purges and shops full of goods

by Abby Tan
Rangoon

Abby Tan, Gemini's experienced Manila correspondent, was one of the first outside journalists allowed into Burma by the military in 1992. Her report was widely used as a result. Tan's account balances a hard-hitting description of intimidation by the government with a recognition that living standards have risen with the arrival of a market economy. (17 April 1992 – GN 33764)

The military government of Burma has sacked 15,000 civil servants in its latest purge of disloyal elements.

Diplomats in the capital say they have counted 150 teachers in the premier Rangoon University and 72 others in educational institutions elsewhere who lost their jobs in recent months.

Thousands of teachers below professor-level have been sent to re- education camp in the Central Institute of Public Services in Phaunggi, 25 miles north of Rangoon.

The four-week drill course of exercises and lectures, begun in January, is patterned on China's Red Guards rural re-education in the Sixties.

Intimidation is still relentless and the pledge of a new constitution by the junta holds no promise that the flowering of a democracy, nipped in the bud in 1988, is possible.

A senior academic, who heads a think tank in Rangoon and is a key economic adviser to the government, confirmed the sackings, and called the exercise unfinished business by the regime in consolidating its power.

The academic refused to be named. 'The government has handled the

51

students, the politicians and the Buddhist monks', he said. 'Now it must address the civil servants who also joined the students' strike'.

The strike in 1988 was costly for democracy. Bloody riots by students, communists and liberals against socialist one-party rule prompted the armed forces to step in. All popular dissent was crushed when it imposed martial law that September.

The army's omnipotent presence is evident at major road junctions in the capital of this devoutly Buddhist Southeast Asian nation.

One big billboard with a red background reads: 'Anyone who is riotous or destructive is our enemy'. Another exhorts: 'Beware of underground and above ground destructive elements'.

And for the benefit of the United States embassy, a billboard in front of its gate declared: 'Down with minions of colonialism'.

The teachers being re-educated are blamed for the behaviour of students, the adviser said. They were on forced vacation for three years until mid-1991 when schools re-opened.

The military authorities shut the schools indefinitely once more last December when students rallied in the streets to celebrate the award of the Nobel Peace Prize to their heroine, opposition leader Aung San Suu Kyi.

The loyalty check on civil servants and teachers took the form of a questionnaire. One question asked: 'Should someone married to a foreigner be elected head of state? If yes, what will be the situation of the country'?

The reference was to Suu Kyi, who is married to a British academic. She headed the National League for Democracy (NLD), and has been under arrest since July 1989 in her own house in a leafy suburb of Rangoon.

The junta say she can go free if she gives up politics. She refuses. Last July she realized her guards checked and photographed personal items sent to her, so she gave up all contacts with the family.

The NLD swept 80 per cent of the 485-seat National Assembly in the May 1990 elections, but the junta refused to honour the results.

Diplomats agree that Gen. Saw Maung, the chairman of the ruling junta, the State Law and Order Restoration Council, has exerted stronger control over Burma than any ruler before him.

He promised Burma a new constitution to be drawn up by a national convention, obviously to be handpicked by the military.

In a March speech on Armed Forces Day, the General gave no timetable as to when the new constitution will be introduced.

Rangoon-based observers expect at least four years – enough time to disqualify the NLD parliamentarians elected to a four-year term from the convention. Foreign Minister Ohn Gyaw pledged that the constitution is a reality, once law and order is ascertained. 'What we say, we'll do. We do what we say', he stressed in a recent interview.

In spite of Gen. Saw Maung's promise that the mist will clear 'with the appearance of the sun once the constitution emerges', observers are not sure to what extent democracy will be allowed.

One diplomat said: 'It is fairly obvious there are military men who feel the politicians are not qualified. They have complete antipathy to politicians, who are blamed for Burma's economic backwardness'.

The military could be ensh rined in the draft law, in the way that the Thai and Indonesian military are assured of power sharing.

Gen. Saw Maung and other cabinet ministers insist that the army has no intention of holding on to power. They point out that they had power in 1958 and 1962, but handed back to civilians once security stabilized.

Gen. Saw Maung made no mention of civil liberties or human rights in his speech, but pointedly insisted that the junta's main objective is to look after the three basic human needs – food, clothing and shelter.

Diplomats agree that martial law has done much to lift the Burmese standard of living. In 1988 the junta ended the 26 years of socialism that had brought Burma to economic ruin. The government asked the United Nations to downgrade its status from a developing country to 'least developed'.

A dirty, grotty, dull Rangoon city, which looked as if it had been asleep for years, suddenly woke up to a market economy. The capital is clean and painted up. Foreign investments have brough in more employment opportunities. Rangoon shops are full of consumer goods. There is no starvation in the country because Burma is self-sufficient in food.

Following the logic that discipline brings prosperity, the junta is unfazed by international condemnation of its deplorable human rights record. Many elected opposition legislators are either jailed or being harassed. One died in prison due to poor medical care.

Human rights watchdog groups say about 2,000 dissidents are in jail. Non-political prisoners have been forced to become army porters, made to walk ahead of Burmese troops to clear landmines in insurgent areas.

It is acknowledged that civilian courts have become more professional and fair in handling non-political cases, while human rights groups say abuses have also been committed by rebels in Karen state.

With state apparatus firmly in the government hands, a limited form of democracy with a built-in Buddhist respect for authority is the most probable in the long term.

As Brig. Gen. David Abel, who holds the most important cabinet economic portfolios for planning, finance and trade, put it: 'We're going to become a democratic state within an acceptable social structure'.

Water dampens peace hopes and whets the appetite for war

by Barry Chamish
Bet Shemesh, Israel

This is an example of an analytic piece, devoted to one aspect of the Middle Eastern peace process, where good information can result in a prophetic exclusive. Chamish is editor of 'Inside Israel', a monthly intelligence newsletter, with privileged sources. Environmental issues, in which Gemini has increasingly come to specialize, are now serious politics. (23 August 1994 – GV 219)

As the Middle East peace process moves forward, an old problem blocks its path: water.

Dividing the region's scarce water supply between Israelis, Jordanians, Palestinians and possibly Syrians is a critical problem. With technological solutions such as piping water from Turkey or desalination too expensive, what water there is must somehow be shared or no peace will ever be reached.

The water issue is stumping the Israeli planners of the current peace process. It is intractable already but the growth of population in Arab countries will, according to a government report, cause such a shortfall by the year 2010 that armed conflict is a real possibility.

'The likelihood of war over water is there', says Gideon Tsur, Israel's national water commissioner. 'But after the war ends, there still won't be enough water to go around'.

A confidential report by Tel Aviv University's Institute of Strategic Affairs predicted in 1991 that any future peace negotiations would be confounded because the 'other side will demand every last drop of water'.

It has proved prophetic. General Uri Saguy, head of Israel's Internal Security Services, told the Cabinet recently: 'The problem of water cannot be solved by diplomatic means'.

Of the 1.8 billion cubic metres of water in rivers, lakes and acquifers to which Israel has access, the Jordanians and Palestinians are demanding 1.3 billion cubic metres, he said. 'If the Syrians enter the negotiations, the total amount demanded will be more than the entire supply'.

Israel's 5.4 million people use substantially more water annually than the 1.5 million Palestinians. But Tsur insists this does not mean Israel is acting recklessly. Israel uses only a third of the water per capita of Syria and gets by through careful conservation. While only 12 per cent of Israel's water is wasted, the figure for Jordan is 50 per cent.

Jordan is making claims on all the water that flows into the Sea of Galilee and Jordan River from its side. To get King Hussein to sign a non-bellig-erency treaty, Israel had to offer four million cubic metres of water as a one time gift.

Tsur says: 'At the multilateral talks on water, I said, "Let's now divide the water. Of course, we all know there isn't enough water so the end result for both of us will be zero". The Jordanian delegate, Muntner Haddadin answered: "In that case, we want half of zero"'.

The Israelis are also squaring off with the Palestinians over water. Avraham Ben Oz, the country's chief negotiator over water at the peace talks, accuses the Palestinians of 'mixing religion with their water. Their position is that rain comes from Allah and that since practically all of Israel's coastal rivers and wells originate from West Bank rain, we are stealing their rainwater'.

The Palestinians have demanded that Israeli repay them for all the water stolen since 1948 (when Israel was created in what had been Palestine) – over 40 billion cubic metres. 'I told them to get off their high horses and start being serious', Ben Oz says. 'Their compromise was a demand for repayment of all water used by Israel since 1967' (when Israel occupied the West Bank and Gaza Strip).

A Palestinian delegate to the water talks with Israel, Rejwan Hadad, argues that 'the Israelis want everything to stay the same. They'll keep pumping all they need and we'll get a fifth the amount they use per person'.

Adds fellow delegate Riyad Khodari: 'There will never be cooperation as long as they still treat us like an occupier. They are offering us rights over land and airspace and we are demanding the same rights over water'.

While the Israelis, Palestinians and Jordanians are deadlocked over the fact that there just is not enough water available to support three societies, the inclusion of Syria into the equation could make concessions impossible unless the Syrians show great sensitivity to Israel's needs.

Thirty per cent of all the water in the Sea of Galilee drains in from the streams of the Golan Heights. In 1966, Syria tried to turn northern Israel into a desert by damming the water. Israel responded by bombing the dam sites, an act which contributed to the outbreak of the Six Day War the following year.

In the past decade Israeli farmers have greatly increased the efficiency of the Golan waters by constructing a series of reservoirs that conserve practically all the rainwater that falls on the Heights. By doing so, they block as much water as they formerly used, thus keeping the Sea of Galilee in balance.

Few doubt the great threat to peace posed by the water debate. Martin Sherman, a geologist and political activist, believes that if the Syrians took over the entire Golan Heights they would use the reservoirs to capture all the rainwater flowing to the Sea of Galilee.

'They'll claim they have the right to do what they want with rain that falls on the Golan', he says, 'and there will be another war over water'.

3 The developing world and the new information order

A major debate, in the second half of the 1970s and early 1980s, surrounded the international flow of news and opinion. The debate crystallized in calls by developing countries for a New International Information and Communication Order, a project in which UNESCO became heavily engaged, and which led to a bitter campaign of hostility by certain US and British-based media corporations, backed by conservative bodies such as the Heritage Foundation. A great number of issues became enmeshed. Although Gemini was not an international player on a par with Associated Press or Reuters it was significant because of its Commonwealth provenance, and because it was almost alone in Britain in advocating and practising a grassroots distribution of 'news power' to journalists in developing countries.

The proposed information order was argued for in terms not dissimilar to those used about the proposed New International Economic Order at the same time. Both were inspired by the sight of the oil-exporting governments, in the OPEC cartel, acting together to reverse the global balance of power. The Third World, which now represented a majority of the votes though not of financial contributions to the UN, UNESCO and other international bodies, wanted a more equal South-North news flow. Its spokespersons pointed out that it was neocolonial for the agenda of news and views to be set by powerful Northern agencies, unaccountable to those they wrote about. Such agencies had a tight grip on global communications, not seriously challenged by the Soviet Tass or Chinese Xinhua. It was demeaning for governments and peoples in independent states to be forced to see themselves not through their own eyes, or the lenses of journalists from other developing states facing similar problems, but as summarized by editors and journalists from the North. Such editors and journalists brought their own prejudices, ranging from prior Cold War commitment, to an interest in commercial exploitation and even racism.

Against such arguments the powerful media corporations of the North replied by quoting the need for free speech as a human right endorsed by UNESCO itself. Their apologists focused on the lack of media freedom in countries of the South; these were often one-party states with a controlled press where expatriate journalists were expelled if they abused their sufferance.[1] In practice, they would continue, anything other than free international press activity would lead to the government-organized exchange of information which would be boring and not credible to readers.

In fact the debate about the New International Information Order petered out in the 1980s, certainly in its original form. This was partly because the parallel claim for a New International Economic Order was rebuffed by the conservative Reagan–Thatcher axis at the Cancun summit in Mexico in 1981. Political fashion in the Anglo-Saxon world was moving rapidly in favour of deregulation and privatization at the national level (which led, for instance, to a reduced public service and increased commercial emphasis in television, and a multiplication of cable TV channels). Internationally, the rich states which fund the UN system started to apply financial sanctions to inhibit policies which might threaten their interests. And technological change – data transmission, fax, satellite television – made it harder for any government to isolate its country in the global village.

Gemini reported the debate, and was also part of it. For Ingram, whose natural inclination was to support a free press and the maximum freedom under the law for journalists, there was a need to balance this approach with a sympathy and understanding of nation-building needs in the South. The ambiguity showed in an article he wrote in the first part of 1971 following an International Press Institute conference in Helsinki. It was given the punning title, 'Stop Press: Lee in Helsinki'.[2]

Lee Kuan Yew, Prime Minister of Singapore, came to Helsinki after quarrelling with three papers on the island: the *Eastern Sun*, which he accused of being supported with Chinese communist funds; the Chinese-language *Nanyang Siang*, where four executives were jailed for abusing Lee and using pro-Mao material; and the *Singapore Herald* which had been closed after its licence was withdrawn. Lee, who was talking on 'The Mass Media as Seen by World Policy Makers' gave as good as he got, and said that he was worried about communist, Malay and American influence in Singapore as well as American pop culture.

Ingram reported that Lee asked the head of the CIA in Southeast Asia to give him assurances that an agreement he had reached in Washington some years earlier, that the CIA would not interfere in Singapore, was still being honoured. Ingram's comment showed sympathy with Lee: 'Just as Westerners have come to accept, slowly and reluctantly, that Western-style democracy is not transferable to every kind of society, so the question has to be asked and considered whether if a country is plainly seen to be fighting for its independent existence (and that must be the proviso) it can allow its media to be in any kind of hands.'

Interestingly, one of the very few cases known of Gemini not publishing an article for reasons of political caution occurred two years later and concerned Singapore. Chris

---

1. As recounted in Chapter 5, two contributors to Gemini and *The Guardian*, John Worrall and his son Nicholas, were separately expelled from Rhodesia (John, by Ian Smith), and from Zimbabwe after the end of UDI (Nicholas, by Robert Mugabe). Although these governments could not have been more different, each had reacted drastically to embarrassing reports.

2. Service number GN702.

Mullin, a British freelance journalist who was later editor of *Tribune*, the left-wing weekly and who afterwards became a Labour MP, talked to members of the Singapore opposition on a visit there. Some had been detained by Lee. But Ingram told Mullin that it would be impolitic to run the piece.[3]

Gemini, through its editor, became publicly involved in the issues behind the New International Information Order when Ingram read a paper to the Royal Society of Arts in London in December 1975.[4] He pointed out that while in Britain this was a year when all but one of the national newspapers were losing money due to a recession, in the wider Commonwealth there had also been substantial changes. In India, following the Emergency, censorship was introduced. With the takeover by President Kaunda's government of *The Times of Zambia* there were only two papers in Commonwealth east and central Africa which were left in private hands. In Nigeria the military government had taken over the *Daily Times* and the *New Nigerian*. All the main newspapers were now owned by the government in Bangladesh, Guyana, Sierra Leone, Ghana, Uganda, Tanzania, Zambia and Malawi.

But he went on to say that the situation of the media cannot be divorced from the whole question of world political and economic development. The deep divisions of outlook between the industrialized rich and the mainly poor but developing parts of the world were reflected in attitudes to the press, and the way in which news is currently disseminated. A monopoly of news distribution is in the hands of the rich agencies which primarily serve markets in the developed world.

Ingram quoted, as an example of the distortions that resulted, the fact that he and others attending a Commonwealth Finance Ministers' meeting in Georgetown could not find out what was going on at the fifth conference of non-aligned countries, taking place simultaneously in Lima. Only the barest reports reached Georgetown, and they focused on a coup in Peru. (Jonathan Fenby, then running Reuters and in 1993–95 editor of *The Observer*, challenged this: he said that 10,000 words had been filed from Lima on the conference, of which 6,000 had been distributed to Guyana. Nicholas Harman, director of information for the Commonwealth Secretariat, who was chairing the event, came down on the lecturer's side.)

Ingram gave other examples of the failure of Western agencies to serve the interests of developing countries – exactly the failure which Gemini was trying to remedy. He quoted a seminar of Third World journalists which had run in parallel with the recent UN Seventh Special Session on the New International Economic Order. It 'concluded that the New International Economic Order requires a new framework of world information and communications. I agree', commented Ingram.

Ingram criticized the imprisonment of journalists without trial and added that state ownership of titles was incompatible with a free press. But he pleaded for more under-

3. Interview, Chris Mullin.

4. 'Commonwealth Press: The Years of Challenge', 11 December 1975, published in the *Journal of the Royal Society for the Encouragement of Arts, Manufactures and Commerce*.

standing of situations which were quite unlike those in a developed country – situations where a casual comment in print could set off inter-ethnic conflict, or where an adversarial approach by the press made little sense if a country had to pull together to escape from poverty. In small countries state ownership was often the only realistic alternative to foreign ownership, and ownership by a private local group could challenge the then commonplace commitment to socialism.

Gemini regularly reported the media debate[5] and Ingram himself returned to the issues periodically.[6] In 1988, for instance, he wrote a useful round-up of the subject for the United Nations Association in Britain, which suggested that although the Cold War had sunk the new information order the debate had helped set up a Nonaligned Newspool based in Belgrade and PANA, the Pan-African News Agency. But for the journalists who contributed to the service, and the papers which took it, it was what Gemini actually did that carried most weight.

For the journalists the key benefit was the world-wide by-line, something very gratifying to someone who might feel rather lonely on a paper in a developing country. Mehr Khan, now head of information for UNICEF, New York, began writing for Gemini in the late 1960s when she was with the Associated Press of Pakistan:

> My work with Gemini enabled me to write on issues about Pakistan for a foreign audience. While the stipend I was paid was small, the work was very important to me because it allowed me to build up a portfolio of international stories. This gave me confidence that enabled me to get a job as a stringer with UPI.

> Later, the articles I wrote for Gemini influenced the decision by the East West Center in Honolulu to award me a Jefferson Fellowship for study and travel in the United States. The East West Center experience led to other useful opportunities and were a factor in enabling me to work with UNICEF, which I joined in 1976.[7]

Abby Tan, Manila correspondent for Gemini, had covered the tumultuous history of the Philippines for 17 years by 1994. Friends in other Asian capitals remarked on several of her Gemini stories, such as those she wrote on Burma (Myanmar) after a visit to Rangoon in April, 1992, when the military regime was testing the water for foreign correspondents. They noticed too a lighter piece she wrote, on an eccentric vigilante, Jun Pala, who lived in Davao city in the southern Philippines. The UN publication, *Development Forum*,

---

5. For example, Brij Khandelwal from New Delhi reported in Gemini's Asia column that the Non-Aligned Movement was planning a Third World news agency dedicated to development journalism at a Colombo meeting starting on 9 August 1976 (Service Number GAS211).

6. In March 1977, in the *UK Press Gazette*, Ingram advocated that a Third World news press agency should be set up based in the Third World. In 1980 (GR36) he reviewed for Gemini a book by Dr Oliver Boyd-Barrett, *The international news agencies*, London: Constable, 1980, which focused on the dominant role of the big four – Associated Press and United Press International (US-based), Reuter (British), and Agence France Press (French). In an article he wrote for the 20th anniversary of Gemini in 1987, he speculated that Gemini itself might be based in a developing country in future.

7. Mehr Khan (formerly Mehr Kemal), letter to author, 18 March 1994.

reused a piece she had written on a children's TV show, *Batibet*. 'That gave me an idea that Gemini had a wider reach than I realized'.[8]

The scale of influence that Gemini correspondents could reach in a single country where the leading journal was heavily dependent on the service was illustrated in its most dramatic fashion in Zambia. The Friday 5 December issue of *The Times of Zambia* in 1969 carried ten substantial Gemini pieces, with by-lines from Wellington, Singapore, Ibadan, London, Nairobi, Mar del Plata, New York and Suva. These ranged from political stories (about the Nigerian civil war and Peking's influence in Africa), to fashion items and social issues ('Villagers starve in South Sea islands drought' and 'A race relations stir over a Scottish porridge cook').

As a matter of policy the articles written by correspondents were not normally sent back to subscribers in their own country, so they only saw cuttings of articles which were used elsewhere, which arrived much later. The policy was designed more to avoid boring editors with material they already knew, and with stories that might already have moved on, than to protect contributors who might have criticized local vested interests or who did not wish to advertise their Gemini work. For some journalists the relationship was solely with the London office, and there was little sense of camaraderie as between Gemini contributors. But quite a number were led to write for Gemini by others who were already doing so.

For instance Philip Short, the BBC correspondent who was writing for Gemini in his freelance days in Africa, remembers encouraging a young man at the Bank of Malawi to do features for the service when he was working in Malawi between 1967 and 1970.[9] In Zimbabwe, John Gambanga began writing seriously in 1980, after a colleague on the *MOTO* weekly newspaper in Harare had passed on the address.[10]

Journalism for Gemini was always a delicate art form, because ambitions to topicality had to be balanced by the constraints of the post.

Contributors soon realized that an article for the service had to have a life of as long as a month – it might take ten days to get to the office, it might wait there for a week for editing and to form part of a balanced package, and it could take another ten days to get received and used by a subscriber.

From the 1980s Gemini ran various training workshops and seminars for journalists (described in the chapter on its educational work). But long before that the service had been seeking out indigenous correspondents and encouraging them to contribute. Postal delays, and the modest rates paid by Gemini to contributors, meant that there was less checking back by the London office with correspondents in the field than is common with First World news agencies.

Nonetheless Gemini sought to provide a training and development element in its day-to-day relationship with correspondents. Partly this arose because there was always a greater

8. Abby Tan, letter to author, 24 January 1994.

9. Philip Short, letter to author, 22 February 1994. The man concerned was subsequently arrested and imprisoned for several years under President Banda.

10. John Gambanga, letter to author, 23 April 1994.

supply of material than the service could take, and rejection letters offered an opportunity to explain. For example Gambanga, who went on to become a regular contributor from Harare, had his first article turned down. It was on tribalism in Zimbabwe, and Ingram told him it was too shallow. Later on, when Gambanga wanted to move from the Zimbabwe Broadcasting Service to become a feature writer on *The Herald*, he reckoned that it was a Gemini cutting – of a feature he had written about Dambudzo Marachera – which helped get him the job.[11]

Christmas and other round-up letters from London praised particular correspondents and focused on criteria for successful articles. In the 1980s the office tried to send a monthly letter to correspondents with their payments, but this did not often reach the more irregular contributors. Nelson carried on this tradition after he took over as editor. In a detailed analysis of the March 1994 service, for example, he specified: good on-the-spot reports; topicality and a fresh angle; an apparently minor upcoming event which is ignored by mainstream media, but has a wider significance; a rapid response to a new situation; a report on a country or issue which has dropped off the agenda of the international media; important non-political issues (such as health, social trends, culture, gender); sport, environment, media, business; profiles; and humour. He was more guarded about the value of wrap-ups of rapidly changing situations, or reports after an event.

In an earlier *Guidance for Correspondents*, issued when Gemini was a *Guardian* subsidiary, Ingram advised that, because of the postal delay, it was necessary for writers to anticipate events, or to react to an event with a forward-looking angle or side-angle. 'You should assume that the reader has heard the hard news developments you are referring to, and only needs to be reminded of them in passing.' In the case of major set-piece conferences, where the graphics might need careful preparation, the office needed copy three weeks in advance.

Gemini provided quite a lot of technical advice. Articles should normally be around 900-1,200 words in length and Ingram in particular laid stress on the 'stand-first' – an introduction of around 60 words which gives the reader (and sub-editor) a welcoming gist of an article. Authors must provide 30 words of biography and date their pieces. Paragraphs are to be kept short, often only one or two sentences. Such devices, though they reflected Ingram's experience on the old broadsheet *Daily Mail*, also helped readers and journalists for whom English was a second or third language.

One of the things which became apparent from the early days, and which did not alter, was that Gemini articles were usually run as they stood by subscribing papers. This was in contrast to international news agency reports which were more often cut, edited and merged. In the case of Ingram's own lengthy year-end analyses of world news – a popular feature for editors – these were sometimes run on successive days.

But perhaps the most instructive aspect for correspondents was to see how their copy was edited in London. This could be quite drastic where Gemini homed in on material which the correspondent had buried in the story. It was not at all the case that what a correspondent

11. Gambanga letter, *ibid*.

wrote emerged from London in the same form, and in this respect Ingram stayed true to habits learned on the *Daily Mail* (traditionally a sub-editor's paper) rather than those ascribed to *The Guardian* (traditionally a writer's paper, where specialists had been known to kick up a fuss at the excision of a comma).

Given that many of the Gemini correspondents were new to international exposure this was a necessary discipline. It was, however, tempered by a democratic approach in the office under which different staff members reread and reedited the same copy – a practice which caused one temporary staff member to raise his eyebrows when he saw a a relatively young Canadian rewriting copy already handled by the editor.[12] Where London was not totally on top of material in a particular region there was always a risk that correspondents could lift an item straight from a local paper and send it unaltered to Gemini.[13]

Although the price paid for articles seemed low in developed countries, and no correspondent could expect to write that many articles each year, Gemini was important too because it built long-lasting ties with its contributors. The Ghanaian writer Cameron Duodu – born under a Gemini star sign like Ingram and Carruthers – believes he has contributed to the service every year since its inception. He came to London as an exile in 1965, continued to write when he returned to Accra, and has provided reports and commentaries on trips to Africa since he came back to London. Yet in no year did he write more than six articles.[14]

What, then, is the nature of Gemini journalism? Looking back at the end of his time as editor, Ingram said, 'Even today I find it quite difficult to describe in a few words to people the exact nature of Gemini's coverage, although you and I and others in the office know instinctively what is (or what ought to be) a Gemini story. This partly springs, I suppose, from the fact that I have always been anxious that Gemini should not be put in any specific category – namely, a Third World news service, a Commonwealth news service, an alternative news service etc. I dislike *World Press Review* (in New York) calling us a Third World-oriented news service and have told them so....

> All this springs from my firm conviction from the outset that Gemini should be considered a mainstream source of copy. I wanted it to be seen by the big boys (*Toronto Star, Melbourne Herald, Straits Times* etc) as a bona fide news agency, small of course, but nevertheless a competitor to the big agencies. That was the case for calling it a 'news service' and not a 'features service.' 'Features' is a slow word.

> Gemini would thus always have a newsy edge and not bypass the big events as though they had not happened. In fact, the only way to get into the bigger papers was to maintain topicality, peg stories to the news.[15]

---

12. Interview, Cedric Pulford

13. Interview, Mike Urlocker, who spotted that material from an Indian journal had been sent almost unaltered to Gemini. Where the London office found out, use of such a correspondent was normally discontinued.

14. Interview, Cameron Duodu. The veteran British journalist, William Forrest, was contributing into his 90s.

15. Memo, Ingram to Nelson, 1993.

There was, of course, no way that Gemini could compete with the international agencies in spot news and its stories were frequently placed on features rather than 'hard news' pages. This was specially appropriate when the stories had a strong opinion or commentary quality, but in many developing countries newspapers were not so sharply compartmentalized as they are in Britain or North America. In putting out a balanced packet of material Ingram never forgot that some clients were almost wholly dependent on his agency for their world news.[16]

Over time the output of Gemini unquestionably changed. In its first phase, during the Ingram–Carruthers partnership, it was more like a smaller, more specialized version of a major international agency which was seeking to compete on all fronts (including with crosswords, horoscopes and knitting patterns). It had its specializations, with the Commonwealth and an interest in good news about development, a particular strength in Africa, and a willingness to tap Britain and 'Swinging London' for material. Its London Line column, usually written by Ingram, actually ran into the 1980s but was not continued after the restart.

During the period as a *Guardian* subsidiary the service consolidated its position as a specialist in the mutual reporting of the developing world. In those days quite large chunks of the globe, for instance eastern Europe and the Soviet Union, rarely featured except insofar as superpower rivalry impinged on the South. However southeast Asia and the war in Vietnam were thoroughly covered. A series of articles on Vietnam by Chris Mullin, a British journalist, treated American claims for the 'domino theory' with suspicion, and pointed out that one reason why refugees fled Vietcong-controlled areas was because the US forces promptly declared them 'free fire zones.' His article in April 1975 titled 'The Vietnam Offensive that never was', when the PRG occupied 18 out of 44 provinces almost without resistance, did not however indicate that the Communists were about to enter Saigon.[17]

Gemini had difficulty always in balancing its sympathetic coverage of development stories – one of the reasons why editors on government-controlled papers in the South could run its service without anxiety – with its reputation for independence and objectivity. Even when pressure for a New International Information Order and a New International Economic Order was at its height the reality was that there was home-grown tyranny and corruption in some parts of the Third World which had little to do with the North.

One of the most interesting examples of Gemini's success in publicizing awkward realities came from Argentina. Andrew Graham-Yooll, part-Argentine news editor of the *Buenos Aires Herald*, had seen the first packets in the late 1960s with his editor. But with the Argentine peso depreciating under a military government the service seemed too expensive. Ingram asked him to keep in touch and in the early 1970s he wrote his first article, a tame piece about the British in Argentina which nonetheless was used all over the world including by the *Fiji Times*. He recalled:

16. In 1993, Ingram believed that the *Tanzania Daily News* did not take any other international agency and relied wholly on Gemini for its world news.

17. Article, GN1590.

The result was a dream.....I was famous, read all over the world, as far as Fiji.

From that start, I moved on to Argentine, and Latin American, politics. Argentina was short of news about itself. That is the problem with military dictatorships: they destroy information about themselves by preventing its publication. The press was not publishing many of the incidents that were taking place. People were not yet beginning to 'disappear' by the score, but there had been one or two nasty incidents, and also reports of torture of political detainees.

The press ignored those victims, because the individuals were not important, not 'one of us'. I began to keep a chronological record of such incidents. Years later the chronology became first one book, then two books, and then a jumbo compilation of the two, plus succeeding events. The books, chronologies of events, without comment or analysis, were banned and the author, not the perpetrators, declared subversive.

That was later. Before that, I had begun to publish short chronologies of events in the *Herald*. The paper was cautioned by the Press Secretariat that such publications were seen as disruptive, because they would alarm the public by the number of incidents recorded. We published anyway, and were cautioned again.

It seemed best to get some of this material out of the country. A chronology of Latin American abductions, of civilians suspected as guerrillas, but principally of diplomats and businessmen, kidnapped by urban terrorists all over Latin America, went into the post to Gemini. The number of these actions, and the rise of terror and counter-terror, had become alarming. Of course governments did not want such information published; the frequency of terrorist events, by guerrillas and paramilitaries throughout the continent gave a picture of growing instability.

The lists, with a short accompanying narrative, went to Derek Ingram with an apology. This was not good journalism as I had read in English newspapers, I confessed, but I hoped he would not spike my copy. Rather, would he keep this in a safe place, for reference and use, because somebody had to keep it.

Again, to my surprise, Gemini came back with a revelation. The chronology had been reproduced as a feature on the classic blue paper, accompanied by one of those remarkably helpful Gemini maps, pin-pointing the places where the abductions were taking place. And weeks later, the cuttings were sent to Buenos Aires from London: again, amazing, people in Colombo, in Canada and in African capitals thought this was useful information and worth publishing.

For about five years Gemini took similar pieces from Graham-Yooll on Argentine and Latin American politics until one day in 1976, with his successful young architect wife and their three children, he was forced to flee the country with a criminal trial pending and threats of all kinds ringing in his ears.[18]

18. Andrew Graham-Yooll, letter to author, 21 May 1994.

In 1976 too Gemini reports did not mince their words about the hardship involved in Pol Pot's forced evacuation of the Cambodian cities.[19]

The agency always liked to put out some human, humorous or off-beat stories. A few correspondents, such as Gamini Seneviratne in the early days or Nicola Cole later, specialized in such pieces. But with many, who found writing about politics either more engrossing or easier, the office had a continuing struggle to persuade them to broaden their range. Some regular readers of the output also felt that it ought more often to have run stories about political and commercial corruption, which had become major problems in the South.

In the 1980s there was a gain in depth, as a result of the rural reporting initiative, improved environmental coverage and maybe also the increased confidence of the journalists nurtured by Gemini. Issues, such as those affecting women and children or the debt crisis, were brought to life. At the same time there was a questioning of ideologies as people like Nelson and McParland encouraged correspondents to 'tell it as it is.' The rather wide-eyed series on the changes wrought by the Chinese communist leader which Gemini had run at the start of 1972, 'And then came Mao', would have been unthinkable 15 years later. Human rights issues received attention all over the world.

The momentous changes triggered by the arrival of Gorbachev in the Kremlin, and the fall of the Berlin Wall in 1989, caught Gemini at somewhat of a disadvantage. Eastern Europe had never been a major part of its parish, although events were to show that the region had more in common with the developing world than the East-West rivalry had let people realize.

But the agency was well-placed to score as the knock-on effects of the collapse of communism became more obvious – in the drive for multiparty democracy in the South, and the UN intervention to eject the Iraqi invaders of Kuwait. (A series of three articles in November 1991 on the Gulf crisis warned that the West was making a hero of Saddam Hussein in the Arab world, that marine wildlife faced annihilation, and that the disruption in oil output could impoverish poorer countries.)

Elias Nyakutemba, a correspondent in Zambia, returned home in 1988. 'I sent my first piece to Gemini unravelling (President) Kaunda's hypocrisy over sanctions against South Africa which he said he stood for while he traded with them at night!' Since then he wrote regularly, almost as a participant-observer. 'I lashed out at the one-party dictatorship. I pushed the point home about the unworkability of Kaunda's centralized economy. I covered the collapse of health, education and social services. I tackled regional issues such as the plight of refugees, the environment, human rights, sport and music. Most of these stories had special human interest and development angles which Gemini liked and used, I think, with great success.'[20]

The impact of Gemini, in providing information and opinion, tended to be greater in the smaller, poorer or more isolated countries. David Robie, who began writing for it when

---

19. See for instance GN 1817, 'The First Year of Peace in Indo-China', Chris Mullin.

20. Elias Nyakutemba, letter to author, 25 May 1994.

he was night editor on the *Rand Daily Mail* in South Africa, carried on elsewhere in Africa, in New Zealand and from Papua New Guinea, where he is now lecturer in journalism at the University of PNG. In 1994 he assessed its reputation in the Pacific:

> Gemini has played a unique role in the South Pacific, especially during the formative years of the news media in the region in the 1970s and the 1980s. Most of the media in the smaller Pacific countries were unable to afford paying for wire services and the Gemini service was a godsend – it provided international articles on major issues and development dilemmas backed up with strong graphics tailormade for their needs. Also, it provided far more refreshing perspectives on world and Commonwealth events than were usually available through the wire services.

> Even after Pacnews, the Honiara-(Solomon Islands)-based Pacific regional news cooperative was established in 1987, the need for Gemini's distinctive style of journalism continued. While Pacnews provided a daily smorgasbord of news morsels edited for radio consumption, Gemini continued to provide the in-depth and interpretative articles needed in the region.

> There are many loyal Gemini subscribers in the Pacific – among them the daily *PNG Post-Courier* (Rupert Murdoch-owned) published in Port Moresby which with a circulation of 41,000 is by far the biggest newspaper in the Pacific. It uses Gemini articles almost daily, plus two or three in the paper's *Weekend Magazine*. Gemini articles have played an important role in informing and educating Papua New Guineans about their region and the world about them.

> Among other keen users have been the Solomon Islands Broadcasting Corporation and Radio Vanuatu which have used the articles for current affairs programmes. The *Cook Islands News*, now a daily, has been a frequent user and the *Fiji Times* was always an enthsiastic user until a change of editor in 1992 when the service was used less frequently.[21]

In assessing the contribution of the service it is of course important to remember the great variations facing media in the developing world. Whereas a modern press did not emerge in parts of the South Pacific until the 1970s and 1980s there are English-language newspapers in India with a continuous record of publication since the mid 19th century. In the Caribbean there was a strong and independent press by the Second World War. By the 1980s, when British newspapers were still struggling to adopt computerized production, newspapers like the *Daily Gleaner* in Jamaica or the *New Straits Times* in Kuala Lumpur were already well-advanced in the electronic revolution.

The environment in which Gemini was working changed sharply in the 1980s and 1990s. Whereas it seemed acceptable and efficient in the 1970s to mail packets of articles round the globe, by the late 1980s it was beginning to look out of date for developing as well as developed country media. Gemini's technical and financial problems in distributing

---

21. David Robie, letter to author, 13 March 1994.

material electronically became more of a handicap. The ambiguous impact of instant news TV – the 1991 Gulf War over Kuwait seemed like the apotheosis of Ted Turner's US-based Cable News Network – penetrated the South by means of government offices, hotels and local media themselves.

TV in the South was beginning to take the market for spot news, and to stimulate a demand for more immediate comment or perspective pieces. Yet broadcasting in the developing world remained, by and large, under government control. Hence these trends also strengthened the case for a service of the kind provided by Gemini: more oriented to the needs of the South than the TV provided by Turner, Murdoch or even the BBC World Service, more balanced and thoughtful, and more independent of government propaganda than the national broadcasting services.

For the press the late 1980s and early 1990s also showed contradictions. Newspapers in South East Asia, for instance, were getting richer but were not necessarily more critical in their reporting. The burst of multiparty democracy in Africa had temporarily strengthened the diversity of expression there, but had not always guaranteed the financial resources or political experience to make new or newly-independent papers viable.

On the whole Gemini had had to sell its service on the basis of exclusivity, so the arrival of new papers in the developing world did not necessarily mean more outlets. (In Zambia, however, both *The Times of Zambia* and the *Zambia Daily Mail* were taking the agency.) Competition was also strengthening as newspapers like *The Guardian* downloaded up to 25 stories of news and news features each night to Africa by satellite, picked up by African papers equipped to take them.

Curiously enough the growth of the regional news services in the South – CANA in the Caribbean, Pacnews in the Pacific, PANA in Africa – did not challenge the niche service provided by Gemini. Ingram had at one point speculated in an anniversary piece that the agency's headquarters might move to a developing country, but its bona fides were well enough established for this to be unnecessary on public relations grounds. It happened to be in London, but it was not perceived as being Northern. (By the 1990s a lot of distinctions between developing and developed economies, which had appeared absolute 30 years earlier when Japan itself was hardly a world economic power, were beginning to blur.) It had shown more staying power and was less exposed to charges of editorializing than the Rome-based Inter Press Service, which had had various changes of control.

It had also fought off a direct challenge, from the Compass feature service which had been backed by the formidable resources of the Aga Khan, and which expired in the early 1990s after seven years of losses. 'I really don't think the international market was big enough to support two fairly heavyweight alternative/independent Third World-oriented news services, and probably Gemini survived because they were in the field first and had established their footprint. They also had a good product,' Gerry Loughran, the managing editor of Compass, concluded afterwards.[22]

Although a small player Gemini had sought to make a reality of the intentions behind the

---

22. Gerry Loughran, letter to author, 4 July 1994.

New International Information Order. Its service had been direct and, with regard to journalists from developing countries, often personal.

In an early message to correspondents, when the office was in John Street, Holborn, Ingram invited them to call round for a pot of tea or something stronger in the pub downstairs whenever they came to London. More recently John Gambanga from Zimbabwe remembers 'when I first visited Gemini offices at Angel, and the editor took me to lunch. I found him to be a very fatherly figure, friendly and very willing to assist.'[23]

Ingram, who lived in a small mews house in central London, frequently offered it as a place to stay to correspondents who were short of foreign exchange. On one occasion Gamini Navaratne, visiting from Sri Lanka where he had chronicled the ethnic conflict between the Sinhalese and the Tamils, locked Ingram out of his own house at midnight by mistake.[24] The Gemini service, though it might look fragile from some perspectives, was backed by a more than commercial commitment.

---

23. Gambanga letter, *ibid*.
24. Gamini Navaratne, letter to author, 2 April 1994.

4 An eye on world events

lthough it was a small service, in terms of resources and the quantity of its output,
Gemini was anxious to avoid being seen as marginal or too specialist. It felt it had
a duty to comment on and contribute towards the main global stories, bearing in
mind the knowledge of its contributors and the needs of its subscribers.

How could it best do this? The answer lay in a variety of methods. Its indigenous
correspondents had special insights. Its perspective, especially from the 1980s, was that
of the developing countries: what was the impact on them, and how did they interpret an
event which concerned the big powers or which dominated world media? Some of the
most widely-used articles, put out by persons like Ingram, Tom Aston and Daya Thussu,
were outspoken opinion pieces based on media analysis and media critiques.

Constraints of the post enforced other disciplines. Gemini writers, if their copy was to be
usable three weeks after they wrote it, had to get into a subject, stand back from it or project
it forward in a fashion that a 'spot news' journalist, tied to immediate topicality, could not
afford. They also had to remember that they were writing for audiences whose educational
levels might be modest, and for whom international affairs might seem far away.

All in all the agency was obliged to evolve a kind of art form and style of journalism in
which 'backgrounders' had to seem like 'foregrounders' for editors and readers of
subscribing journals, where a trend or event had to be made meaningful in quite varied
societies. Much of the East–West struggle which occupied column inches in the North
from 1967 to 1989 was quite remote from the concerns of newly independent states
engaged in construction, national development and basic survival. Yet battles over aid,
votes in the United Nations, and socialist versus capitalist approaches could impinge on
them immediately. Even Pacific islands suddenly found themselves in the vortex as a result
of US and French nuclear tests.

The following excerpts from the service give a flavour of Gemini coverage of issues and
events of international interest. As in Chapter 2 they are reproduced here without
abridgement, with a brief introduction.

Did he ... or didn't he?

by Cameron Duodu
Accra

Published by The Guardian *on 24 July 1968 and reproduced throughout the world, this Gemini report by Cameron Duodu, Ghanaian novelist and journalist, persuaded the Nigerian military to produce Wole Soyinka alive. Soyinka subsequently won the Nobel Prize but has never ceased campaigning against his country's unelected governments. (Service number unknown)*

I was having a drink at Accra Continental Hotel with a couple of girls. Pretty, vivacious, but not, I am afraid, girls I would have considered well read.

Yet to illustrate a point about the lack of masculine prowess in some men, one of them said 'Did he ...?'

I was puzzled, but the girl caught her meaning and repeated "Or did he ...?' They then both burst out laughing.

Since I was still in the dark, one of them asked me, 'Why, didn't you see *The Lion and The Jewel*?' In this play by the Nigerian playwright Wole Soyinka, a young school teacher tries to woo a pretty girl called Sidi. But the chief of the village also wants the girl, though he is over sixty and has many other wives.

The chief realises that he stands very little chance, and therefore hits on a stratagem – he sends Sadiku, one of his old wives to the girl with a story that although he, the chief, is clearly impotent, he still wants Sidi, the girl, to come and 'have supper' with him.

But when Sidi goes, the chief shows himself quite capable of the greatest exertions. Here she is telling Sadiku what happened.

'He told me ... afterwards, crowing,

'It was a trick.

'He knew Sadiku would not keep it to herself. That I, or maybe other maids would hear of it

'And go back to mock his plight

'And he laughed.

'How his frog face croaked and croaked,

'And called me little fool.'

It is at this point that the young school teacher, Lakunle, in spite of what Sidi has been saying, makes the comical statement:

'But Sidi, did he ...? I mean ...

'Did you escape?

'Speak Sidi, this is agony.

'Tell me the worst; I'll take it like a man.

'Is it the fright which affects you so,

'Or did he ...?'

Soyinka's ability to accentuate memorable comical situations is unsur-
passed and although I had always admired him as a dramatist, novelist and
poet, it took my 'ordinary' drinking companions to show me how far he has
really succeeded in joining the immortals. To be quoted by simple minded
folk, when most modern writing is so complex and demanding that even
'lettered' people find it difficult to understand, is an achievement that in the
African context is comparable to Shaw's. This duality was recognised by
Penelope Gilliatt of *The Observer* in reviewing Soyinka's *The Road* during
the Commonwealth Festival in London in 1965.

'Soyinka does for our napping language what brigand dramatists from
Ireland have done for two centuries, booted it awake, rifles its pocket and
scattered the loot in the middle of the next week.'

But what thanks has Soyinka got for doing more than perhaps all of Nigeria's
missions to put his country's name on the map? The Nigerian Federal
authorities arrested him very shortly after the civil war broke out, imprisoned
him without trial and told the world to go hang when protests were made
about his arrest. The last that was heard of him was that he had been taken
away from Lagos, the Nigerian capital, to the North. Since Mr Soyinka is a
Yoruba and the North is populated by Hausas and the Hausas dislike the
Yorubas almost as much as they dislike the Ibos in Biafra, Mr Soyinka's
transfer was greeted with misgivings by all who heard about it.

Now reports circulating in diplomatic circles here say that Mr Soyinka in fact
has died in prison and that the sad event took place in December 1967.
The reports are persistent and one is forced to give them credence because
although the Nigerian High Commission in Ghana is extremely vociferous
in 'putting the record straight' about anything that is said in the Ghana press
that relates to Nigeria, it has not said one word about a letter that I wrote to
the Ghana *Daily Graphic*. Personally, I quite simply fear the worse. For if
he is alive, why is he not brought to trial? And if he had done nothing that
could be used to bring him to trial, then why hold him in gaol? Surely the
Federal authorities must have some concern for the good name of the 'One
Nigeria' which they say they are fighting to preserve.

It is hard enough in Africa to break through the indifference of one's
countrymen and the misunderstanding of foreign publishers and get something into print that is worthwhile. When one is able to do this and one'e
efforts are greeted with delight as Soyinka's have been, the glory goes to
one's countrymen as well as to oneself. It rends one's heart to think that
good brains, ever in so short supply in Africa, should be so lightly spilt.
Already in the Nigerian civil war, one of Africa's best poets, Chris Okigbo,
has perished. Chinua Achebe, the finest novelist the continent has produced, recently told the East African magazine *Transition:*

'I hope I have not retired completely ... But I was writing something which
suddenly seemed irrelevant to me. What seemed important to me at the
time as a subject matter for a novel seemed unimportant compared with
what was happening; and also I think even if I felt like seeing my way through
to a brilliant novel I might, in fact, not find the emotional or even the physical
convenience to do it."

Of course, in the face of the starvation that is taking place in Biafra, it seems
unimportant that artists and their craft should be preserved. Only the
thoughful will realise that it is artists, through their ability to form the

consciousness of people, who can prevent the same horrid thing from being repeated a hundred years hence. To borrow again from *The Lion*:

What is a jewel to pigs?
If now I am misunderstood by you
And your race of savages, I rise above
taunts
And remain unruffled.

The way of life down Pumpkin Lane

by Chris Mullin

This was the first in a series provided by a journalist who later became editor of Tribune *and a Labour MP in Britain. Gemini put his articles out under the title 'And Then Came Mao'. It caught the interest generated by President Nixon's visit to China, and the US rapprochment with the communist regime. (January 1971 – GX 20A)*

Wang Fou-ching pushed open the rickety door of a shack little bigger than a rabbit hutch. It was put together with bamboo matting and driftwood snatched from Shanghai's filthy Whampoa river.

Wang pointed to the empty darkness in the doorway of the hut: 'Twenty years ago this was home for my family and I. We lived here for many years and we were very poor. And then came Mao'.

We were on a housing estate known as Pumpkin Lane in a suburb of Shanghai, the city of ten million people on the teeming East coast of China.

As housing estates go there is nothing very special about Pumpkin Lane. It is just a series of neat little three-storey apartment blocks with washing drying from balconies and little girls playing hopscotch in narrow alleyways. Little boys play basketball and occasionally somebody's window gets broken.

But Wang, a retired rickshaw puller, has lived in Pumpkin Lane since the days before the Revolution. In those days there were no three-storey apartment blocks. Only row after row of rabbit hutch houses.

The three we were looking at have been preserved so that the kids who play basketball and hopscotch will never forget that life could have turned out very differently for them.

Back in his spotless two room ground floor home Wang told me about his life in the days before the Revolution: 'I was born sixty-nine years ago in the countryside province of Kiangsi, 400 miles from Shanghai.

'My father and mother were beggars and for food we usually lived on wild vegetables and the boiled roots of trees. Sometimes these made us very ill. I had no education and when I was about eight my two sisters were given away to be slaves of a local landlord. I never saw them again.

'When I was sixteen my father died of starvation and with the three remaining members of my family I walked to Shanghai where I found work pulling rickshaws'.

It was then he came to Pumpkin Lane, which at that time was in the area of Shanghai owned by France. In 1930 Wang married and in the rabbit hutch house at Pumpkin Lane his wife gave birth to two of their three sons.

Several years after the Revolution in 1949 the shanty town was gradually demolished and the people were rehoused in flats like Wang's.

There is nothing particularly exceptional about the story of Wang's early life. It is just a tiny part of the huge catalogue of suffering which was an accepted part of Chinese life in the days before Mao.

Of all the people I talked to in 4,000 miles of travelling in China there was scarcely one who did not have a relative who had died of starvation, perhaps in the great North-West famine of 1928–30 in which six million died; others had relatives who had drowned, perhaps in the Yangse River flood of 1933 which killed three million; some of those I met were the sole survivors of families who had been butchered at the hands of Chiang Kai-shek's troops or the Japanese who conquered the whole North and East of China in the 1930s and early 1940s.

All these and many others are among the greatest disasters recorded history. They went almost unnoticed in the rest of the world.

What has happened in China in the last twenty years can only be properly understood if it is viewed in the context of her terrible history. To do that you need only talk to anyone over thirty in the fields and villages and factories of modern China.

Wang now shares his flat with his wife and the family of one of his sons, who is a Shanghai policeman. For this they pay 7.40 Yuan (£1.40) a month in rent.

Since his retirement at the age of sixty Wang now receives a monthly pension of 21 Yuan (£4). In addition his son and daughter-in-law, a factory worker, have a combined income of 108 Yuan (£20) a month and his eldest son, a professional soldier living away from home, sends 40 Yuan (£8) each month.

The family of seven, therefore, lives on a total income of about £32 a month, Not much by Western standards, but it goes a fair way when you consider that all prices in China are fixed by the State and there has been virtually no inflation for the last fifteen years.

Every household has about two or three main rooms usually shared by about three people. There is no such thing as a living room. The beds simply convert into a place to sit during the day.

Each home displays its portraits of Chairman Mao and its little frame of family photographs – the ones of the children probably taken at school.

The pavement plays an important part in the social life of the average city dweller in China. No family sits at home on sultry summer evenings. Instead they squat outside playing cards, drinking tea, gossiping and perhaps sucking penny lollipops.

All eating is done at the doorstep with ricebowl and chopsticks in hand. Should anything interesting appear, such as a sun-burned Englishman for example, they just get up and follow him for a few miles, chopsticks, rice bowl and all.

Most of the younger children outside of Peking and Shanghai have never seen foreigners before and two of us walking on our own in a city suburb could pull a crowd of up to a thousand within minutes.

Traffic on the wide roads is almost entirely human. There are no private cars in China. Apart from embassy vehicles in Peking, a city of seven million, the only motor vehicles are taxis, buses and the occasional lorry. Bike is the main form of transport and most of the heavy loads in town and country are still carried by donkey carts.

Mao is the biggest industry in China. Wherever you go there are pictures of Mao, stones that he sat on, houses he lived in. *Mao Chu-hsi wan sui*, Long live Mao Tse-tung, is carved on the side of impregnable mountains. In the cities there are little girls with pigtails and red arm bands who spend their spare time from school shouting his Thoughts to passing traffic through loud-hailers.

Sometimes Mao-worship strays into the positively ludicrous. One of his slogans pinned above the waters of the moat on Peking's Imperial City screams: 'Criticise Selfishness, Fight Revisionism. No Fishing'.

All other forms of religion have been abolished. One of Peking's six cathedrals has been converted into the mess of an electric light bulb factory.

Religion or not, a rigid form of moral code applies throughout China. It is quite impossible to lose anything, let alone have it stolen. Things you forgot or abandoned days before will suddenly reappear in your baggage hundreds of miles later. One girl in our party was regularly embarrassed by the continued reappearance of a pair of paper panties she kept trying to dispose of.

In sharp contrast to Russian and other East European countries no-one queues for food. Large department stores sell everything up to cameras, transistors and fairly sophisticated toys – all made in China.

China is a paradise for women's lib. It comes as a bit of a shock when you are walking down a street in Peking or Shanghai and you come across a really beautiful girl – wielding a pick-axe among a gang of navvies.

One of the most refreshing things about China is that, although there are many attractive girls, no-one tries to exploit their looks. There are no advertisements and no pin-ups.

I remember meeting Chou Chu-shiu, a lovely peasant girl in the mountain village of Mao Ping in the far south of China.

Chou was 23 with hazel eyes and black hair bound tight behind her head in thick plaits leaving only little wisps free to curl over the temples. She had never left Mao Ping in her life and worked eight to ten hours a day in the fields alongside her parents.

Like all Chinese girls she wore no make-up, her pink and white chequered shirt was loose fitting and her grey trousers were baggy. She had never heard of Coca Cola or the Beatles.

When a friend of mine tried to compliment her on her looks the interpreter refused to translate saying that Chou would be very insulted.

Although the legal age of marriage is 18 for both sexes Chou will probably wait until she is 25 or 26 to get married. She told me: 'I want to devote my youth to the socialist construction, then I will marry and have a family, but it will be a planned one'.

A huge programme of birth control is underway in China and I found evidence of it even in the most remote villages.

Almost all women go out to work and there is fairly generous provision in factories and communes for maternity leave with full pay. Although equal pay for women is the rule laid down in Mao's *Red Book*, I came across a number of instances of women earning less than men.

It is just 22 years since Mao seized power over that quarter of the human race who had apparently been abandoned by God to a terrible conspiracy of natural calamity and human wickedness.

If you were to ask Wang Fou-ching where he and the millions of others like him would be today, were it not for Mao, he would tell you: 'In the rabbit hutch house at Pumpkin Lane'.

Putting God above Ugandan politics

by Fred Mpanga

Fred Mpanga, a former Attorney-General of Buganda, came to London in the 1960s as an exile from President Obote. He found work at Gemini, initially as a messenger and handyman, later as a contributor on legal matters and humorous British customs. He returned home after General Amin took power, an event which he and others welcomed at the time. He visited London four months later and wrote this report. Sometime afterwards he died in Uganda due to lack of medical care. (10 June 1971 – GG 3021)

Uganda's General Idi Amin is not only in control of the whole country, following his coup in January against President Obote's government, he is also on his way to becoming a father-figure. Just what Uganda wanted.

Recently the Pope sent a personal representative to a religious leaders' conference Amin convened in Kampala. This fervent Muslim soldier told the religious leaders, assembled from home and abroad, to love one another and to fear God.

In delivering those timely words Amin was still wearing a General's uniform in which he had just climbed the pulpit in a Protestant church at Namugongo – the Uganda Martyrs' shrine near Kampala. His message was simple: love and unity. His sincerity, even to cynics, was compelling.

There are three main religious groupings in Uganda: the Roman Catholics, the Protestants and the Muslims. Obote caused dissension and bitter wrangle at the leadership level among the Protestants and the Muslims.

This was a move of divide and rule on Obote's side. It, however, went well beyond innocent division: in at least one quarrel over a mosque in 1968 several Muslims died.

Religious adherence in Uganda is a great deal fiercer than political party membership. That is why when ex-President Obote was fast losing popular support, he turned to church and mosque leadership. This was, paradoxically, his own undoing.

Amin, a regular mosque-goer, did not like the idea of splitting Muslims and other groups, for political ends. When Amin, then commander of the armed forces, called upon his boss Obote, then Head of State to repair the gaping cracks in Muslim leadership, Obote, a Protestant, demurred.

Obote's plan was to persevere with the National Association for the Advancement of Muslims (NAAM) under an octogenarian Sheik called Semakula.

At the beginning of 1970, the chasm between Obote and Amin suddenly assumed the proportions of a canyon when Amin publicly made it known that his loyalty was not with NAAM. He implored Obote to make amends with Prince Badru Kakunguru, leader of the Uganda Muslim Community since 1921.

Obote would not listen and Amin continued to say his Friday prayers in Prince Badru's mosque at Kibuli, near Kampala. The misunderstanding between the two men could not have been more clear cut. Obote, who viewed the NAAM as a necessary political arm, resented his General who regarded the political manoeuvres as meddling in matters strictly religious.

As a good Muslim, Amin wanted to go on a pilgrimage to Mecca, in September last year. He cut his journey short in Cairo and suddenly returned to Kampala. It is believed that Obote was going to replace Amin in his absence.

Here was a mistake of double magnitude on the part of Obote. Amin had support among the Muslim rank and file. And by saying his prayers at Kibuli, Amin was close to Prince Badru, the late Kabaka's (King Freddie) uncle.

In this apparent defiance, Amin had the undivided popular support of the Baganda, which was Obote's main weakness – he had failed to win the Baganda over to his side.

Amin's successful coup has taken religious undertones. The General would prefer to think that his military take-over was God's own act.

That is why he stresses Uganda's motto – For God and my Country. That is why also he wants to bring about reconciliation not only among the Muslims but also in the Protestant Church, whose headquarters are at Namirembe, near Kampala.

It would be self-deception for any Ugandan leader to expect political peace while there were fierce quarrels in the Church and the Mosque. That is why Amin is so keen on a genuine reconciliation ecumenically and within the religious sects themselves.

At the religious conference Amin told the nation over the radio and TV that his greatest desire was to unite Uganda spiritually and nationally.

His performance towards this goal so far, is very impressive. Within the past four months, the General has toured the entire country, including distant Karamoja among whose naked tribesmen Obote never went. (Amin suggested to them that they should wear trousers like their brethren in the rest of the country).

Amin has recently revealed a dream he had in 1952, when he was a mere struggling corporal. Among the many things that have now come true, the voice in the dream told Amin that he would be Uganda's Head of State. He now believes that he is going to die on the date mentioned or revealed in that dream.

That presumably is going to be many years to come for he has not told the nation the day forecast and he continues to smile like a big daddy.

'I quit' Williams now says 'I stay'

by Trevor McDonald

Eric Williams was the father of independence for Trinidad, and a notable historian. Trevor McDonald, now well-known as newscaster for Independent Television News in Britain, was freelancing for Gemini and other outlets at this period. His involvement with Gemini led later to his chairmanship of the governors of NewsConcern International Foundation. (17 December, 1973 – GN 1287)

Dr Eric Williams' decision to stay on as Prime Minister of Trinidad and Tobago at least until a general election is held – probably early in the New Year – means his ruling People's National Movement is bracing itself for the toughest fight of its political life.

Elections are to take place in 1974 – most likely under a changed constitution – (a commission is to submit its report by 31st December) – and their importance transcends the question of the mere survival of the PNM.

For many years now Trinidad has been virtually a one-party state. Elections should afford the opportunity for the two-party system and for consensus politics to reassert themselves.

When Williams announced he was resigning the PNM leadership and the premiership Trinidad was plunged into a state of great political uncertainty. Not for the first time, his opponents were confused, and for a while even the Prime Minister's most persistent critics seemed bewildered and uncharacteristically speechless.

The uncertainty was caused partly by the dramatic suddenness of the Prime Minister's resignation. Having resigned, he promptly dropped out of circulation, went on vacation, and for some days, it was not known how or by whom the affairs of the country were being looked after.

It was left for a Member of Parliament, after a visit to the Governor- General, to announce to an anxious press that the Prime Minister 'was attending to matters of state'. The Governor-General could not, however, tell the MP when the Premier's 'vacation would end'.

Although, in retrospect, Williams' resignation was foreshadowed by his ill-disguised general 'disenchantment', and more specifically by his frosty approach to preparations for the annual party convention (we know now that at least part of the Prime Minister's time was taken up in writing a bitter and stinging indictment of Trinidad society), when announced it produced a massive shock.

There followed the predictable rash of political obituaries, instant judgements of Williams' 17 years in office, and an orchestrated demand from loyal party members that he should not resign. Williams' response to the initial requests were coolly negative.

Today, a Minister of the Government, Kamaluddin Mohammed, and a former Cabinet colleague, Karl Hudson-Phillips, are struggling for the party leadership. There is no clear line of succession to Williams, and in recent years he fudged the leadership issue deliberately by naming *three* deputies, instead of one.

In nearly every respect the nature of the leadership crisis in Trinidad is a derivative of the way in which Williams led his party and ran the country for nearly two decades.

Unlike any other party in contemporary Commonwealth West Indian politics, the PNM was a monolith. Loyalty was its watchword and the authority of its leader was important above all. This is not to imply that the premier was a dictator, although many of his detractors would so describe him. He did not need to be. State decisions were taken collectively at Cabinet level and there was never any doubt about whose word was law.

Ministers were deferential and the party appeared sycophantic. In a series of weekly press conferences in the Sixties Williams roundly criticized political commentators for their lack of prespicacity, even their lack of basic intelligence and soon the press was running scared.

Additionally, the opposition in Parliament was virtually non-existent – divided, split, ineffective.

For a long time, the leader of the Opposition lived and taught in London, 4,000 miles from Port of Spain. Calypso singer, Mighty Sparrow, the country's most reliable political analyst of the period, said of the Prime Minister's authority that when he speaks 'no dog barks' in protest.

The truth of the Mighty Sparrow's observation is seen in the rise and fall from grace of Karl Hudson-Phillips, the man still thought the stronger of the two challengers for party leader.

He emerged as one of the few voices of authority in April 1970 when the Government was almost overthrown by an armed revolt and became the darling of the party and heir apparent.

Then he sinned against the highest canons of party discipline. He talked about the party's future, its attitude to young people, its relationship with the trade unions, and its need for revitalization. Pointedly snubbed by the Premier on his return from a trip abroad, he resigned his Cabinet post, and put all his cards, face up, on the table.

To Williams the challenge from his brash young Minister was the 'unkindest of all'. That is one reason why Williams is said to favour the other main contender Kamaluddin Mohammed.

If this is so, it would be a turnaround. Ten months ago, in a Cabinet reshuffle, Williams took over the important Ministry of External and West Indian Affairs from Mohammed and appointed him to the Ministry of Health and Local Government. The move was interpreted then as demotion.

But even more important than who becomes leader of the party, is the broader political picture.

If the Hudson-Phillips – Mohammed contest becomes vicious, it could split the PNM permanently.

If the Wooding Constitution commission recommends the sort of electoral changes which would convince them that elections would be fought openly and fairly (some parties have maintained that the voting machines have rigged) there could be more than one party in Parliament again after Williams goes, and ironically, Williams probably always envisaged a vibrant two-party democracy.

Joy and anxiety as the wives wait for their freed menfolk

by Mehr Kamal
Karachi

A good example of a Gemini descriptive piece on the aftermath of a big international story – the breakaway of Bangladesh from Pakistan. Most international media had lost interest by this stage but a Pakistani correspondent, close to the human experience, brings out the joy and anxiety in the exchange of prisoners and civilians. (8 October 1973 – GG 5404)

The agony of separation has given way to anxiety over reunion as thousands of Pakistani families wait for the arrival of husbands, fathers and brothers kept prisoner for nearly two years.

The first train from India carrying soldiers and civilians captured in Bangladesh in December 1971 steamed into Pakistan on 28th September. On board were 800 prisoners. Thousands of families waited to find out if their man was on the train.

No advance list of names was received and no one knew who was coming. They only knew that the train carried men from Camp No. 38.

The anxiety of the waiting families was increased by the knowledge that India is holding back 195 unnamed prisoners wanted by Bangladesh for trial pending an agreement on this issue between Pakistan and Bangladesh.

A number will never return home. Forty-eight prisoners were killed during captivity. They were said to have been trying to escape. Another 96, including seven officers, died in the camps.

About 6,000 prisoners are unaccounted for. Major-General Qamar Mirza, Chairman of the Prisoners of War Welfare Committee, said Pakistan had definite information that 75 army personnel were in Dacca Central Jail and 2,800 were held in two camps in Dacca and Chittagong. Another 43 Pakistani policemen had recently been transferred from an Indian camp in Benares to a camp in Bangladesh.

Pakistani authorities expect the repartriation to take about four months. For the men in the camps and their families in Pakistan this period may well seem longer than the 21 months they have already spent in the camps.

The wife of a Pakistani journalist, on hearing that her husband was coming, rushed from Karachi to Lahore and waited for hours on the border with her two children only to be told that her husband had been offloaded as a more seriously ill prisoner had to be sent home.

She said: 'What I went through that day is more than enough for a life time. I would never like anyone else to go through anything like that'.

The joy of imminent reunion is tinged with apprehension. No one knows what these men have gone through in this long period and what to expect.

Another journalist who is in an Indian camp wrote to a colleague in Karachi a few months ago: 'Do not be surprised if a bearded man leaning on a stick walks into your office one day. Don't turn him out, he is your friend.'

The mother of one prisoner told a correspondent: 'As the hour of reunion draws closer, I feel more and more depressed.'

A father said: 'I just don't know. I have never been so impatient, so restless, so nervous.'

A brother remarked: 'It is like I had walked many many miles during a transport strike late one night and felt faint when I saw my house. I could not have taken another step then. I don't have the nerve and energy to wait a moment longer now.'

For 21 months there has been no joy or celebration in about 90,000 homes all over Pakistan. Three 'Eid' festivals have gone by uncelebrated and have served only to make the pain of separation more acute. Babies have been born and loved ones have died.

Many families have denied themselves the basic comforts of furniture, good food, and new clothes because their loved ones have been deprived of these.

For weeks, since the 28th August signing of the Delhi Agreement on the repatriation of around 350,000 persons stranded by the 1971 war in the sub-continent, Pakistan has made hectic preparations to receive 90,000 prisoners of war and about 80,000 Pakistanis mostly confined to camps in Bangladesh.

Up to 200,000 Bengalis, including defence personnel, who were living in West Pakistan before the war, are also going home. Teams of social workers and medical personnel have been touring areas where most of the prisoners come from, talking to families, getting them ready to receive their relations, and solving their problems.

New reception camps have been built in Lahore for those returning. Civilians and armed personnel are being housed in separate camps. The soldiers undergo a medical examination, are given two months' advance salary and leave to go home before they are required to report for work.

The arrival of the prisoners has cast into the shade another two-way-repatriation that is in no way less emotional for those going home. Chartered flights are flying home Bengalis from Lahore and Karachi to Dacca and bringing back Pakistanis from there.

With the returned people on each side go a host of problems, for them personally and for their country. Problems of adjustment to a changed environment, and in many cases the problem of finding new jobs in countries that already have severe unemployment.

The most poignant situation, however, is that of men and women from two different parts of the divided country who intermarried. One chartered flight that took a Bengali contractor, who had lived in Swat for 15 years and married a Pathan girl, and his family to Dacca, brought back a West Pakistani with his Bengali wife and children.

World Bank choice will prove US intentions

by Daniel Nelson

Gemini, and Daniel Nelson from the London office in particular, kept a close eye on the international debt issue, seeing beyond the technicalities to the damage inflicted on developing countries and the net transfer of precious resources to the lenders. A cartoon by Paddy Allen, which went out with this article, satirized the process pointedly. (24 November 1986 – GE 8811)

It is a measure of the reduced level of hysteria about international debt that there has been so little reaction to Nigeria's decision to put a ceiling on the amount of money it is prepared to pay back to the banks.

Or that on the final day of last year Poland failed to make a $550 million interest payment due to Western governments.

Or that Brazil has been trying to get agreement on debt restructuring without a formal International Monetary Fund (IMF) programme.

Or that US Treasury Secretary James Baker's debt rescue plan has run into resistance from private Western banks.

Part of the reason is none of the moves are as dramatic as they seem.

Although Nigeria says it cannot afford to repay capital, it will continue to pay interest – an arrangement already adopted by many Latin American countries, and nowhere near as stringent as Peru's earlier decision to limit repayments to 10 per cent of export earnings.

Poland has not only maintained interest payments to banks – a far more sensitive issue than payments to governments – but has even begun to repay some the principal.

Brazil is trying to go-it-alone, which it may be able to do because of its uniquely self-sufficient economy and booming exports, but it is hoping to agree a compromise under which the IMF will not formally monitor the economy but will give a nod and a wink to private banks to show that it approves the Government's policies.

And though Swiss, Canadian and other Western banks have expressed reservations about the Baker proposals, (as have for different reasons the Cartagena Group, the African Development Bank and other institutions representing Third World interests), all will join in because there are no other plans on the table.

A more important reason for the muted response to these developments is that at long last there has been a shift of focus in the way the debt problem is perceived which offers a glimmer of hope for its solution.

It has changed from being seen as a crisis in which the key issue is bank balance-sheets to a crisis of development in which the key issue is the economic advancement of the debtor countries.

This moves the emphasis from the previous case-by-case approach in which banks could lean on particular countries and insist on the implementation of policies which however sensible individually were unfeasible collectively to one which tackles the overall situation.

Fig. 11.

And the overall situation, of course, is absurd: a net transfer of capital from the poor countries to the rich.

Ending that anomaly is the top priority for any reform. The anomaly arises because the private banks, having helped create the problem by lending indiscriminately on the assumption that sovereign debtors would never default, and having failed to spot the mounting crisis through incompetent monitoring, then made it worse by reducing their lending when it was most needed.

As was pointed out by Jacques de Larosiere, managing director of the IMF, commercial banks are jeopardizing the economic recovery of developing nations by cutting back on lending.

The Baker Plan addresses the problem by proposing that banks should lend an additional $20 billion to some 15 developing countries in 1986–88.

It also envisages that the World Bank and other development banks will increase their lending in the same period, and play a bigger role in helping developing countries implement policy reforms aimed at boosting longer-term economic growth.

US Treasury Secretary Baker and other Washington politicians realize that the combination of low growth arising from previous IMF prescriptions and the present reverse flow of resources represents the real debt crisis – one that could lead not just to defaults on a big scale, but to a questioning of the whole international financial system.

Unfortunately, Baker's efforts have not been backed by other parts of the Washington maze.

Japan and West Europe have already expressed dissatisfaction to Washington over the mediocrity of some of the names being canvassed to take over from Bank president Tom Clausen in July.

They point out that William Middendorf, US Ambassador to the European Community, lacks standing in the financial markets; John Hennessy of the First Boston Corporation lacks weight because of his comparative youth; and John Petty of the Marine Midland Bank lacks political clout.

An appointment needs to be made soon, because the lack of leadership at the Bank since the Baker initiative was mooted at the annual meeting in October is already becoming evident.

Pressure is thus on the Reagan Administration to signal its support for the Baker Plan by making a decision, and making a good one.

Concern about the American position has been exacerbated by a Washington proposal that interest rates should be introduced on loans made by the International Development Association (IDA), the soft-loan arm of the Bank.

Bank officials hope that the annoyance over this move will not mar the atmosphere during the negotiations for the next replenishment of the IDA. They had hoped that the new consensus among Western countries over how to deal with debt would avoid the damaging split between America and the rest which occurred during talks for the previous funding facility.

Nevertheless, for the US to be advocating a bigger role for the Bank, which it was formerly trying to cut down to size, and putting an emphasis on growth (the Baker initiative stipulates that additional financing would be conditional on policies for growth, adjustment and inflation control, in that order) is a breakthrough.

And it is not surprising that Washington has a split personality on the issue: at a time when it is telling the world that the path to development is paved with private enterprise, it is being forced to intervene to avert a disaster caused by the unregulated lending of private banks. It's a hard act to swallow.

(g)   Clean-cut, ambitious shock troops of the Right

by Kevin J. Kelley, New York

The 1980s saw a marked shift in the international agenda of the US and Britain as the

Reagan–Thatcher axis propagandized for anti-communism, free markets and against UN bodies which were thought to have fallen prey to socialism and Southern interests. Gemini sought to explain what had happened and focused on the lobbying of the conservative Heritage Foundation in a series of four articles, of which this was the second. (26 March 1987 – GS 4303)

The Heritage Foundation was launched in 1973 by two Capitol Hill functionaries, Edward Feulner and Paul Weyrich. They shared a belief that the Republican Party establishment had become complacent and unimaginative, more interested in preserving the political status quo than in vigorously advancing rightist ideology.

The Republicans controlled the White House, but were then a minority in Congress and did not seem, to Feulner and Weyrich, willing to challenge a domestic and foreign policy consensus largely shaped by liberal Democrats during the previous 40 years.

Some wealthy benefactors, mostly from the nouveau-riche Sun Belt states in the South, shared Feulner's and Weyrich's disgruntlement with the country's condition and the lacklustre Republican response to it. Among them was Joseph Coors, a millionaire Colorado beer brewer and sponsor of far-right causes.

Coors gave Heritage a $250,000 start-up grant, and the Foundation began cranking out position papers that at first attracted scant attention outside the ranks of a small but energetic group of rebellious reactionaries.

The Foundation and the New Right movement of which it was a part steadily gained ground as the Carter administration slid into political disrepute.

Heritage and other combatively conservative forces outside the Republican Party helped set the stage for the electoral triumph of Reagan, one of their longtime heroes, and for the shift in the Senate from Democratic caution to supply-side, laissez-faire enthusiasm.

No sooner had the most conservative president in 50 years taken power than Heritage's troops were distributing a detailed battle plan for the next four years.

By 1982 Foundation president Feulner – Weyrich having left to run another rightist advocacy outfit – was proclaiming that 62 per cent of Heritage's hundreds of policy proposals had been favourably acted on by Congress or by the administration.

Early on Heritage recognized that ideas mean little in Washington unless they are properly marketed. In this way, it bears little resemblance to the previously more prestigious American Enterprise Institute, a staid collection of conservative scholars who produce heavily footnoted tomes intended to be slowly digested in the bureaucratic maw.

By contrast, the 250 or so studies released annually by Heritage are each designed to be read in 20 minutes. Nor do they moulder in forgotten filing cabinets; the Foundation's publicity apparatus distributes thousands of copies, hand-delivered in some cases, to journalists, key congressional aides and mid and upper echelon federal officials, all of whose names and specialities are stored in constantly updated computer banks.

Heritage also maintains its own news service, which distributes original

The Heritage show

Fig. 12.

op-ed (leader page) articles to newspapers across the country, and it publishes a variety of journals and bulletins, as well as organizing regular issue seminars and legislative briefings.

Researchers – many of them under 40 – are meanwhile expected to proselytize actively for the reports. Foundation staffers spend much time on the luncheon circuit, cultivating personal contacts with departmental policymakers and congressional committee aides.

Feulner describes his young and eager employees as 'the shock troops of the conservative movement'. They often come to Heritage out of the iconoclastic contingents who have been trying to shatter the liberal hold on college campuses in the US for the past decade.

Ambitious and clean-cut, this conservative new wave is at least partly attracted by the Foundation's reputation as a job clearinghouse for the

Reagan administration. Feulner proudly acknowledges that 'several dozen' contributors to Heritage's 'Mandate for Leadership' policy compendiums are now in federal posts.

About 40 current or past employees also hold full or part-time positions in the government. Some are fairly prominent, such as the head of a White House task force on welfare reform.

Many more labour in relative obscurity, shaping policy behind the scenes and acquiring the job titles and seniority that will make them immune from political replacement by a future administration.

On most domestic issues, Heritage's positions derive more from right- wing libertarian philosophy than from fundamentalist dogma. Like the ideologues who have inspired Britain's Margaret Thatcher, Heritage theoreticians envision a harshly competitive, fiercely entrepreneurial society in which government welfare programmes play little or no role.

Thus the Foundation gave early help to Charles Murray, a social policy analyst who would cause a major stir with the 1984 publication of *Losing Ground*. That volume, heatedly debated for months, argues that Lyndon Johnson's 'war on poverty' and the institutions it spawned have proven ghastly, hurtful failures.

Welfare should essentially be abolished altogether, Murray contends, with the poor thereby being weaned from their 'dependence' and from the 'incentives to fail' inherent in the public assistance system.

Heritage has likewise argued against increased government attention to the burgeoning problem of homelessness in America. It maintained in a 1985 report that long-term aid projects would only 'throw money at the symptoms while creating a new federal bureaucracy'.

Heritage focuses much more attention on economic causes like privatizing parts of the social security system than it does on the 'social issues' favoured by the religious right. It is more likely to espouse wholeheartedly the Thatcherite initiative of selling off government-built flats than to take up forcefully the demands for outlawing abortion and mandating prayer in the schools.

The think tank's role as importer of Thatcher-style conservatism is also apparent in its advocacy of 'enterprise zones'. Stuart Butler, a British-born Heritage economist who helped establish a similar institute in London, proposed in 1979 that special districts be designated in urban ghettos where private companies could operate free from any tax and labour restrictions.

Butler borrowed this concept of unfettered capitalism as the salvation of the slums from Sir Geoffrey Howe, the mid-Seventies' leading architect of Tory economic policy.

The enterprise-zone idea was then adopted by Congressman Jack Kemp, who has made it a central plank in the platform he is building for the 1988 Republican presidential nomination.

Reagan's similarly warm endorsement of the proposal shows how much clout Heritage wields in domestic policymaking circles in Washington.

It is, all in all, a remarkable success story – the kind that's possible only in America, as shaped by Ronald Reagan.

Britain's isolation may strengthen the Commonwealth

by Derek Ingram
Vancouver

Ingram's round-up at the end of the 1987 Commonwealth Heads' Meeting typifies his commentary style, and his sympathy for the majority of Commonwealth countries on the divisive South African issue. No other journalist by then had his range of experience of the association, and few were as willing to take it seriously. (28 October 1987 – GN 32815)

In Nassau in 1985 and in London in 1986 British Prime Minister Margaret Thatcher distanced herself from the Commonwealth on South African policy. Now in Vancouver she has put herself totally out of mainstream thought and action on what is still the central issue in the Commonwealth and likely to remain so long into the future.

This is a watershed in the history of the Commonwealth, but not the devastating blow that some observers may be predicting in the weeks to come.

The new situation could prove in the long term to be a strengthening factor, showing that the Commonwealth is not dependent on any single member, even one that has always seemed as central as Britain.

The division on the issue of South Africa was as wide as it could be. Thatcher not only argued that sanctions had proved either ineffective or counter-productive but that the right policy was to create a strong South African economy because only then could the apartheid system be changed.

Britain admitted it was isolated and said it was not bothered about that. The other countries said they had not tried to change Thatcher's mind because, in the words of Indian Prime Minister Rajiv Gandhi, 'that would have been a waste of time'.

The argument was bitter and the meeting was notable for new tactics adopted by the British. Instead of, as in the past, holding briefings for British journalists only, the Prime Minister's press secretary, Bernard Ingham, gave what were virtually public performances three or four times a day with all journalists invited.

At these, the Thatcher line was repeated *ad nauseam* on the basis, it seemed, that the more something was said the more likely it was to be accepted as right. At her press conference after the meeting, Thatcher persisted with her arguments in the same way.

The British tactics were highly aggressive, reflecting the Thatcher style of international diplomacy and embracing highly questionable insinuations against Canada and other Commonwealth countries which no-nonsense Australian Prime Minister Bob Hawke called disinformation.

Hawke quoted Thatcher as saying at the meeting that she didn't feel at one with the rest of her colleagues on the whole issue of South Africa. It was all, from her point of view, a waste of time, and she would have nothing to do with the Commonwealth on the question of South Africa. This took her much further down the road to isolation than did her performance at the London mini-summit of 1986.

89

Fig. 13.

Not since the early days of the Rhodesia crisis in the mid-Sixties have such strong words been heard inside and outside a Commonwealth meeting. In those days African leaders often attacked Britain for its policies *vis-a-vis* Ian Smith. Now, not just black leaders are at loggerheads with Britain, but the prime ministers of the so-called old Commonwealth as well.

Canada's Prime Minister Brian Mulroney and New Zealand's David Lange take the Hawke view of Thatcher. There has never been a Commonwealth meeting where Britain has put itself so completely out of line with the rest of the leaders.

What was impressive in Vancouver was the unity of the rest. At a memorable press conference given by President Kenneth Kaunda of Zambia and prime ministers Robert Mugabe of Zimbabwe, Gandhi and Hawke there was complete harmony on what needed to be done.

The Commonwealth has set up a committee of eight foreign ministers – from Australia, Canada, Guyana, India, Nigeria, Tanzania, Zambia and Zimbabwe – to be chaired by Canadian External Affairs Minister Joe Clark, Britain refused to take part – one of six points made in the communique with British disclaimers.

The committee is to meet periodically to monitor and review progress on sanctions but also with a wide remit to react to developments as they unfold in South Africa.

A study is to be made of South Africa's relationship with the international financial system and high priority will be given to counteracting South African propaganda and censorship.

Thatcher made big play of the fact that the Commonwealth is not proposing any new sanctions and gave this as proof that the sanctions campaign is running out of steam. The others point out that the Commonwealth sanction list came into operation only at the beginning of this year and that it is important that these are working properly before embarking on anything else. Evasions by third parties need to be investigated.

But the meeting was not just about South Africa and Fiji, and on other issues there was much agreement. Fiji is out of the Commonwealth because the Governor-General has resigned and a change from monarchy to republic requires a reapplication.

Currently there is no properly recognized government.

The Commonwealth has offered its good offices if Fiji wants help in resolving its problems on a basis 'consistent with the principles that have guided the Commonwealth'. India in particular will be anxious that a new constitution does not discriminate against Fijian peoples of Asian origin.

Thatcher wants to see Fiji back in the Commonwealth as soon possible, but it may not be so easy. The situation may take months to resolve.

Vancouver was notable for the concern everyone showed for the man-made climatic changes now affecting a number of countries, especially those with low-lying and marginal agricultural areas like Bangladesh and the Maldive Islands.

The threat of rises in the sea levels is causing great concern in the Maldives, whose government has already put in hand a study. The Commonwealth Secretariat was asked to convene a group of experts to examine the implications for member countries of possible climatic change and to include the problem of flooding. Even as the leaders talked, temperate Britain was hit by an unprecedented wind storm which did huge damage.

The Commonwealth is also to develop a long-term programme of action on conservation and development as a result of a study it has done on desertification and deforestation.

It is to take a much closer look at women's affairs. A group will examine the impact of structural adjustment – that is, the major changes now taking place in ways of running the economies of many countries – on women's lives.

The first Commonwealth meeting of ministers responsible for women's affairs took place this year in Zimbabwe. Now such meetings are to be held every three years, the next in 1990.

As a result of a Commonwealth report on youth unemployment, a problem of alarming proportions in many developing countries, exchanges between governments, employers and labour are to be encouraged.

The most important development of all in Commonwealth cooperation at Vancouver came with the agreement to take the first steps towards establishing a university of the Commonwealth.

A university and college network for distance education is to be set up with headquarters in Vancouver. Canada will pay half the funding for the first five years and at least ten other countries will contribute, including Nigeria, India and Brunei.

The idea is that 'any learner anywhere in the Commonwealth shall be able to study any distance-learning programme available from any *bona fide* college or university in the Commonwealth'.

Small countries were pleased to hear that the office set up for their United Nations missions in New York with financial help from other Commonwealth countries, notably Australia, is to be enlarged. This unique idea allows small

Fig. 14.

states in Africa, Asia, the Caribbean and the Pacific to run their tiny missions out of a single office. Without this facility they would not be able to keep representation at the UN.

The leaders in Vancouver spent as much time on economic matters as they did on South Africa. Protectionism, low commodity prices, the debt problem – all came under examination. Good news came for Kenya, Ghana, Nigeria, Swaziland, Zambia and Zimbabwe when Canada announced it would forgive $347 million in outstanding development assistance loans to them.

If Thatcher went away from Vancouver disgruntled, no-one else did. In two years the leaders will assemble again Kuala Lumpur. It will be the first time the meeting has been held in Southeast Asia since 1971.

The venue is a surprise. When Dr Mahathir Mohamad became Prime Minister of Malaysia he took a jaundiced view of the Commonwealth. He did not even bother to go the Melbourne summit held in 1981 just after he came to power.

In Vancouver he took part in all the main discussions making valuable contributions from his lively mind. He said he found the meeting so productive and enjoyable that he just had to ask everyone back to his country.

How the West has made a hero of Saddam

by Tom Aston

This opinion piece by Associate Editor Aston, on the eve of the Gulf War, was falsified by events: the US-led coalition suffered modest casualties and the allied victory led indirectly to the Palestinian-Israeli peace talks. But his trenchant attack on the hypocrisy of the West was widely appreciated and Gemini's war coverage included radical analysis of the Western media (especially TV) and reports from affected capitals. (11 January 1991 – GAR 148)

Whether or not it comes to war, the Gulf crisis marks a turning point in the post-Cold War era. The ideological East–West war between communism and the 'free world' is over; the war between the developing world and the highly industrialized nations – the West, or the North – is just beginning.

Saddam's Iraq is the nightmare of this new era for the West – an emerging state armed with conventional, chemical and possibly biological weapons bursting in on the rich man's banquet. Even worse, the West finds itself confronted by the leader it so readily armed during the ten-year Gulf war in an attempt to use him to crush the Islamic revivalism of Iran.

Saddam has not only laid bare the soft oil-dependent underbelly of the Western economy, but also capitalized on the weakness of the selective Western appeal to morality and international law to preserve an unjust status quo.

Crying foul over the breach of Kuwaiti sovereignty rings hollow given the long US record of military intervention in the Caribbean and Latin America.

US moral outrage looks skin-deep – for instance, in May 1987 Washington was only too ready to forgive Iraq for an Exocet missile attack on the frigate USS Stark in the Gulf that left 37 American seamen dead. Saddam was regarded as a good guy bolstering the forces of light against the darkness of Ayatollah Ruhollah Khomeini.

And yet, even then, Baghdad's pogrom against Kurdish separatists was being carried out as brutally as today, torture and arbitrary imprisonment was widespread, political opposition within Iraq was as non-existent as it is

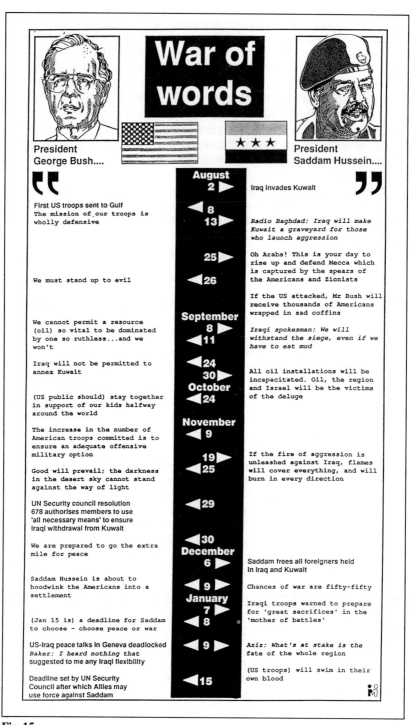

Fig. 15.

now. To wheel out these arguments several years later as a justification for military intervention in the Gulf betrays the bankruptcy of the Western case.

Washington has overpersonalized the crisis, daubing Saddam as an international devil in the mould of Fidel Castro and Colonel Gadaffi. Saddam has responded with dexterous manipulation of international television to defuse this image and called for a Holy War against the Infidel West.

The West has few real friends in the Middle East and Saddam has played the card of Arab nationalism masterfully, weakening the resolve of even the closest US Arab allies by threatening to draw Israel into any conflict and repeatedly demanding some resolution of the Palestinian question as a condition of a settlement over Kuwait.

Seizing on the opportunites created by the virtual withdrawal of the Soviet Union from the Middle East stage, Saddam has opened a political Pandora's box, leaving the US and its Western backers looking flat-footed. Decades of arrogant manipulation of the politics of the region have finally come home to roost.

Just as the victory of the Vietcong over US forces in Vietnam marked a military turning point in the post-World War Two global order – Uncle Sam was no longer regarded as invincible – so Saddam's invasion of Kuwait marks a turning point in the post-Cold War era, for he has demonstrated the economic vulnerability of the West.

While the Organization of Petroleum Exporting Countries (OPEC) nations were able to muscle in on the West's booty with the huge oil price rises of 1973–74, Saddam has gone a step further and, abandoning economic means, simply taken what he wants by force.

In the eyes of many in the developing world, he has done nothing worse than adopt the bullyboy tactics that the West has been using for a century or more to ensure a ready supply of cheap labour and raw materials from Asia, Latin America, the Caribbean and Africa.

There was profound symbolism in the embrace shared by Saddam and Zambian President Kenneth Kaunda, for long an unofficial spokesman for the poorer nations, in Baghdad just two days after the failure of the Geneva peace talks.

And this despite the fact that it is the economies of the developing world that have suffered most from the fall-out of the crisis and would be so badly hit economically if war was to occur. Overnight Saddam has become an international hero in continents he has rarely, if ever, expressed any concern about.

Saddam's success is the result of the failure of the rich nations to nurture a vision of an economics and politics allowing for the growth of the poorer nations.

This Western indifference has backfired for it has created the conditions in which Saddam could become powerful enough to invade Kuwait, in which such an invasion could actually become conceivable and even, just possibly, practical.

His move has been so radical that it has taken London, Washington, Brussels and Paris by surprise.

And his diplomacy has been so cunning that the Western alliance has been left with little option but to threaten to bludgeon him to death – the nightmare scenario – despite the huge price it will have to pay militarily and economically in doing this.

Apart from the global environmental impact of a war, which is likely to hit the developing countries worst of all, an attack on Saddam is likely to leave the West with a legacy of profound Arab hatred even amongst the peoples of its so-called allies.

The real horror of such a war has yet to permeate the minds of the Western public, mainly due to the blinkered media coverage given to the military build-up in the Gulf. Time and again British and US servicemen have been interviewed on television and radio describing the war as 'a job that's got to be done, so let's get on with it'.

Reports have pointed to the battle-readiness of the Allies' air and ground forces, emphasizing their technical superiority, largely ignoring the terrifying reality of modern warfare and the battle-hardened Iraqi forces that Allied troops will have to flush out of extensive trench networks.

The civilian casualties of a conflict would run to hundreds of thousands, yet those who have questioned the necessity of war have fallen victim to the anachronistic label of 'appeaser'.

It is ironic that the West is not more prepared to give economic sanctions against Iraq a chance to bite, for any war would ultimately be about retaining the economic benefits for a considerable time after hostilities ceased.

Politics has been reduced to its most crude level – that of brute force – and as both sides sound the drums of war, both are seen in all their ugliness. The failure of Western policy in the Gulf has never been more stark for it has made an unlikely hero of Saddam in much of the developing world and revealed the lie on which the affluence of the North is based.

To resort to war to try to conceal this failure would, in the long-term, only exacerbate the instability of the North-South divide. In the short-term, peace through sanctions would be a safer option.

In the long run 'a new politics' is needed in Washington, London, Paris, Brussels and Bonn so that another Gulf crisis becomes an impossibility. The North must tear down the economic Berlin Wall it has built around the South and give up its ostrich-like indifference to the genuine needs of the developing world.

This century has seen the rise and fall of Fascism and Communism, but the current upheavals do not signify the 'end of politics', as Francis Fukuyama, formerly of the US State Department, has put it, and the beginning of a global evolutionary trend to the free market and liberal democracy.

Rather, global politics have been transformed. The West can no longer regard the developing nations simply as a resource to be exploited and manipulated, or, if it does, then it is at its own peril. Saddam is ample proof of that.

Why so much about the Gulf War proved wrong

by Daya Kishan Thussu

Aston's successor as Associate Editor had co-authored a book on Third World news exchanges, Contra-Flow in Global News[1], *and shared Gemini's interest in media manipulation from a more academic standpoint. A year after the Gulf War, Thussu reflected on the uniformity of Western media coverage and how truth became a casualty. (25 February, 1992 – GM 62)*

Just as the Western world was marking the first anniversary of the Gulf war with assessments of its historic significance, a much-quoted media story in the pre-war campaign to demonize Iraq was exposed as a fraud.

The story told how in one atrocity in occupied Kuwait Iraqi soldiers snatched 312 newborn babies from incubators in the city hospital. The incident was included in an Amnesty International report, issued soon after the Iraqi invasion of Kuwait in August 1990.

Politicians, Middle East 'experts', religious leaders and editorial writers and columnists quoted it copiously, especially the incubator outrage.

After the liberation of Kuwait, the story was thoroughly investigated by human rights activists and, according to Andrew Whitley, of Middle East Watch, was a 'complete hoax'.

But it was a crucial element in the war of words which preceded military action. The story was repeatedly cited in the United Nations Security Council.

During the debate in the United States Congress on the war resolution, the incubator story was mentioned seven times, while Congress and the US public opinion was hanging in the balance.

The story received credibility from a witness to the US Congressional caucus on Human Rights. Nayaira, a 15 year old Kuwaiti 'escapee', gave a first-hand account of the incubator outrage. She was in fact the daughter of Nasir al-Sabah, the Kuwaiti ambassador to the US and a member of the Kuwaiti royal family.

A video of the Congressional hearing was part of the professional public relations package produced by the biggest US public relations company Hill and Knowlton.

They had been retained by a coalition for a free Kuwait (backed by the Kuwaiti government) to 'sell' the war to a reluctant American public.

According to a programme made by the Canadian Broadcasting Corporation and shown on British TV in February, 10 million dollars – equivalent to a US presidential election expense – was spent on the propaganda war, using all the promotional techniques, such as providing videos to various news organizations.

The media generally underplayed the considerable opposition to military action within the US, reflected in the close vote in the Congress.

1. Oliver Boyd-Barrett and Daya Kishan Thussu, *Contra-Flow in Global News:International and regional News Exchange Mechanisms.* London: John Libbey, 1992.

According to a New York-based media monitoring group Fairness and Accuracy in Reporting (FAIR), in the run-up to the war, the three major American TV networks, ABC, NBC and CBS, devoted less than one per cent of their airtime to organized opposition to the Gulf policy.

Few journalists asked any critical questions about why the democratic West should go to war to safeguard undemocratic sheikhdoms.

Hardly any reference was made to other policy goals, such as to keep control on supplies of cheap oil; to justify the continuation of the arms trade in the post-Cold War age, and the long-standing US desire for a permanent military presence in the Gulf.

Already since the end of the war the West has sold arms worth $30 billion in the Middle East region. The media once again made little of last September's Kuwait-US defence deal which ensures that US forces can stay in Kuwait.

During the war itself, double standards persisted in reporting the military action. The Western missiles caused 'collateral damage', whereas the Scuds caused 'civilian casualities'. George Bush was 'at peace with himself, resolute, statesmanlike, assured' while Saddam Hussein was 'demented, defiant, an evil tyrant, a crackpot dictator'.

The West had 'reporting guidelines', while the Iraqis had 'censorship'. The coalition had 'press briefings', while the Iraqis had 'propaganda'.

The 48-hour news blackout before the ground war raised practically no media protest. Little was reported about the large-scale killings by B52s of retreating Iraqi soldiers (many of them in fact Kurds).

The war exposed a deep strain of racism. Mostly an image was projected of the Iraqi people as abstract and disposable. Iraq and the whole Middle East was largely dehumanized. By allowing that to happen the media facilitated the political aims behind the war.

Many saw the media as submitting willingly to censorship, repeating the military's information uncritically. Wrote John Naughton, in the London *Observer* newspaper: 'What was galling about the coverage was the supine tractability of many journalists ... It was hard to avoid the impression that they saw themselves as part of the Allied war effort'.

One key 'fact' repeated throughout the crisis period and the war itself was that Iraq had the world's fourth biggest army.

As the *World Defence Almanac* shows, before the Gulf war Iraq was in seventh place after the Soviet Union, China, the US, India, Iran, and Turkey.

This exaggeration of Iraqi military capability could be seen to justify the continuous bombing of a retreating, largely conscript army.

Alfonso Rojo, of Spanish newspaper *El Mundo* who also filed for London's *Guardian* newspaper from Baghdad, was close to the truth when he said after the war: 'Journalists have to figure at the top of the list of those who lost out by the Gulf war. We allowed ourselves to be manipulated and we confused the public. There did not exist an Iraqi army of a million men and Saddam Hussein's power was deliberately exaggerated'.

Last April the annual assembly of the International Press Institute in Kyoto, representing more than 2000 newspapers and broadcasting organizations, unanimously passed a resolution condemning the media management techniques used during the war, which had 'prevented a balanced picture of events, including the full extent of human suffering'.

These wrong images of the war were not only for 'allied' consumption, but shown across the world. Unlike Radio Baghdad or the Iraqi News Agency INA, which lack credibility even within Iraq, the US-dominated Western media have global reach and influence. Most international news is disseminated through Western news sources.

The American Cable News Network (CNN) reaches nearly 100 countries. In countries where CNN is not available, Visnews and Worldwide Television News (WTN), the world's two biggest television news companies and both owned by Western organizations, provide TV news.

The powerful *Voice of America* and the *BBC World Service*, with their domination of radio frequencies, can be tuned into anywhere in the world.

The four biggest international news agencies – Associated Press (AP), United Press International (UPI), Agence France Presse (AFP) and Reuters – are Western, the first two American.

They wield great influence in setting the agenda of world events, reflecting Western strategic interests – as do such US publications as *Time* and *Newsweek*, both with global readerships.

Articles and editorials from Western newspapers are syndicated to newspapers in many developing countries.

There remains, as was so often argued during the debate in the early Eighties on a New World Information and Communications Order, a virtual Western monopoly on news and information available to shape public opinion internationally.

One year on, the Western media seem to have lost interest in Iraq. While the regime of Saddam Hussein unabashedly triumphs in its 'victory' over the West, thousands of ordinary, powerless Iraqis continue to suffer the excesses of dictatorship.

As the al Sabah family celebrates the first anniversary of Kuwait's liberation, the human rights of millions of Iraqi children are being violated by the UN (read US)-dictated sanctions without any legal reason. Why has Iraq ceased to be newsworthy?

5 The journalists and artists

At all times in its history Gemini could call on 70–80 regular contributors, and a wider pool of almost double that for occasional pieces. Particularly in its early, entrepreneurial days it appeared to have an expert correspondent on every conceivable subject. In 1971 Bruce Bedford, writing about a direct assault on Mount Everest which had failed, was described as the Gemini News Service mountaineering correspondent. He was also, readers learned, the editor of *Descent*, a caving magazine.[1] Nor were the experts necessarily resident where one might expect: Geoffrey Lindop, the space correspondent, was an astronomer to be found living by Britain's Solway Firth, from where he kept an eye on space probes and satellites.

In fact those who contributed to the service came from different walks of life and with different motivations. The agency was, in some countries, able to recruit contributors who were already prominent journalists. This was true of India, for example. Kuldip Nayar, whose exclusive interview with Mrs Gandhi went out in the first Gemini packet was followed later as Delhi correspondent by D.K. Joshi who had been a journalist since 1946, written two books and was then working for the *Indian Express*. During his world tour of 1966, prior to the launch of the service, Ingram had been able to find a number of prestige figures who welcomed the extra international exposure.

However the service had not been running long before younger, ambitious journalists outside Britain, who were looking forward to making their names, saw it as an avenue for wider expression and for cuttings that would help their career. A number of able young Caribbeans, attracted also by the non-metropolitan perspective, typified this trend. Among them were Tony Cozier, later to become well-known as a cricket correspondent, who in 1970 was writing from Barbados about the region's tourist industry.[2] Another was Mohamed Hamaludin of Guyana, a teacher who had been writing short stories before joining the *Guyana Chronicle* in 1968.

> The way I remember it, I got into contact with Gemini News Service around the 1970s through the then Guyana correspondent, Hubert Williams ... I did occasional pieces for Gemini and eventually became the Guyana correspondent.

1. GG3030

2. See, for example, GG2003

Writing for a foreign medium has always had a particular kind of cachet for journalists in small states. In my case my links to Gemini and such other media as *The Economist* and the *Financial Times* provided me with a sort of buffer against political interference and intimidation and allowed me to develop skills that would not have been possible if I had been confined to writing for the local newspaper alone.

I never rose to any great heights as a journalist but whatever abilities I was able to develop came largely through the work I did for Gemini. I was captivated by the fact that Gemini allowed its correspondents to write stories their way, from their knowledge of the issues, and never tried to impose journalism structures on the writers.

In the truest sense, the agency provided – and still does – a forum for sharing information among developing countries, in particular, about what is going on. This developmental orientation no doubt became necessary because of the fact that this was a niche in the profession that was not being filled by the international media. A vast number of stories of great consequence about the developing world that came through Gemini was not of the sensational kind. But they have helped document the human experience in places where it mattered, where life-and-death struggles are a daily occurrence.[3]

Hamaludin was too modest. Following a move from Guyana to Miami he became managing editor and then editor of *The Miami Times*, the American South's largest black weekly. *The Miami Times* uses much Gemini material, but he emphasises that the subscription is not a matter of altruism. The ANC's anti-apartheid struggle in South Africa, the efforts at self-sufficiency of rural villages in Africa, and the plight of black Brazilians (a two-part Gemini series at the time of Rio's 1992 Earth Summit) were all examples of items of concern to his readership.

Hamaludin's transition from contributor to user was not, unfortunately, universal. Andrew Clark, as a young Australian journalist, had written for the service in the early 1970s. Twenty years later, when he was editor of *The Sun–Herald* in Sydney, he looked back with fondness to that earlier time, recalling pioneering articles from Gemini and a piece he himself had written on the Green Ban Movement among Australian trade unionists, which had anticipated later environmental concerns. But from his editorial chair now he was also hard-nosed:

> Gemini is a fine service with some lively journalism. However, its broader rationale of the Commonwealth as a coherent source of news and features, has little drawing power in this country. All metropolitan Australian papers have extensive sources of foreign news from their own correspondents, Reuter, AFP, AP, UPI and at least two or three services drawn from the *New York Times*, *The Guardian*, the *Financial Times*, *The Daily Telegraph*, *Los Angeles Times* and *The Washington Post*.[4]

---

3. Mohamed Hamaludin, letter to author, 14 January 1994.

4. Andrew Clark, letter to author, 8 March 1994.

Much of the authority in the Gemini copy lay in the authenticity of its contributors. Elias Nyakutemba, a Zambian who did not begin writing for Gemini until after he attended a course in Berlin in 1988, describes his own background:

> I was born as Kayombo Nyakutemba on 28/12/51 in a remote village near the Zambia–Angolan border in North West Zambia. I'm the second child of Chief Chiteta Jose Nyakutemba, one of many Luvale (tribe) chiefs whose lands and peoples were divided by the colonial border.

> The missionaries christened me as Elias and I'm stuck with it! I'm married with four children, the youngest, Kahilu ('back to life') is just over one month today. My old man died in 1971, at the age of 41! My mother is still alive at 61 and just arrived to see the baby, as is tradition, the other day.

Nyakutemba joined the Zambia Information Services in 1974 which he worked for until he took early retirement in early 1994. His writing at home and abroad had by then upset the 'new democracy' of President Chiluba, and he feared that he might be sacked and lose his pension. 'Now I'm scratching a living trying to freelance, thanks to the ties blended largely by Gemini News. I now write for half a dozen London-based African magazines whenever I have a story, also for the BBC African service.'[5]

He had been put on to Gemini by Frank Barton, one of the lecturers on the course at the International Institute for Journalism in Berlin, who had told him over a beer, 'Your stuff is good, it can sell, try Gemini News'. Ingram and Nelson's wide range of contacts meant that they were in touch with many journalists who might at some point contribute. (For much of his 27 years as editor, Ingram was travelling outside Britain for three or four months each year.)

An example of this kind of burgeoning relationship was with Kabral Blay-Amihere, editor of *The Independent* of Ghana. He was first in touch with Ingram in 1986 when he was secretary-general of the Ghana Journalists Union and Ingram was president of the Commonwealth Journalists Association. He subsequently became a correspondent when he was on a one year attachment at the London School of Economics. He has since written about four items a year, including economic stories and coverage of the Non Aligned Movement meeting in Accra, and has looked after a Gemini Regina award-holder in Ghana.[6]

However the knowledge of a single country and an ability to communicate information from it is not the only qualification. Some of the most successful Gemini correspondents have been those from developing countries who have travelled more widely, or who have taken up residence in another. Two such are the Pakistani Mehr Khan (who also wrote as Mehr Kamal) and the Singaporean Abby Tan, who made her home in Manila.

After working as Assistant Editor on the Foreign Desk of Pakistan's Associated Press Mehr Khan, whose Australian husband John Williams also wrote for Gemini, joined

---

5. Nyakutemba letter, *ibid.*

6. Interview, Kabral Blay-Amihere

UNICEF in New York. But she continued to contribute items for the service as she travelled: for instance about Fiji women making handicrafts for tourists in 1977, or land reform and the changed priorities of independent Zimbabwe in 1981.[7]

Abby Tan moved from the secure, regulated society of Singapore to the dangers and unpredictability of the Philippines. She has freelanced for many publications but has steadily put her experience and insight at the disposal of Gemini. Of the war zones she says, 'Whenever I go to the Moro National Liberation Front territory in the south, I am always at risk of being shot at or I can walk into an ambush.' But her most dangerous time was probably during the December 1989 attempted coup which nearly toppled President Corazon Aquino, when the bullets whizzed past her.

> Two fully armed rebels entered my office on the tenth floor to ask if they could watch the events outside unfolding on TV. I had to firmly say No, because the secretaries on my floor were too scared, screaming 'They are here! They are here!' then fled and slammed the doors. The rebels understood and didn't demand further.
>
> For the next few days the building was raked by machine-gun fire and rockets. The British Embassy above me on the eleventh floor was rocketed as well. I had to be the one to call the British Ambassador in his house to inform him his office was damaged. 'Oh dear, how dreadful', he replied. I continued filing on radio and for newspapers amidst the rolling thunder sound of mortar rounds.
>
> On the third day everyone was evacuated from Makati. On the fourth day we, the press, were allowed back to Makati centre to meet the rebel leaders who were negotiating to surrender.
>
> The ceasefire was only for three hours till noon. While we the press were being ushered out to safety, I decided to go back to the office to retrieve my computer. It was so eerie. I realized I was the only one walking on Ayala Avenue from the rebel headquarters in one building to my office a few blocks away. I walked quickly and prayed I won't get shot. I couldn't run with my computer, it was an old laptop that weighed 10 lbs. After what seemed like eternity, I reached the safety zone. The shelling resumed in the afternoon.
>
> At one instance I stood on Edsa Highway watching the rebels on top of the Nikko Garden Hotel. At dusk the rebels gave the customary round of fire to signal the end of the day. I walked away, then a security guard less than two feet away from me suddenly fell writhing to the ground. A bullet struck him in the leg. It could have been me.[8]

Although Gemini was always sympathetic to positive stories about developing countries, and their hard-won achievements, its contributors could nevertheless find themselves the

---

7. 'Fiji's women cash in on the tourist boom', GG6174 and 'Where life's no longer just a bowl of cow peas', GA 366

8. Abby Tan letter to author, 21 January 1994.

objects of suspicion from governments. Two who suffered most were Luis Tricot, correspondent in Chile during the military dictatorship of General Pinochet, and Min Thu, Burma (Myanmar) correspondent under another military regime. Letters from each of them, sent respectively in November 1987 and November 1988, told the London office of their plight.

Luis Tricot wrote to Nelson on 3 November 1987 from the prison hospital at Pedro Montt, Santiago:

> Dear Daniel,
>
> Thanks for your letter. You've no idea how much it means to get a letter in a situation like this.
>
> Well, I'm alive, and in a country like Chile this becomes something of an achievement.
>
> My plaster-cast has just been taken off, so I can sit a little. The pain hasn't gone away yet but at least I'm able to move a bit more. I've been in bed for two months now.
>
> Needless to say I'm stuck in prison. Knowing the 'impartiality' of the Chilean military justice system, I'm likely to spend a long time in here. In other words, it's just another frame-up. But people do care. Solidarity with myself and my wife (five months pregnant at the time of her arrest) has been enormous. Both here and abroad, people from all walks of life have been pressing the authorities for my release and for the detention and prosecution of those who tortured us.
>
> But my own pain and suffering become insignificant compared to that of my people. Fourteen years of dictatorship have transformed the country into a living hell for millions. It breaks my heart to see hunger, poverty and misery all around us.
>
> How can anyone deprive a child of his childhood?
>
> How can happiness be the privilege of a few?
>
> Has the cult of death triumphed over the beauty of life?
>
> I think not. That's why I'm full of hope for the future, for noone, no dictatorship, has ever been able to halt the advance of a fighting people.
>
> Do write whenever you can, it's an important form of support.
>
> I'm sure we'll see each other again in the not too distant future.
> Regards,
> Luis[9]

Tricot had been arrested, beaten so badly that his back was broken, and had to learn to

9. Ingram Archive.

walk again. The beatings and electric shock treatment he suffered took place during the same month that President Pinochet signed the Inter-American Convention to Prevent and Punish Torture. It was 14 months before he got out of jail, but he has continued to write for Gemini, contributing not least on the failure to bring torturers to justice after Chile returned to civilian rule.

From Rangoon Min Thu wrote to Gemini on 14 November 1988 after 17 months of silence:

> I am sorry that I was unable to leave any message for you when authorities came for me May 22 1987 in connexion with my story on the 25 years of socialist construction here and threw me behind bars in an 8' x 10' cell in the Insein jail from where I was released last July 15 – that was why I 'disappeared'.
>
> On my release I found other problems – I became homeless and penniless. The landlord sold off the flat during my detention and some cash left behind was 'dead' because of the last demonetization.
>
> As I was kept incommunicado I was unable to send a message while under detention under a law which translated would read 'law to protect the state from the dangers of destructive and anti-state elements...' that empowered the government to detain a person up to three years without trial.
>
> However I managed to find a room from where I banged the typewriter for my first story which is enclosed.
> Yours sincerely, Min Thu[10]

Expatriate correspondents could always be expelled, as happened to the South African Johnny Maseko, a Gemini correspondent and editor of *The Mirror* in Lesotho. Tom Thabane, Secretary to the Military Council of Lesotho, burst into Maseko's office to complain about a story in *The Mirror*; one of his complaints was that he had not given permission for his photo to appear alongside another person's, Chief Retselisitsoe. Maseko was first charged with criminal defamation, then deported.

Resident nationals were always more vulnerable, particularly when a regime was getting shaky. Various Gemini writers had problems in Zambia towards the end of President Kaunda's one-party rule. Augustine Phiri, a Zambia News Agency reporter who had cabled a story to his editor stating that a five month old baby had been trampled to death in a mealie meal stampede outside a state-owned shop in the Copperbelt was charged with publishing false information with intent to cause fear and alarm. He was acquitted. Phiri also had the distinction of being denounced by President Banda in the Malawi parliament for a piece he had written.

Kaunda himself issued instructions to interrogate Fred Chela, who had chronicled the deteriorating Zambian economy. Thereafter Gemini ran some of his stories under the pseudonym of 'John Street', a rare decision.[11]

---

10. *Ibid.*

11. Fred Chela, letter to author, 21 February 1994.

Sometimes a government backed down, as happened in Sri Lanka in 1983. Three judges of the Supreme Court gave a verdict on a fundamental human rights case against the then President J.R. Jayewardene and his government. The next day the judges' houses were stoned by members of the ruling United National Party in a well-orchestrated affair. The police were nowhere to be seen and could not be contacted because the judges' phone lines had been disconnected.

Gamini Navaratne wrote an article about what he saw as a disgraceful episode, insulting to and intimidatory of the Sri Lankan judiciary. His Gemini report was widely published and on 29 March the government brought in a parliamentary motion, naming him for alleged breach of privilege. He could have been tried at the bar of the House:

> I went to the best tailor in the city and ordered a suit. After all, I could not go shabbily dressed to the august assembly where the people's sovereignty is supposed to repose. Forget that this Parliament had once been called a den of thieves by an Opposition member, who got thrown out when he refused to apologise and withdraw the reference.

> I telephoned the Minister who raised the issue and said I was ready for the trial and asked whether he was ready. That was the end of the matter.[12]

Navaratne, who was himself Sinhalese but had won a reputation for the objective way in which he reported the fighting in the Tamil north, successfully faced down a threat to his own and Gemini's reputation. His article could not have appeared in Sri Lanka at the time.

From the viewpoint of the London office there were some countries with a plethora of correspondents, such as Zambia, Tanzania or Kenya, and others, like Malaysia, Nigeria or even Australia where it was difficult to get regular coverage of a high quality. This was partly a function of the system of standard payments – still only £60 per article in 1994 – which were unattractive for higher earners or in higher income countries. It also arose because many correspondents needed nurturing to produce better copy and this was time-consuming and labour-intensive for a small head office. Finally a number of freelance journalists in developing countries were so fixated on politics that they were unable to supply the kind of cultural, environmental, gender, human rights and offbeat stories that were increasingly crucial to Gemini's niche in the 1980s.

Genuine specialists rather liked the agency. Bob Holmes, an Australian sports enthusiast who came late to journalism, always appreciated the fact that Gemini encouraged him when he approached them, even though his first story was spiked.

> Indeed they have a unique place in my heart as the only people from the *Writers' and Artists' Yearbook* not to have sent me a rejection slip!

Holmes, based in Sydney, soon got the hang.

> Liking the offbeat as well as the underdog, I always knew there was an outlet when I came across a one-legged, Western Samoan weightlifter or an Algerian woman

---

12. Ingram Archive.

sprinter who could not show her legs in public in her home town. More seriously, I was encouraged to do some in-depth previews to major Games such as the Olympics, World Cup football and cricket and, of course, the Commonwealth Games.[13]

By the 1980s the perception of Gemini was that it was largely concerned with developing countries and mostly written by journalists indigenous to them. Also, some of the most useful types of contribution came from journalists from the South who were placed in newsworthy situations, such as the Ghanaian Charles Quist-Adade who was reporting from the Soviet Union. However Ingram had always resisted stereotyping the service and the fact was that Gemini still made use of pieces and writers who were British, writing either from Britain or as a result of stays in other places. (In the late 1960s Gemini had used much more material of British origin and prominent journalists like William Forrest, who had covered the siege of Madrid in the Spanish Civil War, had written regular commentaries on European politics and diplomacy.)

Gemini was particularly keen to avoid the dangers of 'parachute journalism' – where a reporter jumps into a different society and opines at short notice on the basis of first interviews and pre-existing prejudices. But the modest rewards available, and the flair of people like Ingram and Nelson in picking out contributors with genuine knowledge and commitment, helped to guard against them.

So what sort of people were the British contributors who helped Gemini? Seven who give a flavour of this strand in Gemini journalism are Philip Short, Andrew Lycett, Christabel King, Nicola Cole, Cedric Pulford, David Spark and Chris Mullin.

Philip Short, who went on to have a distinguished career with the BBC – he had a nasty brush with Idi Amin's regime in Uganda and served in China and Japan for the BBC – started writing for Gemini and its associated magazine, *African Development*, soon after he set up as a freelance in Malawi in August 1967.

> I was the only freelance 'foreign correspondent' (really too grand a title for the infant reporter I then was) in Malawi, having 'bought out' the strings, goodwill and associated commercial photography business of a Yorkshireman called W.G. Farnworth – 'Bill' as everyone called him, who'd been in Malawi for years and had decided the time had come to move back to Britain; the business cost me £600, which I had to borrow. That was a huge sum then. A young journalist joining the *The Daily Telegraph* or *The Times* in those days could expect a starting salary of less than £1000 a year. Until I took over from him, Bill Farnworth had likewise been the only freelance in the country ... So it was a very small pond.

> I continued to write for Gemini until I left Malawi in March 1970, and then again from March 1971 to March 1973 in Uganda. Soon after that I left Africa and the connection was broken.[14]

---

13. Bob Holmes, letter to author, 15 February 1994.

14. Short letter, *ibid.*

Andrew Lycett and Christabel King were examples of British journalist-travellers who wrote just occasionally for the service. In early 1979 Lycett, who was a freelance and later was to become the biographer of Ian Fleming, wrote a piece titled, 'After 13 years ... good news out of Chad'.[15] King, who was a scion of one of the most famous press families in Britain, the Harmsworths, was in the late 1970s travelling round Africa as a partner of Nick Worrall. Worrall's father John had been a friend of Ingram. Both John and Nick contributed to Gemini; John had been expelled from Rhodesia by Ian Smith and Nick was subsequently expelled from Zimbabwe by Robert Mugabe.

King was working chiefly as a radio reporter but says, 'I was freelancing for everything that moved.' She knew that Ingram was on the lookout for offbeat pieces. Finding herself in Egypt in 1978, on the eve of the historic Camp David meeting which led to peace between Israel and Egypt, she managed to interview Mrs Sadat, wife of the Egyptian president who was subsequently assassinated. She sent something to Gemini. It was exactly the sort of topical but different article, unlikely to be overtaken in the vagaries of a postal service, which bolstered the agency's reputation.

Nicola Cole, by contrast, has had a long connection. Now resident in Norfolk she has provided a series of lighter pieces from Britain which have helped prevent Gemini being seen as too worthy or problem-oriented. In a letter to Ingram marking his retirement as editor she commented, 'Gemini has helped educate, feed and clothe my girls, pay my mortgage and generally keep body-and-soul together.'

She also recalled a sequel to one of her stories.

> 'Can you assist in our inquiries?' the Scotland Yard detective asked. 'Certainly, if I can', I replied, wondering what I'd done now. Yet it wasn't me 'in the frame' but the owner of a London art gallery whom I had interviewed five years earlier. It transpired he was wanted for international-scale fraud; was there anything in my notes about people he dealt with, countries he visited, which might provide a clue as to his present whereabouts?

> It was one of the few occasions I've regretted my practice of keeping interview notes for no longer than three years. I was unable to help...[16]

Cedric Pulford, a *Guardian* sub-editor who created his own career as an international consultant in the training of journalists, has written for the service on his travels and also filled in at the London office. He wrote two alternative stories about the restart in 1983, to go out in the service, and Ingram decided to use both. His succinct and breezy style was illustrated in a piece he wrote about Cyprus in 1992, when he focused on the run- down nature of Turkish-occupied north Cyprus. The fourth paragraph ran:

> The partition of Cyprus could not be more bad-tempered. The ramshackle wall that bisects Nicosia Old Town is guarded by three lines of soldiers – Greek, Turk

---

15. GN2486.

16. Ingram Archive, letter of 31 December 1993.

and United Nations. From the Greek side you can phone anywhere in the world, except Famagusta down the road.[17]

Pulford was British, but he had seen Gemini used in many other countries and was sympathetic to the developmental and training bias it had acquired. The same was true of David Spark, formerly with the Westminster Press (a British regional press group), a key figure in the Development Journalists' Group in London and editor of the Commonwealth Journalists Association newsletter.

Spark thought that Gemini's practice of referring to men and women simply by their surname, long before it became standard practice in British papers, might have explained a rough reaction to one of his articles.

> In the early 1980s I interviewed a Scotsman who was a pioneer of holidays in Vietnam. My article was used by Gemini and published in the *Bangkok Post*, which received a letter from the Scot claiming he never gave the interview. He was sending a copy of the letter to his Vietnam contact. The interview and article appeared to me innocuous. Perhaps the contact did not like being referred to simply by surname, without even a Mr. [18]

Chris Mullin, now a Labour MP, contributed to Gemini throughout the 1970s when he was freelancing and then working for the BBC World Service. He stopped soon after he joined *Tribune*, the left-wing British weekly, which he edited from 1982 to 1984. He ceased regular journalism on being elected to Parliament. He had started out as a trainee on the *Daily Mirror* training scheme and in 1971 went to China on a trip paid for by the *Mirror*. But the paper did not want to use any of his articles, perhaps because they gave too rosy a picture of Mao's country after the Cultural Revolution.

However Ingram snapped up the series 'And then came Mao' in the context of President Nixon's visit to Beijing. From then on Mullin became a frequent writer on Asian topics. While some of his pieces offered political analysis, especially of the winding-down of the Vietnam war, others were lighter. He wrote, for instance, about the suspicions aroused by long-haired travellers in Southeast Asia, and Gary Davis' 'World Service Authority' passport.

His contacts with the office were usually with Ingram or his secretary. They wrote to him when he was overseas via poste restantes. After Mao's death in 1976 Mullin provided quite a severe appreciation of the life and work of the Great Helmsman.[19]

Although most people associated Gemini with Ingram, and Ingram's wide network of friends and contacts provided contributors and informants, the office was never a one-man band. The role of the assistant editors (from the appointment of Nelson onwards the usual title was associate editor) and of the tiny London staff was essential. It strengthened the

17. 'Passing through the looking glass in Cyprus', GU4001.

18. David Spark, letter to author, 5 January 1994.

19. Interview, Chris Mullin. See Asia Column, GAS220, for his piece after Mao's death.

professionalism of the agency, and added ingredients which Ingram alone might never have thought of.

In the first phase of the service people like Richard Hall, Oliver Carruthers and Alan Rake had a strong understanding of Africa. Hall, especially, was one of the best journalists of his generation and he left Gemini to edit *The Observer* colour magazine. Zambia, where Hall had been based before he returned to Britain, was one of only four African countries to recognize Biafra. He twice went to Biafra, writing strong copy about the starvation he saw there. On his last visit, on the eve of the secessionist state's collapse, he had to take a kitbag of food for himself; he flew in with Holy Ghost Fathers, drinking Irish whiskey, on New Year's Eve, 1970.

A few days later he flew out of Uli airstrip – in reality a stretch of main road – to São Tomé with two Irish nurses in a Stratocruiser flown by Icelanders. It was impossible to leave without an exit visa, even though the state was crumbling. The exit visas were green and Hall, who didn't have one, waved his American Express card in front of officials before boarding the plane:

> One of the Icelanders said to me, 'I think there is some trouble there'. I said, 'You won't be going back' General Ojukwu, the Biafran leader, fled from Uli the following night.[20]

Someone like Hall, beavering away as writer and sub-editor, was an inspirational figure. Around 1969 he went on a selling trip for Gemini to Yugoslavia, Greece, Lebanon and Egypt, designed to persuade papers and other media to take the service. He was a friend of Ingram's but witnessed the growing frictions between Ingram and Carruthers. He concluded that Gemini was too under-financed to be able to go on getting international exclusives, and also that journalists were perhaps not very good at running a media business.

Like others he too was impressed by Gemini's reach. He once wrote a piece about Eduardo Mondlane, the leader of Frelimo, the Mozambican liberation movement. It was put out by the agency after Mondlane's assassination. Quite some while later he had to go into a Kensington hospital with a collapsed thorax. There, in a lavatory, he inexplicably saw a copy of the *Sarawak Times*, and there was his piece. 'It was surreal, but that sums up the Gemini experience', he recalls.[21]

Another journalist with a genuine commitment to Africa, preexisting experience and real staying power was Alan Rake. He joined the Gemini group in 1968 at the age of 35. For some years he had been editing the East African edition of *Drum*, the celebrated magazine for South Africa's urban black population which Anthony Sampson had built up. He recalls Ingram pointing to a pile of old *African Development* magazines, cuttings and press releases and saying, 'Would you like to make a magazine out of this?'

Gemini had bought the African Buyer and Trader company and its almost extinct giveaway

20. Interview, Richard Hall.

21. *Ibid.*

publication, *African Development*. Hall was initially put in as editor but, with his other commitments, left much of the work to Rake who in March 1970 became editor in name also. Rake built a network of correspondents in Africa – sometimes Gemini stringers also – and ran more investigative and analytical pieces. Instead of puffery for British exporters it gradually became a respected monthly, charging a cover price, and with a sympathy for African needs. (Rake and the magazine stayed with Carruthers when the split in Gemini occurred; in 1978 he organized a palace coup and the magazine was bought by Afif Ben Yedder, a Tunisian.)[22]

If Carruthers fancied he was a better journalist than he was, Rake like Hall added a ballast of competence to the early Gemini. With the designers Cliff Hopkinson and Peter Clarke they completely changed the look of *African Development*, switching from a two column format to a more modern and dynamic three or four columns to the page.

In these early years there was also that unlikely Ugandan staff member – Fred Mpanga, former Attorney General of Buganda, who had fled to London with the Kabaka in 1966. Carruthers had known him in Africa, discovered he was hard up, but could initially offer him only a job as a messenger. But soon Mpanga was writing breezy articles about Jack the Ripper, London sex shops and legal cases which caught his fancy. As a refugee from Obote he returned home in 1971 when Amin offered a welcome to such exiles after taking power in Uganda. In a touching farewell piece for Gemini Mpanga said that 'my own experience is that for an exile there is nothing like journalism.' Sadly he died not long after in Uganda.

After *The Guardian* took over Gemini in mid 1973 there continued to be liaison with GeminiScan and *African Development*, even though the news service was financially separate as a *Guardian* subsidiary. One of the key editorial figures over the next few years was Dickie Walters, Ingram's deputy, who did much of the subbing.

Brana Radovic, who was working as a graphic artist, remembers Walters as a man in his sixties – 'a real RAF type, with a very short fuse. He loved Derek, but he also used to fight him.' Walters had been a copy boy who rose to become a copytaster on the *Daily Mail*. He joined Gemini on retirement and had a severe heart attack towards the end of *The Guardian* period. He was paternalistic to the young Radovic, used to complain about the poor levels of pay at Gemini, and was the person who pointed out a *Financial Times* advertisement in the *UK Press Gazette* which led to Radovic's departure for over twice as much money as he had been getting.

It was, of course, a very small show then – with only four or five people in the office including Radovic and the secretary/receptionist. But Ingram's caring style with staff, the sense of doing something important, and the high regard which famous visitors had for Gemini, gave an ethos of excitement.

They also had some laughs. Radovic recalls that, when Gemini was housed in John Carpenter House, there was a space behind the building overlooking the offices of

22. A useful account by Alan Rake of the early history of *African Development* appeared in the September 1992 issue of one of its successor titles, *New African*.

Weekend magazine. An executive and his secretary were having a torrid love affair in a room with frosted glass windows, unaware that they were remarkably visible to the Gemini staff across the way. Work stopped at Gemini when the two got together until one day the man opened a window for air, and saw a lot of faces looking down at him.[23]

In the 1980s, after the restart, the editorial people in London seemed more youthful. This was partly because of the contribution of the Canadians, covered more fully in the educational chapter below. The interests of Daniel Nelson and Kelly McParland, for example, were not just in the content of the service but in the professional growth and training of the contributors. The rural reporting initiative, run by McParland, was a difficult concept. Developing country journalists, who had seen going to their capital and covering government and other 'national' activities as a key to promotion found it hard initially to understand that spending time in villages could produce reportable material.

There were difficulties of other kinds too. A rural reporter from northern Namibia, covering a Damara district called Gainachas in the south of the country in 1992, told the office that problems began at the Windhoek railway station:

> We met a man in the train who was so hostile to us when we told him that we were going to Gainachas on such a programme. He asked us why we had chosen to go and do rural reporting in the south as we were 'Ovambos' – from the north. He said that he was suspicious and he did not believe we were on a 'reporting' programme. He said that we were sent by the government to go and do 'something else'.

> We spent more than R200 on transport (to and fro). Fortunately we arrived and got an accomodation at 85-year-old Oupa Higoam's house.

> Though Oupa Higoam's family welcomed us well in their home they did not trust us. After a week with them, his wife asked us if we were sent to spy on them. They said it was their fear and that of the whole community that we may be police informants. They explained that this state of affairs was common during the previous regimes.[24]

McParland explained the rationale of the rural reporting initiative in a way which implied also that it demanded a skilled and sensitive relationship between Gemini and the journalist.

He wrote:

> The journalists are told to approach the assignment without preconceived notions of what they will find, and to leave behind a list of stories they feel in advance will require reporting. They are likewise encouraged to avoid wherever possible basing their articles on the musings, pronouncements or declarations of local politicians, aid officials, development workers, experts or other authorities.

23. Interview, Brana Radovic.

24. Ingram Archive.

> The point is to reach beyond this familiar level of secondhand information and go to the sources themselves. It is hoped the journalists will learn to appreciate that the real concerns of villages are not always understood or accurately reflected by authority figures, and often have little or nothing in common with matters that preoccupy city-dwellers.[25]

McParland was an IDRC fellow from Canada who stayed on at Gemini to become an assistant editor. Like Nelson he had been radicalized in his understanding of the world by his travels in the South. The unequivocal commitment to the interests of developing countries by Gemini in the 1980s, which had attracted the support of donor agencies in the North, was fuelled by a more militant spirit in the London-based staff.

McParland's Gemini fellowship had involved a long trip to Kenya and Zimbabwe, in the course of which he managed to take in other countries as well. He landed at Dar es Salaam airport, which was large and impressive but had almost no air traffic. He found an even bigger, newer and cleaner airport at Gaborone in Botswana, then served by an Avis rental dealer with a huge fleet of cars for only one international flight a week.

He asked:

> Why would anyone build a hugely expensive airport 20 kilometres from a town of 35,000 which no-one wanted to visit? The answer, as with Tanzania, was of course that a foreign donor had paid for the airport out of aid funds, on the inane idea that if the airport existed, maybe someone would use it. By the time I arrived the support for megaprojects among the world's foreign aid donors was waning, but by that time millions had been spent on dams and roads and airports that served noone. You had to wonder: if the donor countries had been so wrong first time around, why should anyone believe they could get it right in the future?[26]

There were some who did not stay long, like Tom Aston, who was briefly associate editor at the end of the 1980s. His background was in TV, and he wrote perceptively about TV coverage of the Gulf War. He had other means, and was therefore not too worried by Gemini salaries, and a Buddhist. One Canadian IDRC fellow said he was the first angry Buddhist she had come across.

In the 1990s, reflecting the quiet internationalization of the office, Gemini acquired an Indian associate editor in Daya Thussu. He had come to Britain in 1988 on a Commonwealth scholarship after working for the Press Trust of India and obtaining a PhD in international relations at the Jawaharlal Nehru University in Delhi. Before joining Gemini he had done media research at the Open University, analysing how Reuters covered South Asia.

His was an editing and commissioning job, but he was writing two articles a month by 1994, sometimes based on books. His subjects included the arms trade, GATT and the activities of the World Bank; they were mostly commentary pieces. He wrote about NATO

---

25. From McParland article on Gemini and the Commonwealth, *The Round Table*, 1986, pp. 395–402.

26. McParland letter, *ibid*.

Did life originate in space?

Professor Wickramasinghe: looking heavenwards for the beginning of life

Fig. 16. Non-photographic portraits, often with other types of information included, evolved in the earliest days of Gemini. Three more recent examples include Professor Wickramasinghe and stellar space (March 1986).

Hong Kong

10mls/16km

China

Mirs Bay

New Territories

Kowloon

Lantau Is.

Hong Kong Is.

Lamma Is.

South China Sea

Hong Kong Island ceded to Britain 1842. Kowloon peninsula ceded 1860. New Territories (975 sq km) leased 1898 for 99 years. All returning to China 1997.

Governor Chris Patten

Fig. 17. Chris Patten with Hong Kong (October 1994)

planes being deployed outside the NATO area, maintained an interest in South Asia, and was keen that Gemini should continue to avoid a CNN news agenda.

He was critical of Gemini's more spur-of-the-moment and amateurish traditions, but enthusiastic about its training role. He had taken part in workshops for journalists from Bangkok to Malawi. It was possibly due to his influence that some African users of the service in the 1990s thought that Asia was getting more attention than their own continent, though Thussu himself welcomed his exposure to African concerns.[27]

And throughout the years of Gemini until the end of 1993, when all due allowance is paid for the contribution of others, Ingram remained the editorial rock. Good in a crisis, swift as a sub-editor, willing to share his contacts, he had a clear view of the agency's purposes and was able to inspire others. There were those who felt he found it difficult to relate to some women, especially the more challenging feminists who emerged in the 1980s. But he was genuinely interested in people and maintained his journalistic curiosity.

Boxing promoter Don King
Finding a fight for Tyson

Fig. 18. A caricature of the US boxing promotor Don King (October 1994).

Young Canadians, as well as journalists from developing countries, treated him as a guru. By the late 1980s he was perhaps not quite as hands-on for all parts of the service as he had been in the 1970s (when he was regarded as the quickest-fingered collator of paper on press days). But he was still writing a lot of copy, travelling frequently for Commonwealth and other reasons, and talking to actual and potential contributors. He also lived up to his own admonitions, for instance about the importance of humour. When *The Times* of London was closed for a year in a showdown with the print unions he wrote a witty piece about the misery for *Times* readers who could no longer tell the Editor, through the correspondence columns, that they had heard the first cuckoo in Spring.

27. Interview, Daya Thussu.

Finally, in painting a picture of the men and women who made Gemini, it is vital to pay attention to the artists and designers. Very rapidly, and perhaps surpassing Ingram's expectations, its graphics became the trademark of the service. Maps, diagrams, and faces of political leaders combined with information went out with most articles. They were both simple yet recognisable. Feedback from users suggested that it was the graphics that often gave Gemini the edge over competition.

The key person who got the service off to a good start was Cliff Hopkinson, who had been with *The Observer*. It was a former colleague of his, Richard Leadbetter, who designed the black-and-white twins which symbolized both Gemini, and its desire to communicate across racial and national barriers. Hopkinson used the logo on every print item emanating from the office.

At the 20th birthday of the service Hopkinson stated:

> The symbol was the first move in the development of Gemini's worldwide reputation for striking graphic design. The maps were next. Before the launch of Gemini I was asked by Derek Ingram, its founder, to specify a style for maps: he anticipated that if really well-designed they would find a ready home in newspapers of many countries. How right he was.

> I had developed a style for maps in *The Observer* which lasted unchanged for more than a decade. For Gemini the problem was more difficult. We needed maps that would be striking, would convey information easily and would reproduce adequately in all newspapers, no matter how primitive their printing processes; maps that could be reduced to a simple column or blown up across several.[28]

Hopkinson worked with Peter Clarke, an immensely creative artist who is best known now for his portraits in *The Guardian* and the Yugoslav Serb, Rade Radovic, who drew many of the maps. It was with Clarke that Hopkinson developed GeminiScan as a design business, with all its educational kits and *Orbit*, the educational magazine for Zambia. But their bread-and-butter activity was to provide design input for the news service.

Hopkinson himself indicated what was needed. Quite soon he came to rely on Radovic to draw up the detailed maps, and it was Radovic who developed the illustrations of leaders and celebrities. Radovic was a find of Carruthers, in the first weeks of Gemini. He had been working with the Zebra Trust, which housed African students in west London. He was brought in as something of a handyman, but soon turned out to be a person of many talents and a workaholic.

Radovic was only 16 when the Second World War broke out. He was a pilot and shot down. His father had been a wealthy landowner and he had wanted to be an artist if the war had not intervened. In 1944 he was in Rome, delivering papers to the last royalist Yugoslav embassy. When the war ended he was in a displaced persons' camp in Kiel, north Germany. Offered a choice between going to Britain or the United States he chose

28. Cliff Hopkinson article, 'The faces behind those famous graphics', in anniversary folder, *Celebrating 20 Years*.

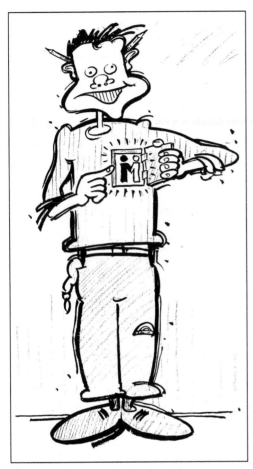

Fig. 19. Self-portrait by Paddy Allen, expressing delight in his Gemini years, which he gave colleagues when he left.

Britain. He came to Chichester, where he met and married an English girl who was in the Land Army.

Thereafter he did many jobs, but never lost his love of art. Working in a car factory in Birmingham, for instance, he also managed to put on an art and sculpture exhibition. Quickly on arrival at Gemini he turned his hand to anything that needed doing – running off the sheets of paper, building office furniture, rewiring electrical appliances. At home he did the sewing, made trousers and shirts. But at Gemini he was often the first to come and the last to leave. He still had time to assist friends who needed help.[29]

He worked on the charts with Hopkinson. These were sometimes simple graphs, bar-charts or pie-charts. Usually they were a striking amalgam of drawings and words which set out to give a simple explanation of a topical if complex subject.

'If I felt like a Svengali, briefing Rade in the style of these exciting new graphics, he quickly became their Midas: he touched the ideas with his drawing pen and they turned to gold. Usually these graphic units were designed in a rectangular, boxed format occupying most of an A4 sheet. Like the maps before them, they infiltrated newspapers around the world', stated Hopkinson. Sadly Radovic died in harness, not long after Gemini had become a *Guardian* subsidiary, with a stroke at the age of 53. But his son Brana Radovic stepped into his shoes in the late 1970s.

Some felt that the Gemini designers had been influenced by the pop art of the 1960s. But they were more influenced by the need to keep things straightforward for their customers. This heavy commitment to graphics was out of keeping with Fleet Street practice in Britain at the time. In an age of Letraset rather than the computer it was also necessary not just to have any artists but to have good artists. Gemini was extraordinarily lucky.

Brana Radovic worked for Gemini from 1975–79, making only gradual changes to the styles which had been established. He remembers a free and easy spirit in the office, wholly

---

29. Information from his son, Brana Radovic.

Fig. 20. Didi, worldly wise cynic, was a versatile cartoon character dreamed up in the 1980s by Paddy Allen, artist, and Daniel Nelson and Kelly McParland, ideas men and jokesmiths.

Fig. 21. Didi cartoon.

lacking in demarcation disputes. When a Sheffield newspaper wanted to know whether the Gemini artist was a member of the National Union of Journalists before it would take the service the younger Radovic felt he should join at once. When he accepted a job at the *Financial Times* and told Ingram he was leaving, the editor looked pale.[30]

After the restart in the 1980s Nick Geen, who went on to be head of the Press Association graphics department, came in to Gemini. He took the original style and made it less heavy. Then Paddy Allen, an ex-student from the Central School of Art who had been made redundant after eight months by a small paper firm, answered Gemini's advertisement in

---

30. Interview, Brana Radovic.

Fig. 22. Didi cartoon.

Fig. 23. Didi cartoon.

The Guardian. It was a high risk appointment because he was very young. But he was also brilliant.

'To start off with Derek looked over my shoulder, and I thought he was difficult to work with. Eventually I won his trust and I could develop my own way forward', he recalled. He hit it off well with Nelson and McParland, with whom he created the *Didi* cartoon strip. There was always plenty of humour in the office.[31]

The slightly casual way in which people came to work at Gemini, which had been such a feature of its early years, was experienced again in the early 1980s by Jenny Ridley. A qualified nurse who had come back from Canada she drifted into the office to help with the photocopying; she did this because she was sister-in-law to Elizabeth Pritchard, the business manager, and she knew that voluntary help was welcome.[32]

In every spare moment she watched Paddy Allen at work, doing tables, charts, cartoons,

---

31. Interview, Paddy Allen.

maps and illustrations. After she had been around for a while, by summer 1986, a Norwegian travel organization wanted maps of every country in the world and Ridley was asked if she could help. 'My first map was of Madagascar'. She was never on the staff – Gemini got into the habit of having one artist on staff and a second on tap as a freelance.

But she did courses in illustration and typography at St Martin's College of Art and, with her practical experience at Gemini, subsequently landed a good job at *The Guardian*. In fact it was testimony to the quality of the Gemini experience that so many of its graphic designers went on to good jobs elsewhere in the British media. The truth was that there were few other places which were ready to teach quite specialized skills. However, although Gemini was doing so much to help writing journalists in the South it had not found a way of passing on these significant visual accomplishments.

The electronic revolution of the 1980s in Britain, which meant that good computer graphics were available throughout the media, also slightly changed the home environment for Gemini. Allen, who went on to be head of graphics at *The Guardian* (where he found himself working with Clarke and Ridley) says that he acquired various Letraset techniques at Gemini which are now redundant. But what the computer revolution and much improved TV graphics have done is to put a premium on the quality of visual and journalistic imagination. By the 1990s there were some who felt that Gemini graphics needed a new leap forward, while others felt that to abandon their rugged, consistent style would be to give away a unique advantage of the service.

---

32. Interview, Jenny Ridley.

6 Offbeat Gemini

Gemini sought to avoid being stereotyped. It had specialisms, of course, but even as its emphasis moved to development it was still powerfully driven by journalistic values. Variety, the unexpected and the entertaining remained important virtues. No paper had to take its service. Not all the items in the twice weekly packets would necessarily be published by subscribers. In the first place even the editors and sub-editors on subscribing papers had to be attracted if articles were ever to get as far as their readers.

Ingram, Nelson and those who worked in the London office were always on the lookout for pieces that were a bit different. Some of the more purist Canadian IDRC fellows felt that this meant the service could appear unfocused, and professional journalists often found it difficult to write articles lying outside the political and economic tramlines. Humour, the offbeat and the dramatically unusual were nonetheless elements of the service throughout.

Such stories came in different guises. Ingram, Gamini Seneviratne and Nicola Cole wrote about fashion, strange British customs, and media developments with a humorous twist. The press conferences of long-winded political leaders were sent up. Profiles of unusual people, whose lives tended to lie outside the concern of the main international agencies, were another rich vein for correspondents. A slightly quizzical approach to social reporting – instanced below in Charles Quist-Adade's account from St Petersburg and Niala Maharaj's from a Trinidad village – helped Gemini to preserve a reputation for realism without earnestness.

Dramatic first-person accounts, like Sosthenes Mwita's from Dar es Salaam, were not the kind of journalism that an editor could anticipate. It was not a world exclusive comparable to Richard Hall's report of the fall of Biafra. However it had a telling eye-witness quality, and its implied comments on overloaded boats and a lack of safety precautions would have been recognized in other parts of the developing world.

The following set of articles sent out by Gemini gives an indication of a range of items that fell outside the agency's main categories. It is impossible to describe such heterogeneous articles as representative of an ill-defined and unpredictable element in the service. It is, however, an attempt to do justice to a key journalistic aspect.

Baldness? You mean pollution of the pate

by Gamini Seneviratne

Gamini Seneviratne, a Sri Lankan, came to Gemini in London after a varied career on The Times of Ceylon. *His quizzical sense of humour found ample scope in the early years of the agency. (23 September 1974 – GG 3077)*

Bald men are making a nuisance of themselves to church authorities in the ankle of Italy, and there is no reason to believe that their activities will not spread.

The church of Castello near Naples has become the first to drain its stoups of Holy Water. Too many bald men have been wetting their smooth scalps in the hope that the blessed liquid will start up something new.

Shining domes in Latin lands are usually associated with cathedrals, the natives being better known for greasy thatches and nimble fingers.

'It just goes to show', as a London trichologist (one learned in the structure, functions and diseases of hair) said, 'that baldness can happen to anyone'.

What, then, does cause baldness? Is there a 'cure'? Have the egg-heads of Napoli really cottoned on to a good thing?

Unhappily, there is no one answer to any of these questions, not even the last. Hair and humans have been together long before Samson made it respectable. What is more, except in rare cases like Samson's there is no apparent purpose in the relationship.

Some people, like Yul Brynner, are happier without it just as others, like Frank Sinatra, go to all extents to pretend at least that they have some left.

But the thing is that the head has less to do with the relationship than the hair. You may shave your head and even tear your hair, but there is no guarantee that you will lose the stuff for always.

It is small comfort to many that it is relatively easier (for others) to keep hair than lose it. But it is true. And it is also true that growing new hair is as easy as inducing baldness – 'provided one remembers that the new hair is old hair playing dead and the bald head is only apparently bald'.

But why do people go bald? Ah, said the hair expert, why indeed?

You may have noticed, he suggested, that women rarely go bald while it is not uncommon for men. I had.

Well this gave rise to the theory that baldness was all a matter of hormones. The females have it. The males do not. Redress the balance and you eliminate bald men – or quite a number anyway.

There must, the man conceded, be something in this. But, as they found in United States where hormone treatment had waves of popularity until it was outlawed recently, things do not work out quite that simply. Among other things, apart from hair, the treated males often grew breasts. Some even became bald–breasted – that is, bald but with breasts.

One of the nice beliefs which grew out of this line of thought was that if female hormones grew hair then baldness meant an excess of male hormones. Ergo, baldness equal virility.

There could be, it seems something in that too. At worst, it is a cheap and comforting thought to the hairless. But my trichologist happened to know personally, a lot of matted men of outstanding virility and bald men who were decidedly otherwise.

So much for sex, or gender if you prefer. What about food? This clearly has possibilities as well. Certainly the more comprehensive courses of treatment to promote hair growth include dietary supplements.

Medical people have also recently noted that bald patients in alcohol and drug addiction units who are injected with saturating doses of Vitamin B often show signs of hair activity.

This, of course, could be for a variety of other reasons, and I was also cautioned to note that people in undernourished areas of the world 'usually have nice heads of hair'.

The oldest hair hospital in Britain, and one of the oldest in the world, is the Hair Loss Treatment and Hair Weaving Centre Clinic, Soho.

Until a few years ago it was the only place of its sort in London. Today a quick look around the city will throw up a crop of hair growers, hair extenders, hair restorers and even hair raisers, though a company of Hair & Skin traders turned out to be nothing more sinister than bristle merchants.

Edward G. Coppage, a director of the Clinic, is quite clear about how much he, and by implication anybody, can do about getting hair back on bald heads. It can only be done if there is some life left in the old follicle.

If the hair follicle is quite dead then there is nothing the Clinic can do. Certainly it is unwilling to undertake surgery. The now fairly common transplant operation which involves lifting the dead scalp in little patches and covering the spaces with skin (hairful) from another part of the body, usually the back of the neck, does not commend itself to Coppage and company.

It is too expensive in pain and money. It cannot guarantee any more success than a hair transplant (perhaps less, in the long run) and failure means worse than baldness. It means baldness in ugly red patches.

But the people whose scalp is completely dead are few compared with those whose hair follicles are only weakened to a point at which visible hair cannot be sustained.

The reasons for this condition are many and varied. But as far as each individual client is concerned the Clinic, while it would prefer to isolate the cause, gets to work on a broadish front.

Since the hair follicles could be weakened by any number of factors, they give the patient a course of tablets to supplement the diet and make good any deficiency of vitamin and mineral.

But the meat, as it were, of the treatment consists of cleansing the scalp and getting the blood circulating, through manual massage and electrically induced vibration. The idea is to create a scalp-climate in which the follicle can activate itself.

Most baldness, says Coppage, is caused by scalp pollution – creams, greases and such, either self-induced in the name of hair dressing and grooming, or uninivited by way of the environment.

So even Holy Water could work. If you just keep your hair washed the chances are you will keep it on.

How Gemini makes the world go round

by Pat Davidson

Pat Davidson, who had been a press officer for Oxfam, had contributed a piece five years earlier about Katharine Allen, an unusual marriage broker. In this follow-up she remarks on some of the less predictable outcomes of Gemini's world-wide readership. (23 April, 1976 – GG 6006)

In 1971 I wrote a Gemini News Service report about Mrs Katharine Allen, the 'mystery guest' at a society wedding in England. It was Mrs Allen, in fact, who had engineered the happy occasion. She runs a one-woman business as a marriage-broker.

Editors seemed to find the piece interesting, for it was published in newspapers all over the world. After that, I forgot all about it – until the other day. I met up with Mrs Allen again and what she had to tell me about that article made my head spin.

If you have the money, it seems that distance is no object when you are looking for a marriage partner. As a result of that one Gemini article, London-bound jets started getting their quota of engineers, lecturers, tycoons and medical men, homing in from every corner of the globe in search of the perfect mate.

Marriages have been made (and presumably children are being born) as a result.

After the article was published, the letters started to arrive at Mrs Allen's office in Sedley Place, Mayfair. One of the first was from two readers of *Milliyet*, Istanbul: 'We are two Turkish youngs who would like to marry with English girls'.

However, Mrs Allen couldn't, regretfully, help people who only wrote letters. She is, she says, a marriage broker, not a name-and-address swapping agency. An essential part is that she personally meets (and gets to know) every one of her clients.

That didn't deter people. Her first caller as a result of the article was a reader of the *Fiji Times*. He was sitting in an aeroplane bound for Tokyo when he read it. After finishing his business in Tokyo he caught another plane, not back to Fiji but to London. The first of Mrs Allen's jetting bridegrooms was on his way.

In fact in the case of this particular client it took several visits and a lot of introductions before he decided to take the plunge, but his persistence finally paid off and he married a woman from Surrey, England, at the beginning of this year.

'It is', says Mrs Allen, with professional satisfaction and certainty, 'going to be a good marriage'.

Born lucky was the widower who flew into London with a Caribbean newspaper under his arm. He was, says Mrs Allen in some awe, 'tall, handsome, exuding life and dynamism and after an early retirement had built up an immensely successful business'.

In other words, a man who had everything (and it is interesting that people who make use of Mrs Allen's service are not the misfits and also-rans that some people might think. Curiously, they often seem to be more than averagely endowed with looks, talent and money. Mrs Allen has her own theories about that, but this isn't the place to go into them.)

Fortunately, she had someone on her books to match up to such a challenge, a woman executive who had a flat in Mayfair and a house in the country. Two such paragons that Mrs Allen had only one doubt before she introduced them.

'You are so much alike', she said, 'that you will either clash violently or fuse'.

They fused. The only problem she had was in trying to persuade them not to marry too precipitately. She likes people to get to know each other for at least a year first. However they are now married and living in the Caribbean.

The bill for the marriage fee that followed them out (for there are times when a marriage broker must act with discretion) was made out to 'one tallboy and one mirror'.

Faced with the problem of someone flying in from a long distance, with only a short time to spend in England, Mrs Allen has had to adapt. The preliminary interview is longer and even more probing than usual, references are taken up and, when a person has been married before, copies of divorce or death certificates are required.

But once her mind is made up, introductions take place at the pace of a speeded-up movie. Three or even four 'dates' are crammed into a day, and those without stamina need not apply.

The palm for the speediest marriage must go to a reader of the *Nile Mirror*, Khartoum. Within a week of his arrival he was 'madly in love' with a Sussex divorcee with two children. Despite Mrs Allen's entreaties to wait, believing that at least the girl should first go out and visit the Sudan, they were married within six weeks. 'And it's worked', she says (with relief, no doubt).

On the other hand, a *Times of Zambia* reader met no one of instant appeal during his week in London. Nothing daunted in his search for a wife, he subsequently sent his brother over to Mrs Allen for some introductions.

His brother brought back a photograph and a glowing report of one girl in particular. *The Times* reader and the girl corresponded, she later visited Zambia and now they are wed.

But some journeys are wasted. There was the man from Mexico City who had read the article just after his wife's death. Although Mrs Allen felt it was too soon for him to consider re-marriage, she couldn't bring herself to turn him away.

He was soon meeting an English woman and a wedding in Mexico City was planned. But when the prospective bride went out there, the man pulled out. 'I felt very bad about it', admits Mrs Allen.

And, after all this time, even in this jet-propelled age, some people are still courting.

A woman from Toronto is trysting with a man from Washington; a mid-West

American is flying to London twelve times a year but still hasn't popped the question; a highly-qualified engineer from the Sudan has yet to take the final step.

Four readers of the *East African Standard*, Nairobi, (including a woman) are all going steady, but with Londoners, not with each other, which naturally slows things up.

And in São Paulo, Brazil, a man of East European origin is raring to marry his prospective British bride, but is held up by the fact that his perfectly legal East European divorce of some years back is not recognized in Brazil.

Mrs Allen is hard at work trying to untangle that one.

Of all the letters that she received as a result of the article, one absolute non-starter was from a 50-year-old Australian seaman who wanted to meet a girl: 'under-25, pretty, demure, charming, obedient, a good cook, good-humoured and tolerant of my heavy drinking and long absences from home'.

And one woman for whom she could hold out very little hope, was a journalist who worked on a British provincial newspaper. Reading one of her own stories, she happened to see the article about Mrs Allen alongside. She took a train to London to ask advice on how to hang on to her lover. It seemed he was mysteriously meeting other women.

Unfortunately, as the tale unfolded, Mrs Allen realized only too well who was introducing him to them.

'I was. He'd been on my books for over a year'.

Writer with a cockroach-eye-view of life

by John Gambanga
Harare

A forceful account appreciated for the acidic personality of its subject, and for its insight into a reputation stretching from Zimbabwe to Britain. Daniel Nelson told Gambanga at the time: 'Lovely story: such personality/ human interest profiles make a welcome change from the political-economic pieces we usually run'. (13 September, 1983 – GB 3303)

Being thrown out of school and forced to live the life of a tramp may have been the best thing that ever happened to Dambudzo Marechera.

The experience inspired him to write a book. It was an instant success. Now 30 years old, Marechera is himself a success story in his native Zimbabwe.

Marechera is a writer with a difference. He has been described as probably the best Zimbabwean author writing in English. He is the only black Zimbabwean to win *The Guardian* Fiction Prize, with his first novel *House of Hunger*.

'Marechera's writing is pure verbal acid', wrote one critic. And after reading his second novel, one is left in no doubt that the former Oxford University student possess a rare writing talent, especially as English is his second language.

His writing inspires, disturbs and provokes. He describes himself as having, 'a cockroach-eye-view of life'. His writing projects the life of the poor with vivid and defiant exactness.

It is not only Marechera's writing which is unique: his lifestyle and ideas are also unusual. He believes for example that writers and artists should not marry. A writer should keep himself to himself, he says.

Marechera has no fixed abode. 'I don't even know where I am going to sleep tonight', he said as he sat in a Harare bar, his typewriter on the table, beside it a pile of books.

'People think I am insane. That's what they thought of me when they expelled me from Oxford University where I was reading for an honours degree in English. I was shocked at the students' casual attitude to education and life. One of my fellow students was a Lord at only 18 years. Money to him meant nothing at all. What he took for granted to me was expensive. I was confronted with people who saw knowledge as merely an appendage for social success.

'I discovered they were trying to make me into an intellectual Uncle Tom. I was being mentally raped'.

So he tried to burn the college buildings with petrol. The authorities, thinking he was crazy gave him the choice of signing into a psychiatric hospital or being expelled. Says Marechera: 'I had to invite them to expel me'. That was 1976.

Then he began his hard days of street life, living like a tramp with neither job nor accommodation. It was this life that inspired his first book.

He originally fled to Britain after being expelled from the then University of Rhodesia for taking part in a demonstration against the racial segregation of residences on the campus. He subsequently won a British scholarship to continue his studies at New College, Oxford.

He writes in English rather than Shona, his mother tongue, because 'English unites us as an official language. We are fighting for African unity. I don't want my writing to be considered on a tribal basis. I want it to be simply Zimbabwean'.

He began writing while at school and later contributed to a national poetry magazine *Two Tone*.

Marechera holds strong views about the new writer in Africa. He feels writers should know where they stand and not pretend to sit on the fence.

'Books are political and are bound to influence people', he says, 'I don't want my writing to be like political tracts. I feel literature should inform rather than preach. I want to be subtle but forceful'.

Marechera speaks with great concern for the poor and believes writers have a duty to uplift the poor.

He is also concerned about the well-being of his fellow blacks. 'Until Independence in 1980', he says 'the people in Rhodesia, Smith's Rhodesia, were living an abnormal life because the blacks had been militarily dominated by the colonialists since 1890. If you tried to live a "black" life you were either arrested or faced worse consequences'.

He advises every writer in the Third World to realize that their country or government is being attacked for being either Marxist or dictatorial. Writers as people who wield the pen, the most lethal weapon today, should correct this distortion.

They should be part and parcel of society's economic and political struggles. In addition they must write books which are economically viable, because 'publishing is not a charity organization'!

Marechera is concerned too at the erosion of the rights of the writer in Zimbabwe and thinks no one should have the power to decide what people should read and see, not even governments. Within hours of his return from seven years in Britain he learned that *Black Sunlight* had been banned for alleged excessive use of obscenities. The ban was later lifted.

He singles out Wole Soyinka of Nigeria as the most outstanding African writer in English and also gives a high rating to another Nigerian, Chinua Achebe, and to Ngugi Wa Thiongo of Kenya.

He recently submitted two new books to publishers in Harare which should be released before Christmas. The first one is another novel, *Mind Blast*; the second is a collection of five plays about the attitude of whites in Zimbabwe at the time of independence.

Talking the Mengistu way ... on and on

by Teresa Mazzitelli
Addis Ababa

A certain cynicism about politicians comes naturally to most Northern journalists, but in many one-party or military regimes an uncritical or sycophantic style of 'Minister says' reporting held sway in the 1970s and 1980s. Gemini increasingly challenged this, both in its service and via training workshops. (22 July 1988 – GG 69630)

It was him or us. Could he keep talking longer than we could keep awake? He, Mengistu Haile Mariam, was winning. We, the international press corps, were weakening. With good reason: none of us had been subjected to a six-hour press conference before.

The odds were in his favour: he had the home turf advantage, access to 17 selected questions beforehand, a docile gathering of East and West bloc journalists and a conference room full of party officials and one or two bodyguards.

The 25-member press corps finally emerged, exhausted but wiser for having gained an exclusive insight into the Ethiopian political machine. Extracting the news from the hours of rhetoric was daunting, but it led to such precious revelations as: 'The West's negative image of Ethiopa is something that has bothered us. We are astounded. The truth is we are working for human ... prosperity and democracy'.

The sense of occasion was not lost: in his first press conference since May 1986, Mengistu had just hosted the 25th anniversary of the Organization of African Unity (OAU) at a time when Ethiopia walked a double-edged sword of war and famine. With the OAU attracting over 200 foreign media, he was guaranteed an instant, appreciative audience.

It was a surprising show of accessibility, a powerful exercise in oration and a nice public relations move. Moreover, in an impressive display of endur-

ance, the President of the People's Democratic Republic of Ethiopa out-
lasted his guests. One reporter fell asleep, another indulged in a magazine,
many doodled – but everyone stayed.

Broadcasters ran out of tapes only two hours later, others stifled yawns,
contemplated interrupting and surrendered to sifting the chaff from the
news. One intrepid individual faithfully transcribed the lengthy soliloquy in
shorthand. Every hour or so, the conscientious writer would look up to ask:
'What was that last word'? The word repeated, the furious scribbling
continued. Surely she would break down, give up, run out of paper, ink or
patience?

The first question elicited a 25-minute answer, which many mistook for
introductory remarks. The ensuing question, regarding improved relations
with Tunisia, segued into Ethiopia's newly signed peace treaty with Soma-
lia, absorbing another 25 minutes. The pattern was set and would continue
to repeat itself.

The foreign media are ushered into a room at the Shengo (parliament) at
2 o' clock. A panel of three party officials, a translator and a master of
ceremonies follow. Mengistu arrives last. A small man, five-foot-five, from
the dark-skinned Galla tribe, he walks slowly, smiling.

The voice is authoritative but not distinguished. Compared to an earlier
impassioned May Day speech, he is restrained. So are his movements.
Only the eyes move continuously, darting instinctively without pause.
Rarely does he glance at the translator on his right or the audience in front
of him. Like antennae, the eyes absorb without looking out.

'How is it possible that a government that stands for the will of the people
be compared with a terrorist organization'? he exclaims, pausing for translation. The eyes move furiously. 'Believe it or not, we revolutionaries do not
live for ourselves, we live for others.'

The questions, asked mostly in English, were answered in Amharic followed
by a translation. There was no prepared script and no time limit. No-one
interrupted him (between them, the three party officials said three words)
but he corrected his translator often enough that it became obvious he
spoke excellent English. Why then respond in Amharic? National pride or
the presence of Ethiopian television cameras? The session would later be
broadcast in two parts.

A coffee break, two hours into the meeting, offered the chance to regroup
and plan a unified attack on protocol but the unexpected appearance of
Mengistu in the lobby ended any consultation. Worse, the interval led to the
mistaken impression that the half-way mark had arrived.

Quick calculations revealed that with four questions eliminated, the remaining 13 would be dispensed with in 9.23 seconds each – a refreshing length
weighed against an earlier 82-minute response concerning the Eritrean
secessionist movement.

The mathematics broke down but the protocol remained. The conference
was nothing if not orderly: access being limited, reporters signed up for the
closed session and submitted questions beforehand. Edited, filtered and
numbered by the Ministry of Information, one question – on average – was
handed back to each reporter before the interview. In most cases it was
your question. In some cases, it was someone else's.

Government priorities crystallized with time: Mengistu's response to rebel attempts 'to carve out another Ethiopia within Ethiopia' exceeded an hour, recent steps towards the liberalization of the agricultural sector lasted 20 minutes, the controversial resettlement programme ate up 35, the Western media's coverage of Ethiopia consumed another 20 while the battle against drought soaked 40.

On the short end of the hourglass, the Moscow summit and the question of South Africa each rated a scant seven minutes. Bilateral relations with France hit 10.

For the first time, Mengistu accused Arab states of supporting the northern secessionist movement. Previously, the West was the implied financier, but now the rebels have 'embarked on a project of convincing the Arab world of an alleged oppression of the Moslems in Ethiopia in order to invoke the sympathy of the Arabs and invoke the financial resources of the Arabs ...'

The radical states of Syria and Iraq and moderates such as Kuwait, United Arab Emirates and Saudi Arabia are believed to be providing aid. Their intent, according to Mengistu, is to control the Eritrean ports of Assab and Massawa, the only non-Arab ports on the Red Sea.

His desire for better relations with the United States was unexpected considering Mengistu refused to meet with Chester Crocker, US Assistant Secretary of State for African Affairs in January.

'We are really not sure what mistakes we have committed against the government of the United States', he said, adding that possibly Ethiopia's choice of socialism instead of capitalism dismayed Washington. Relations could be improved if America 'accepts us on a basis of equality and respect'.

The translator, visibly tired, was pausing frequently. In the home stretch, questions 13 and 15 were mercifully bypassed, having inadvertently been answered along the way. Indifference began to set in even as the President earnestly said: 'We don't know what we can do to be seen as positive in the Western press'. Shorter press conferences, perhaps?

Rescue! The day I nearly drowned on my way to the office

by Sosthenes Paulo Mwita
Dar es Salaam

It only takes a minute or two to cross the Kigamboni creek in Dar es Salaam, regularly used by 40,000 daily commuters. The accident in which nine persons died was not normally the stuff of international headlines, but a sub-editor on the Daily News *happened to be on the boat which overturned. (3 October 1989 – GS 4377)*

It was a fine, bright Friday dawn in Dar es Salaam. The birds had begun to chirp from the mango trees that dot the Kigamboni area.

My wife, Juliana, woke early. We run a small business in our house and she had to go to the city centre for items to refill the shelves.

Minutes later I got out of bed. Theopister, my elder daughter, made the tea while daughter Rose swept outside the house. Four other children were still in bed.

I showered, ironed and slid into my clothes, drank the tea, picked up some

Ordeal by ferry

Sosthenes Paulo Mwita: 'Keep your nose up'

Kenya
Burundi
Tanzania
DAR ES SALAAM
Zambia
Mozambique

Dar es Salaam
State House
Boat capsizes
Harbour
Ferry route
2249

Fig. 24.

documents and cash and set out for Feri, to cross the 200 metre entrance to Dar es Salaam harbour in a small fishing boat.

I was heading for the *Daily News* offices in the city centre where I am a sub-editor. As usual, many others were also boarding fishing boats and crossing the water to their workplaces.

An elderly relative, Mwita, joined me in the boat, popularly known as *Tukutuku*. He was talking about the hardships of crossing the long neck of sea water which widens to form a head at the end.

Our boat was overloaded. It was designed to handle a few fishnets and fish containers and was not modified with seats and lifebuoys when it was converted into a passenger ferry. Most people were standing. The boat could handle 25 comfortably, but now there were well over 50 and you could not turn around easily.

Under our feet were about ten 50-kilo bags of fresh potatoes, tomatoes and fish. The boat also bore three bicycles and a motorcycle. It was nothing unusual. Boats here are always overloaded.

As we were about to depart I craned my neck and saw the Panama-registered ship *Cosmobil Ace* looming, its mast prominent against the now bright northern horizon.

The operator of the 25 horse-power outboard engine seated directly behind me had it running alright, but one thing was amiss. It was almost out of petrol.

Another man held the tiny plastic container up high to let the fuel run to the engine by gravity. There was hardly an inch of fuel left.

A third man upfront beckoned the operator to take off. I was worried and told him to wait until the ship entered the dockyard. He remained silent, so I repeated the call. Then Mwita said the ship was far off and there was nothing to worry about.

Twenty metres from the other side the engine stopped. The current took charge, turned the boat and took it into the ship's course. The passengers began to panic. The engine would not restart. The operator worked frantically as the current took the boat towards the ship.

Passengers stood on their toes as if ready to jump out. The women, some with babies strapped on their back, started to wail.

The men started pushing one another, not knowing what to do. One elderly woman clasped her hands in prayer. I turned to the operator: 'So, you see. I warned you'. He did not hear me. Everyone was yelling.

Then the ship honked. Everyone rushed for nowhere. The uprights holding the overhead canvas tilted and broke. The boat careened and we all went into the sea – bikes, baskets and loose timber on top of us.

Suddenly there was plenty of elbow room. In the sea you could wallow to any place. A mass of people fell on top of me. I had to fight to get back to the surface. I collided with someone's chest. A barrel of a chest. Our hands met. I was lucky whoever was there did not grab me.

I ducked sideways and got trapped in someone's thighs. Now I was nearly losing control through breathlessness. I disentangled myself and quickly ran into army boots. Some army man was up there kicking a lot. He clawed me in the neck and kicked me away, but I had broken surface.

He swam away as I trod water panting for air. Worse was to come. The monster of a ship, the *Cosmobil Ace*, was heading straight at me.

I scrambled to move away and succeeded, but only just. The tricky current played games. It drew me back to the ship, slamming me against its side.

Now there were no more screams. Everyone was fighting silently. As hard as I swam away from the ship I was slammed up against it again.

I pushed the ship with my left hand, but its surface was slippery. After two more pushes I realized I could not get away. I could only flounder around.

Then a new thought numbed my mind. The rotating propeller could reduce me to mincemeat. Then relief when the ship flashed past – the propeller was not running. The water behind was carpet-smooth.

With the ship out of the way the coast appeared clear. But could I swim? The last time I swam was 20 years ago, in a freshwater lake.

Progress across the vicious current was painful, but at least my nose was above the water. The rule now was: 'Keep your nose in the air'.

Other shocks were to come. As I struggled to stay as far from the floundering pack as possible, a woman suddenly broke from underwater only inches from my face.

She blew water into my hair as she screamed and disappeared under my feet legs-first. My heart took a somersault. I scrambled away, lest she should grab my legs.

I could have grabbed her to prevent her from sinking, but I was not that competent. I needed both hands myself. I also needed my legs, my eyes, my brains, a lot of courage – and God.

As I trod water for a rest I saw a sea of terrified heads bobbing in the water. Beautifully pleated heads, small heads, bald heads, blind heads, courageous heads and dying heads. Among the passengers were three blind people – two old men and a young woman – all on the way to beg in the streets. They swam hopelessly, not really knowing what had happened, all following the current towards the open sea.

I spotted an elderly man swimming gracefully with a splinter of wood. For me fatigue was taking its toll, so I clung to the splinter. The man held it with devotion. I would have agreed readily to give him my house in exchange for his rotting splinter of wood.

Then I saw our boat again, upside down, five people clinging to it, their legs trailing in the water. Three men sat atop. Another was standing, pointing and yelling.

The men on the top, seemingly basking unworried while the rest of us struggled for life, included my elderly relative and the soldier whose boots gave me hell. The standing figure was one of the boatmen.

A tiny fishing boat came around and two men pulled me out of the sea.

Boats belonging to marine police, the harbour authority and government were in the vicinity, but to mount a rescue operation they needed the go-ahead. Bureaucracy ruled.

I fainted and came to in hospital about four hours later. On my way home I went into the offices of the *Daily News* and banged out a front-pager for the paper.

Nine people died that Friday morning – including the two schoolgirls, a child, a teacher, a housewife, a militiaman and businessmen. Life continues, but the Kigamboni creek, only 500 metres from the State House, the home of the President of Tanzania, remains a death trap.

Bed-ridden Baba crusades against Narmada mega-project

by Atiyah Singh
Gujarat border

The building of a series of Narmada dams has caused a lengthy controversy, in India and internationally, with conflicting interpretations of development and environmental needs and a campaign on behalf of tribal peoples who would be displaced. Leading the opposition inside India is a spiritual figure, seriously handicapped, profiled here. (19 February, 1991 – GD6)

At 76, Murlidhar Devidas Amte, affectionately known as Baba Amte, shows no sign of forsaking his crusade against the world's biggest dam project.

The Narmada dam project, in north-west India, involves the construction of dams along the 1,312-kilometre Narmada River and its tributaries passing through Madhya Pradesh (MP), Maharashtra and Gujarat states.

The scale of the project is mind-boggling. Sardar Sarovar dam in Gujarat and the Narmada Sagar dam in MP are the biggest of 3,000 or more dams of various sizes which together form the largest such undertaking in the world.

Although China is building the world's biggest individual dam – The Three Gorges with a hydro-electric capacity of 18,000 megawatts – nowhere else is there such a 'cascade development' taking place at several points along a river as in the case of the Narmada project.

Backers of the project say it will generate around 3,000 megawatts of power and help irrigate at least 1.8 million hectares of land, thereby raising

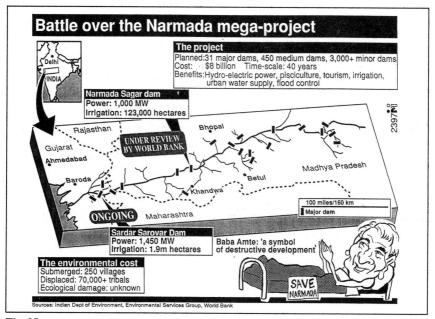

Fig. 25.

agricultural output.

But those opposed say the environmental impact of the project could be disastrous and that its non-financial costs are too high: 250 villages, the homes and fields of around 70,000 tribal people and at least 11,000 hectares of forest will submerged.

Though the Sardar Sarovar dam is being built in Gujarat, the artificial reservoir created would affect large populations in the neighbouring states of MP and Maharashtra.

The tangle of political and economic interests involved in the project has made the debate over it complex and, at times, bewildering.

The World Bank, for instance, has already agreed credit of $450 million for the Sardar Sarovar dam, but is reviewing its involvement in the Narmada Sagar dam. Furthermore, some of this money is earmarked for resettlement programmes for those displaced by the flooding of land due to the Sardar Sarovar project.

The Bank has also made a careful environmental audit which suggests that, overall, the economic benefits of the dam may outweigh the environmental impact.

The anti-dam movement, for which Baba Amte has become a figurehead, faces a powerful coalition of rich farmers, politicians, industrialists and contractors wanting to make money from the project.

There is also international opposition to the dam. The Japanese branch of Friends of the Earth recently persuaded Tokyo to suspend funding for the project this year and sent a delegation to Washington DC to lobby World Bank officials.

In the US, the World Bank has come under fire from the Environmental Defense Fund which opposes the dam, and Survival International, which supports the struggles of indigenous peoples, has launched a campaign backing the tribals who will be displaced by the Sardar Sarovar project.

Even the US Congress has urged the US Treasury Department and executive director of the World Bank to ensure that environmental and resettlement guarantees are made a condition of continued financing of the project.

Despite this level of opposition, the construction of both the Narmada and Sardar Sarovar dams is now so far on that it is unlikely that the state governments can afford to back down. Gujarat state government has already spent 4,000 million rupees on the Sardar Sarovar dam.

But this does not dishearten Baba Amte, 'the grand old man of the environment', as the *Los Angeles Times* calls him. He says he is willing to face *jal samadhi* (a watery grave) if the construction of the Sardar Sarovar dam is not stopped.

To Amte, the uprooting of tribal people is unacceptable. 'I'm for development with a human face', he says.

Scion of a rich family of Warora in Maharashtra state, as a young man he enjoyed food, drink and stylish clothes: he went to the same tailor as the British governor. He drove a sports car upholstered with tiger skin. Fond of hunting and motor racing, he was a successful lawyer, a wrestler and a poet.

That life would have continued but for an encounter with a leper who was writhing in a gutter, his open wounds infested with maggots.

Amte fled in horror but soon returned, determined to conquer his fear. He picked up the leper, gave him food and looked after him until he died.

Amte was transformed by this first experience of altruism. He tore up his legal licence, renounced his share of his father's estate and resolved to devote the rest of his life to bringing hope to the leprosy patients and social outcasts.

Amte's mission started with a mere 14 rupees, 25 acres of scrubland offered by the MP government and six leprosy patients. He was helped by his wife, Sadhana Tai, and two sons, Vikas and Ashok.

Today, the project has grown into Anandwan (forest of bliss) – a hospital and a home for 2,000 leprosy patients.

Amte has become an international celebrity, winning a string of awards, the most notable being the Damien Dutton award in 1973, the Magsaysay Award in 1985 and the Templeton award in 1990. In 1986, India honoured him with the Padam Vibhushan award, the country's second highest civilian honour.

But Baba has been troubled by spinal problems and, after 18 spinal operations, is unable to sit up. Instead, he travels around stretched out in bed with an ambulance in tow. 'I'm a spineless man', he says, making light of his crippling ability.

Amte left Anandwan for good last year, handing over the running of the project to his son, Dr Prakash Amte. He went to live with the people of Harsud village in MP, right at the centre of the area that will be submerged if the Sardar Sarovar project goes ahead.

Despite suffering a minor stroke in January, he continues to join protests in his mobile bed and is convinced his efforts are not in vain. 'Our struggle has already passed a death warrant against all such projects in future', says Amte. 'The people who are going to be displaced by the Sardar Sarovar are determined to fight till the end'.

Western consumerism makes inroads in Soviet society

by Charles Quist-Adade
St Petersburg

No-one could have guessed how rapidly American and western tastes would infiltrate the former Soviet Union. A Ghanaian correspondent, who had been doing a doctorate in what used to be Leningrad, now St Petersburg, describes the fads, greed and naïvete he saw around him after the failure of the abortive conservative coup in August 1991. (18 October 1991 – GL 21)

'Bucks, yes'? the young taxi driver asked animatedly as he pulled at the brakes. I told him I could offer him roubles. 'Go to hell with your wooden roubles'! he howled angrily and sped off.

Before *perestroika*, the mention of the American way of life and anything American or Western invariably provoked cynical laughter among Russians. Not any more.

Having developed a taste for things American – Pepsi Cola, Fanta, rock music, break-dancing, blue jeans and MacDonalds – many Soviet citizens appear to have found magic in the American dollar and the English language.

Foreigners' luck with Soviet acquaintances increases if they speak English and they become instant objects of admiration if they speak English-accented Russian:

– 'Oh! You speak English'?

– 'How do you know I speak English'?

– 'Your accent is nice and soft'.

In the past an English accent would have given foreigners away as real or potential spies. But the demise of communism since the aborted coup in August has changed all that. Now Westerners are admired as having stacks of dollars. No conversation ends without either a hint or mention of the dollar: 'How much is this? Is that in dollars'?

Until last February, it was a crime punishable by fine and or imprisonment for Soviet citizens to be in possession of dollars or any other foreign currency. Many a Russian had never set eyes on a dollar. Only black market operators and privileged Soviet citizens had handled the currency while on tours abroad.

However, a law passed early this year by the Soviet parliament allowed citizens to own small amounts of foreign currency. The law has encouraged Soviet citizens to solicit openly for dollars from tourists and other foreigners.

The Soviet rouble is scornfully called 'wooden' because high inflation has greatly reduced its value.

By contrast, anyone with a US dollar can obtain practically anything in the Soviet Union. Dmitry Gorchak, a self-employed artisan, says: 'You can buy anything here – including our leaders – with bucks'.

The American dollar, he says, is like a magic wand in the hands of its possessor. 'It is an "Open sesame" in corridors of power and influence'.

Many private shops and co-operatives now demand hard currency for their goods and services. And where merchandize is offered for roubles it is priced with the black-market exchange rate for the dollar in mind.

Thus half a litre of Soviet-brewed beer costs 2.6 roubles in government shops but sells for a full 4 roubles on the black market, reflecting the 25-rouble price of a can of imported beer.

Sensing the impending weakening of the state-controlled economy the Dutch multinational giant Philips has opened an electronic appliance shop in St. Petersburg, formerly Leningrad. There, appliances such as video cassette recorders and cameras, television sets and vacuum cleaners are sold for hard currency only.

Georgi Aparkov, the outlet's sales manager, says his customers range from

Soviet millionaires and joint-venture workers to foreign tourists and citizens who have returned from abroad with hard currency.

Many Soviet citizens resent their wealthy compatriots who can afford to shop in hard-currency '*valuta* shops'. Alexander Sizov, a factory worker, calls them 'the thieves and scoundrels of our society. These are racketeers and prostitutes', he says.

Indeed, while the Soviet *nouveaux riche* have unrestricted access to the *valuta* shops and government *beriozkas* – currency shops for foreign tourists – most St. Petersburg residents do not enjoy such privileges.

Boris Sokolenko, a library assistant, complains: 'You can not claim you are building a just democratic society when you allow a foreign currency to divide society into rich and poor, privileged and underprivileged'.

He is angry that democratic politicians have replaced Communist corruption with capitalist exploitation. 'The democrats in Moscow and St. Petersburg', he charges, 'have succeeded where the Communists failed. They have legalized immorality and swindling'.

Sensitive to such public outrage, at least one firm operating with foreign participation has continued to sell products in roubles. But it has gone to great lengths to avoid being swamped with customers.

At LenWest, a joint Soviet-German venture which manufactures and distributes shoes, products are sold for roubles but customers must first obtain coupons which are distributed at workplaces.

'We have done that to avoid pandemonium', an assistant sales manager said, insisting on anonymity. If the shop were open to the general public, he said, queues would rival those outside the MacDonalds in Moscow.

'We could have just as well sold our shoes in hard cash', the sales manager said. 'But when you do that you encourage social injustice. Only a handful of people would be able to afford to buy our shoes.

'We have not allowed the dollar to drive a wedge between our firm and the public'.

Along with the dollar craze another trend among Soviet citizens is a naïve affection for Western lifestyle. Life in the West is now seen as problem-free, a kind of heaven.

Unemployment in the West, for instance, is not generally believed to be a problem. 'The money an unemployed person in London receives is 50 times my monthly allowance', says Sasha Gonchar, a newspaper vendor.

Alla Timoshenko, a factory worker, agrees. 'In the West if you do not work you are paid', she says. 'What could be better than that'?

Democratic politicians argue that the changes which have caused bitterness among some Soviet citizens are normal, an inevitable part of the transition from communism to capitalism. But Communist Party hardliners are angry that 'foreign invaders' have been allowed to 'destroy socialist values and steal our Russian heritage'.

Democrats contend the changes in public perceptions reflect a sudden mass rejection of 70 years of Communist tutelage and spoon-feeding. Communist conservatives retort by accusing the democrats of aping Western standards.

Says a distressed Evgeny Mikhailovich: 'They will soon replace Lenin's face on the rouble with that of Abraham Lincoln's to announce to the world that they are now mature democrats and super capitalists'.

Getting on with life behind God's back

by Niala Maharaj, Matelot
Trinidad

If it is true that a good journalist can find a story anywhere it is also the case that there are many places, like Matelot, where few reporters think of looking. This loving account, put out by Gemini as a special report, focuses on Sister Rosario Hackshaw, a trousered nun who gets things done. (5 July, 1994 – GS 4541)

'Matelot'? people in Trinidad say. 'That's behind God's back'. Not many people pay attention to Matelot either.

Matelot is a tiny village way up in the north-eastern corner of the island, where holidaymakers do not go, telephones go to die and electricity pays only intermittent visits. A satellite dish that ventured up here a few years ago, armed with all the most modern anti-corrosive features science could devise, was quickly defeated by the powerful sea-blast and is now turning to powder.

Progress has met its match in Matelot. It loses its steam as it climbs the hills to the past, past where the trees are charred monuments to 'development', past the holiday retreats of Balandra, the turquoise coves beyond interlinked arms of sea-almond branches, past the turtle-savers shrines of Matura and surfers' paradise of Toco, past the wide, empty curves where waves sweep layered white petticoats over the sand like ballet dancers, past the greying army of abandoned coconut palms on Sans Souci estates, past the vanished rural homes marked by concrete stairways that lead to nowhere, past the sunken sullenness of Gran Riviere, and up again, to the cluster of houses at the top of the hill, the last inhabited hill, the village that refused to die along with the others that once studded this coast.

This is the village which held out and argued back when Progress said that 800 people without Kentucky Fried Chicken, without government interest, a cinema, a supermarket – without even a market – could not survive in today's world.

'Leave Matelot'? asks a young woman sitting at the centre of the village. 'Why'?

She is a walking defiance of modern prescriptions for health and happiness. At 21, she already has three children. Yet her black skin has a glow, her teeth sparkle white and even. She looks like a 16-year-old hanging out at the entrance to a disco.

'It nice up here', she smiles.

You look around at the dilapidated buildings and ask what is so nice about Matelot.

She chuckles. 'We free here'.

It is a statement you hear from villager after villager. We free here. Free of what?

141

'It ain't like in town', she tries to explain. 'In town you have to buy everything. Here, if you're hungry, you could pass in anybody garden and ask for a hand of fig (bananas). And you could go in the sea and dig some packro (shellfish). Or get some seamoss. Look at them fellas there ...'

She points to two men picking large oval breadfruits the clear green of young iguanas. 'That is not their garden, you know. They just ask the owner for some breadfruit to cook. When the boats coming in, you could just go and help pull up and you will get a couple of fish'.

What Matelot people are free of, you realize, is the cash economy. 'The sky, the sea and the People are One', is the village's motto.

Perhaps, where things are free, people also feel free?

'I bought vegetable seeds and taught them how to plant them', grumbles the Roman Catholic priest. 'But when they harvested the vegetables, they gave them all away. They feel food is not something you sell. Sometimes I feel I'm the one who's wrong. When I came up here, the people were in the 15th century. I have dragged them into the 18th. But they were happy in the 15th'.

She sighs.

Yes, you read right. She. For here, behind God's back, the Roman Catholic priest is a nun. The apex of the village is a large church, but the average priest might go stir-crazy from being stuck here too long. So, 10 years ago, Sister Rosario Hackshaw of the Holy Faith Sisters volunteered to take care of this parish.

Possibly she came here to be free as well. As she became engrossed in village life, she began to neglect to put on her nun's headgear. A decade later, having acquired a fisherman's badge and a large maxi-taxi, she bustles about in trousers, collecting the village's fish from a cold-storage depot to sell at hotels in town.

She shrugs off questions about her role: 'I was supposed to help people here with their problems. If they wait for vendors to come to Matelot, they have to take whatever price they are offered. Sometimes they used to give away carite for 50 cents a pound'.

Now, having talked a foreign Church charity into funding the cold-storage facility, she gets the villagers to save up the fish for a couple of days till she can career down the winding curves to find better prices.

'The villagers used to tell me "Things will improve, God willing"', she says. 'I tell them, God is always willing – it's you who are not'.

This is one of the ways she has been dragging Matelot, kicking and screaming, out of the past. You hear the sounds of resistance at village meetings.

Shortly before I arrive, a young teacher brought in by Sister Rosario (or Sissie, depending on the villagers' mood) mentions Darwin's ideas on evolution. Revolt is simmering in the houses between bounteous forest and bountiful sea.

What about Adam and Eve? The Seventh Day Adventists are preparing to go to arms. Theresa, the lady who presides over a few biscuits and snacks in the village parlour (cafe), is an avid Pentecostal Christian. In the midst of preparing a meal for Sister's guest – myself – she takes the nun to task for letting loose this monstrosity of a notion.

Everyone is preparing for the theological bombshell that is going to explode at the next parent–teachers meeting. As we sit on the tiny porch behind the Catholic presbytery watching the sea wash over the rocks, Sister marshals arguments from the Bible.

'They going to qu-arr-el'. She draws out the word gleefully, spooning up some more of Theresa's fish-and-breadfruit with relish, as she recounts tales of earlier parent–teacher meetings.

Debates have been known to end in physical combat, and the ripping off of disputants' clothes. Agreements on a design for the school uniform only came after weeks of discussion, as everyone gave their views on fabric, colour and style. Fishermen almost came to blows at the last school sports, when the judging of the children's raft-race was alleged to be unfair.

'You should have heard the row when I had the primary school rebuilt', she relates, 'They said they had all gone to school in that building and I was destroying their roots. I told them: Sure, you need to preserve your roots. But you don't have to sit down on the roots in the manure. Roots need manure; you don't'. And the nun-turned-teacher-turned-fisherwoman didn't use the two-syllable word 'manure'.

By contrast, life in the bar at the top of the hill is quiet.

I am sceptical.

'The men in this village don't drink and fight and so on?' I ask the women.

They smile in a bemused way, then generously scratch around their memories for isolated incidents with which they might entertain their visitor.

'You know ... long time those things used to happen in truth', concludes Dee-Dee, a solid 39-year-old. 'I think maybe they don't have so much money nowadays to buy rum'.

'They don't beat their wives'?

She looks puzzled.

'Why they will do that'?

I shrug, I don't know why men should beat their wives. I just know that they tend to do so, elsewhere. But here it seems that domestic violence is a rare sideshow in the drama of life. Crime also provides only minor entertainment, amounting to the occasional theft of a chicken to keep the Sherlock Holmes' of the village occupied. People sleep with their doors unlocked.

And yet, when you drive into the centre of Matelot – where the church, the parlour and the school form a ring – the lounging youths look as threatening as any in the urban Caribbean. There are the requisite Rastas, the standard basketball players, the sweaty black muscles that spell testosterone on the loose.

'He'? Sister laughs, after engaging in a raucous slanging match with a giant fisher-youth. 'I will 'fraid he'? I beat him in school'.

In fact, school seems to be the secret of Matelot's peace. The village has two of them, though it contains only about 200 children – the Catholic primary on the corner and a beautiful wooden secondary school across the river to the north. Lack of electricity gave birth to the second.

'With all these black-outs, what can you do in the evenings'? asks Sister. 'One night, sitting in the darkness, we started to entertain ourselves by talking about what kind of secondary school we would want if we could have one.

'We were tired of doing our best with the children at primary school, and then having to send them out of the village to continue their education. Half the time, the bus wouldn't arrive to bring them back in the evening and they would have to walk the 15 miles from Toco. They would be too tired to do homework. And they couldn't get the kind of personal attention from the teachers they got in the village. Electricity didn't come back that night, so we just dreamt and dreamt about what kind of education we could give the children if we had our own school. But the next day, we couldn't see any reason not to begin building it'.

There were reasons, of course – lack of teachers, money, official interest. But Rosario tends not to see some things. And she has a habit of infecting others with her blindness. I know this from personal experience, having myself been subjected to her treatment 10 years ago when she decided to set up a library in the village. Then, she decided that a journalist from the city would be useful to her purpose and abruptly descended on a total stranger with an invitation to spend a fish-filled weekend at the beach. A week later, I found myself begging for bookshelves at a hardware store in Port of Spain.

Today, Matelot has two libraries, God knows how. Or perhaps He does not. He just turns his back and looks the other way when he sees the light going on in Rosario's eyes. Which often happens when the Trinidad and Tobago Electricity Commission (T & TEC) fails to turn on the current.

For that is how this backward village happens to have one of the most modern generating systems at its secondary school. T & TEC wanted to charge some huge sum to extend its services across the river. So Rosario just went out and got a windmill from the Catholic Fund for Overseas Development in London. Then Matelot Community School set about making its own electricity.

It also makes its own fishing boats. Matelotian boat builder Alfred Baldeosingh teaches the kids how, although the Ministry of Education often forgets to pay his salary for months. He can afford to, since you can sell a boat for $15,000 when it costs only $3,000 to build – if you cut down one tree from the forest yourself, that is, and use the right parts of the roots for the inner supports. And if you also know how to make the tools for boat-building.

People come from all over Trinidad to ask Baldeosingh to build boats for them. He does so under one condition: it must not involve putting a foot out of Matelot. He has been 'outside' he says, living and working in urban Trinidad. With his woodworking skills, he can always find a job.

But, he says, in town, 'it is like dog behind Agouti. You always have to be looking behind your back'. (In Trinidad dogs are set on the badger-like 'Agouti' and follow them into their burrows.)

Here, his children can wander into the depths of the forest without him worrying about them. And they have choices. They can do well in traditional school subjects and become bank-managers, or concentrate on subjects that will upgrade the traditional skills of fishing, hunting and agriculture. Experiments in the breeding of rabbits, chickens, ducks, goats and sheep take place behind the school; fish is being converted into animal food. Students who have passed their examinations get tuition at night so they can sit their advanced levels. Those who fail, or are weak, are put into the hands of Montgomery Charles, 21-year-old graduate of Matelot Community School, for evening lessons.

'Matelot has been very good to me', explains Charles. 'I owe a lot to this community, so I want to give something back'.

He is now a full-time teacher at a school down the coast, but he returns every evening and functions as president of the village council.

'I lived in the city for six months', he says 'But I couldn't stand the poverty and crime'.

Isn't Matelot poor as well? He looks horrified at the thought.

'We have fishing, hunting and agriculture. That's not poverty. Any community that can feed itself doesn't have to depend on anybody. We can contribute to the productivity of this country'.

Hence, every child you speak to says she is studying PoB and PoA – Principles of Accounts. Boys train in home economics along with girls. And every single child learns Spanish from day-one in primary school. Grabbing every 'freeness' she can lay her hands on, Rosario encourages young Puerto Rican seminarians to come to Matelot and help her as part of their training for the priesthood.

'When I first came here', recounts one of them, 'they all thought of Spanish as a monster who would eat them up. They would plead with you not to have to do it. Now, Spanish is a friend'.

The school has been so successful that people from lower down the coast, in front of God's face, are now trying to send their children here. The government is also paying unemployed youth from elsewhere to attend Matelot's boat-building programme. Fortunately, since they take up the places of the village children, they don't stay. What is there to do here?

'It have a lot of things here', asserts Dee-Dee.

But she has to stop and think when you ask, 'like what'?

'We have Fishermen's Fete ...' she says, proffering a feeble-sounding example, and then, when she sees the look on your face, tries to impress you with its joys.

'It does be nice! We have our own steelband in the school. And we have our own carnival. We does invite all the other villages on the coast to send entrants to our calypso competition ... It does be good! It does all be on politics. Not just Matelot politics, you know, all kind of politics! And then we have Sports Day – raft race, Iron Man swimming race, relay ...'

And every Sunday it is like a family day at the river. Some play football, cricket or rounders in the space below the school, while the others are swimming. You see girls lugging huge trays of Sunday lunch to the site and then joining the 'blocko' on the ghetto-blaster-infested bridge. Those who have excess energy go deep into the forest to find big pools to swim in, or to hunt for the plentiful wild game.

There must be a catch, you think. Too many clichés spring to mind – nymphs and nymphets gambolling in a glade ... the noble savage ... Man in tune with nature ...

'These children have to live in the 21st Century', Rosario worries, 'not the 18th. Today, computer literacy is what literacy was to us'.

So, if God should only turn his back for a minute or two more, perhaps Matelot might end up with a computer centre – the same way it got its maxi-taxi practically for half-price from local vehicle magnate Sidney Knox, via the Rosario-treatment.

What's next, you tease, the University of Matelot?

'Well, I was thinking ...' she admits, '... of a faculty of environmental science. We need researchers up here to investigate what can be done with the resources all around us. How we can preserve the environment while making the best use of it ...'

Electricity has been off in the village for the last three days. As you sit in the moonlight, with the sound of the sea behind you, there is nothing you can do except think. Soon, you too, begin to spin out the little dreams that you have stored up deep in yourself.

'You know you're a great woman, Rosario'? murmurs a visiting Port-of-Spain businesswoman.

The same bemused expression I've seen on the faces of the villagers when I asked my silly questions appears on the nun's. A look of incomprehension, an inability to find words that people will believe at the end of this century of disbelief.

'I just happy', she shrugs.

7 The Commonwealth

Much of the thinking that led up to Gemini, as has already been seen, reflected Ingram's interest in the Commonwealth. To a considerable extent he envisaged it as a Commonwealth news service, although he avoided using the term. It was a product of his own campaigning, and his frustration that first the British Government and then the Commonwealth Secretariat – which did not have an information programme for the first five years of its existence after 1965 – were doing so little to make the modern Commonwealth known.

So great have been the global changes since Gemini launched in 1967 that it is hard to recall that some still felt at that point that the Commonwealth was the wave of the future. The departure of South Africa in 1961 over apartheid, and Ian Smith's unilateral declaration of independence in Rhodesia in 1965, were treated as major, long-running stories in Britain and other Commonwealth countries. The new Commonwealth Institute in Kensington, opening in a progressive building in 1962, symbolized optimism. Economic development could make the majority of ex-colonies rich. The Commonwealth nexus would mature. It would contain a block of countries which, even if they did not always pull together, represented hopes for peace and stability in a Cold War world. In short, the Commonwealth mattered.

However as the 1960s and 1970s ran on this optimistic view was increasingly challenged both in Britain, and in other significant Commonwealth members. There were several reasons for this, but perhaps the biggest was that national interests were diverging, and there was neither the political nor the economic resolve to maintain the old intimacy, and capacity for united action, in a non-imperial order of independent states. Because of the significance of the Commonwealth for Gemini it is helpful to sketch in something of its evolution.

The 1960s themselves saw the first bout, under Harold Wilson's Labour Government, in a series of struggles between Britain, as the former imperial power, and the bulk of the Commonwealth, especially its newly-independent Afro-Asian members. These last, which had watched British troops intervene in Cyprus, Guyana and elsewhere, could see no reason apart from the white skins of Ian Smith and his followers why Britain should not have put down their rebellion. British attitudes to the Commonwealth were mixed up with a certain loss of face in losing an empire and finding ex-colonies answering back;

with race, at a time when black Commonwealth immigrants were having their entry to Britain restricted; and with political and economic anxiety, as the European Community gained strength, Britain's economy was felt not to be advancing by comparison, and President De Gaulle vetoed British entry.

If British attitudes to the Commonwealth were ambiguous so, sometimes, had been attitudes to the British Empire before it. But one of the real difficulties in Britain was the inability of many to see the Commonwealth as anything but a pale and unsatisfactory shadow of the empire. They were both somehow of the past. Whereas in many newly independent countries, which sometimes joined the Commonwealth before being admitted into the United Nations, the Commonwealth represented freedom and the future, the British were burdened by history. Ingram recognized this problem in a punchy article he wrote in May 1969 for *Overseas*, the newspaper of the Royal Overseas League:

'If anyone thinks the Commonwealth is an anachronism, though, that simply means that he has not discovered what a completely different institution it is from the Empire in every particular. The old Empire and the Commonwealth today bear no resemblance to each other at all, except that they contain roughly the same countries. It is an anachronism only in so far as it has sprung from roots in history.'[1]

The uphill battle was not restricted to Britain. Kuldip Nayar's interview with Mrs Gandhi, which went out in the first Gemini packet in January 1967, had the Indian Prime Minister describing the Commonwealth as a debating forum where leaders aired their views, but nothing more than mutual understanding could be achieved.

'The only value it could have had was in the economic field, but that also is not functioning. I don't really see [in the Commonwealth] any value except that the more the links, the more people can talk together on their problems,' she said.

The situation was no better in Australia. Five months after the service began, in May 1967, Professor J.D.B. Miller of the Australian National University warned Ingram that it was unlikely that any Australian university would subscribe to Gemini. He added, 'As you know, the Commonwealth counts for very little here. In particular, there is practically no interest in the African member-countries, and the interest that does exist in the Asian members is an interest in them as Asians, not members...'.[2] A report filed to Gemini from Canberra by Christopher Reeves in early 1971 described the fifth Commonwealth Education Conference – which had brought 31 Ministers to Australia for two weeks – as 'the case of the conference nobody noticed.'

Nonetheless the Commonwealth was still a big story in the 1970s, even if it was of diminishing importance to some of its bigger members. It nearly broke up at the Singapore Heads' meeting in 1971, overtly because the British Prime Minister Edward Heath wanted to sell arms to South Africa but also in part because of the tensions induced by Britain's dash to join the European Common Market. Nonetheless it held together just – and

---

1. *Overseas*, no. 518, pp. 6–7.

2. J.D.B. Miller, Professor of International Relations, Australian National University, letter to Ingram of 2 May 1967, Ingram Archive.

Singapore also saw a charter for the Commonwealth in its Declaration of Principles, as well as establishment of its aid wing, the Commonwealth Fund for Technical Cooperation.

Through the 1970s the guerrilla war in Rhodesia intensified; the tyranny of Idi Amin in Uganda and his threat of attendance at the London Heads' meeting in 1977 led to the Commonwealth's first cautious work for human rights. But the end of the sterling area and Britain's adhesion to the European Community had knocked a big hole in British interest, and that of others. Developing countries, pursuing a New International Economic Order, saw the Non-Aligned Movement and UN system as preferable arenas for lobbying and action. Opinion-formers in many newly independent countries also saw the Commonwealth as a colonial hangover, a chummy club where leaders chatted amiably but nothing much ever happened. Canada and the Caribbean, for whom the Commonwealth remained a central instrument of their governments' foreign policy, were marked exceptions.

The absorption with southern Africa, which led to a breakthrough towards the independence of Zimbabwe at the 1979 Lusaka conference of heads, took on a more controversial quality in the 1980s. Commonwealth concern with the death throes of apartheid in South Africa was understandable not only on historical grounds, but because Pretoria's policy of destabilization was seriously damaging its neighbours. However the arrival of Mrs Margaret Thatcher as British Prime Minister brought a crisis in relations between Britain and nearly all other member states. She had a strident approach, a Right-wing nationalist agenda, and was opposed to all pressure and sanctions on the white-run regime.

This struggle, though newsworthy, had a number of side-effects. It showed that Britain did not run the Commonwealth, for the association continued to exert pressure and a committee of Foreign Ministers was set up without British participation to oversee sanctions. But it also had the effect of downgrading the Commonwealth in Britain, for it was seen as solely concerned with South Africa, and the British Government – which had a 30 per cent say in the budget of the Commonwealth Secretariat – cut spending on nearly all Commonwealth activities in the 1980s.

By the 1990s, with South Africa moving to post-apartheid elections in 1994 and renewed Commonwealth membership the same year, the association had redefined its purposes. Following a reappraisal, largely conducted by officials between 1989 and 1991, it agreed at governmental level on two broad objectives: democratization, good government and human rights as one; socio-economic development, the relief of poverty and transfer of skills as the other.

However it was still not at all clear that the Commonwealth, despite an energetic role in election monitoring, was capturing the imagination of its citizens afresh. What new vitality was appearing lay mostly in the semi-voluntary non-governmental sector. At the inter-governmental level Australia, Britain and Canada – which together funded around 60 per cent of activity – were still looking for cuts. The Secretariat's Information Division saw its budget reduced in 1993–94, and could do little to remedy a growing ignorance of the association in many of the 51 states.

The increasing pulls of national interest and of regional economic alliances, as well as the

North–South faultline, meant that a frame of reference which had been so important to Gemini in its early years was widely perceived as a diminishing asset.

Nonetheless Gemini, uniquely as an independent international media agency, continued to report the Commonwealth seriously into the 1990s. Indeed in a modest way it helped to keep the concept alive. James Porter, chairman of the NewsConcern governors, commented, 'It is one of the few activities that demonstrates that the Commonwealth has a coherence and an identity'.[3]

There were a number of key features in Gemini's Commonwealth coverage from 1967 onwards. In the first place it was, to begin with, very considerable. Two to four items out of the 12–14 which went out weekly had a strong Commonwealth flavour, often reporting activities of the Commonwealth Secretariat or Commonwealth initiatives of member countries. There was a series of comment pieces – 'What Commonwealth Papers Say.' The coverage of the London summit in 1969 was virtually total, with Gemini transforming itself from a twice-weekly news feature agency to a daily news and commentary service by telex for subscribing papers.

The 1969 coverage was not only political. It included a piece by Alan Rake about demonstrations outside Marlborough House, and another by Gamini Seneviratne about the five bachelor heads of government present. A prescient item headed 'Intellectual Nods and Winks' ran, 'An interesting new generation threesome to watch in the years to come: Premier Trudeau of Canada, Premier Lee Kuan Yew of Singapore and President Nyerere of Tanzania.' These three indeed played a dominant role in meetings throughout the 1970s.[4]

However one close observer considers that there was something of a reaction against the fervour of the pro-Commonwealth crusade and that, by the early 1970s, Gemini was somewhat restraining the quantity if not the enthusiasm of its coverage.[5] By 1971 the Commonwealth Secretariat had, in spite of opposition from the Indian Government, managed to establish an information programme and no longer needed to treat Gemini as a kind of surrogate. Further Gemini's own difficulties, and the threat of Commonwealth break-up at the Singapore summit in 1971, may also have encouraged a greater wariness.

By the 1980s the quantity of overtly Commonwealth material – that is to say articles about the Commonwealth as an organization as against articles about developments in individual countries – had certainly reduced. However Gemini was still providing, through Ingram, regular and well-informed coverage of the biennial heads of government meetings. This was not only through the Gemini packages. He himself, usually by arrangement with a local newspaper which took the service, would write daily commentary pieces in it which were also used elsewhere. From Limassol in 1993, for instance, eight papers round the world were taking this daily input. Ingram would be backed by a special team, including Third World journalists, on these occasions. Given the hectic timetable of press con-

---

3. Interview, James Porter.

4. The series of articles included GGCW22 and GGCW26.

5. Interview, Prunella Scarlett.

ferences – especially when British and Commonwealth Secretariat briefings were competing – it was a heavy commitment.

A second key feature of the Gemini coverage, especially at Commonwealth conferences, was that it took a robustly pro-Commonwealth view. Much of the time, even before Mrs Thatcher became Prime Minister, this was in contradiction of the British government line. For instance Gemini was unsympathetic to Edward Heath's desire at Singapore in 1971 to sell arms to the apartheid government in South Africa, and throughout the 1970s it highlighted the frustrations of African leaders over the continued rebellion in Rhodesia.

In 1979 Shridath Ramphal warned that the Lancaster House talks on Zimbabwe independence, being conducted by Lord Carrington, were in danger of straying outside the parameters agreed at the Lusaka Commonwealth conference. Ramphal, Commonwealth Secretary-General, was publicly rebuked by Carrington. Ingram through Gemini commented, 'The Commonwealth has been fortunate to find such a voice at this time in its development. He (Ramphal) represents the Commonwealth as it really is today, a Commonwealth still not accepted in some of the older member countries, particularly Britain.'[6]

Mrs Thatcher's own love of confrontation and her unapologetic joy in being in a minority – a complete break with Commonwealth habits of consensus – gave a special animus to the debates over South African sanctions in the 1980s. An article by Ingram after the Vancouver heads' meeting in 1987 gave Gemini's perspective:

> In Nassau in 1985 and in London in 1986 British Prime Minister Margaret Thatcher distanced herself from the Commonwealth on South African policy. Now in Vancouver she has put herself totally out of mainstream thought and action on what is still the central issue in the Commonwealth and likely to remain so long into the future.
>
> This is a watershed in the history of the Commonwealth, but not the devastating blow that some observers may be predicting in the weeks to come.
>
> The new situation could prove in the long term to be a strengthening factor, showing that the Commonwealth is not dependent on any single member, even one that has always seemed as central as Britain...[7]

Four years later, at the Harare conference, Ingram was satisfied that the Gemini analysis had been correct:

> Sanctions, however incomplete, have been a success....When Thatcher took Britain her own way at the Vancouver summit in 1987 it strengthened, not weakened, the Commonwealth as an organization. Harare will see Britain begin to move back into unison in a Commonwealth that the majority in the new South Africa will respect for the stand it took.[8]

---

6. GR27.

7. This article, headed 'Thatcher isolated in Commonwealth' was, for example, printed by the English language *Riyadh Daily* on 28 October 1987.

8. GCW103.

But had Gemini's Commonwealth coverage been too uncritical? This was a concern for friends of Gemini and friends of the Commonwealth, over a period when it could hardly be said that the association had been going from strength to strength. It is worth recalling that in 1969 at the time of the London heads' meeting a civil war was raging in Nigeria and in the early 1970s Pakistan split and the old West Pakistan left the Commonwealth; that on two occasions heads of government were actually overthrown during Commonwealth meetings (Obote of Uganda in 1971, Mancham of Seychelles in 1977); that the United States 'liberated' Grenada on the eve of the 1983 meeting in New Delhi; and that Pretoria sought to humiliate the Eminent Persons Group sent in after the Nassau meeting of 1985 with its unprovoked military attacks on three Commonwealth neighbours.

Around the edges of the official Commonwealth, and increasingly reflected in the contributions of Gemini in-country correspondents by the 1980s, there was always dissatisfaction with one-party and military regimes, with corruption and mismanagement, and with development projects which did little to develop. The end of the immediate era of independence encouraged a more clear-eyed assessment of the failures of the new governments.

Gemini, in its more overtly Commonwealth coverage, did respond to some extent to these changes in opinion. Although reports of the 1973 Ottawa heads' meeting had upbeat references to 'a rebirth' of the Commonwealth, the agency did record that it was now recognized that a wrong turning had been taken at Singapore two years' earlier: the Commonwealth was then in danger of becoming a mini-UN, and the arguments about southern Africa had been 'endless.'

By the 1977 London conference, haunted by the shadow of General Amin, Gemini was giving more prominence to human rights issues which the heads would address in private session. A decade later the service would give publicity to efforts by a consortium of Commonwealth non-governmental bodies to push human rights up the agenda.

The service was straightforward, uncritical perhaps, in its descriptions of the work of the Commonwealth Secretariat, its expert group reports on economic and other issues, and so on. Its articles about the Commonwealth Youth Programme or the aid experts of the CFTC treated them from the point of view of developing country readers: they were entitled to know about their Commonwealth, and the assumption was that anything that could help them was valuable.

Gemini also did a good job, especially by aid of its graphics, in explaining the amorphous nature of the Commonwealth. There were expositions of budget, lines of responsibility and even (in 1969) of the table layout at Marlborough House showing which heads and officials sat where. It battled for a word – Commonwealth – that fitted uneasily into headlines. It defended meetings of heads which were like think-tanks, taking no policy decisions and noted with approval Edward Heath's comment in 1973, 'It is accepted that Commonwealth summits are not occasions for making policies or decisions on the big issues. They are an opportunity to exchange views and to influence each other, and this is reflected in policies.'

Ingram himself always believed that, while Commonwealth significance was ebbing in Britain, it was still bright and shining in most other countries. Others were less sanguine, especially after educational and economic links between member countries had weakened. Although the breaches over South Africa were healed in the early 1990s, and South Africa's rejoining gave a fillip to all engaged in Commonwealth activity, there was no sign yet of the political and financial commitment which might breathe new life into the old club. For Britain, supposed increasingly to concert its international and aid policy with European partners under the Maastricht Treaty, quite basic analysis would have to be undertaken.

An indication of how the Commonwealth might mean less to Gemini, especially after Nelson's accession to the editorship, came in the way it reported a coup by young officers in The Gambia in July 1994 which overthrew President Jawara. The report by Rosemary Long[9] from Banjul, the capital, was positively approving.

She wrote that the Anglican Bishop Tilewa Johnson had described it as a 'world record' for a smooth and painless coup; that the new Minister of Youth, Sports and Culture was a 'charming, beautiful young fitness instructor, with her own gymnasium and a personal regime which makes Jane Fonda look slothful' and four other women had been made ministers; that the new head of state, Lieutenant Yaya Jammeh, was a 'handsome, cool-eyed visionary'; that The Gambia's younger set are 'enthusiastic' about the coup; and that 'the grins are back on the faces of the beach-boys.'

Although she mentioned that the US Ambassador and the European Union had called for the return of Jawara and democracy, the only real anxiety she reported was that the coup might upset the tourist trade.

Journalists on a local paper, not wanting to write themselves, had passed Gemini's request for a report onto Long and her uncritical piece had slipped through in the rush of London editing. For what was odd about this dispatch was that it completely ignored the Commonwealth angle. A military coup in The Gambia was bad news for the Commonwealth. Three out of four West African Commonwealth states were now ruled by unelected soldiers only three years after the Harare Commonwealth declaration had sought to underscore a shift to multiparty democracy, and within weeks of South Africa's first election by universal suffrage.

Chief Anyaoku, the Commonwealth Secretary-General had spent a frustrating time on the phone to Banjul, trying unsuccessfully to persuade the young Gambian military that they had to promise elections. The truth was that what had happened in The Gambia could easily occur in a score of other small Commonwealth countries, where a handful of soldiers could hijack a government. While mainstream media quickly forgot The Gambia subsequent reports in Gemini became more sceptical, especially as rumours surfaced of torture in what had been a haven for human rights.

By whatever means President Jawara had consistently won elections since 1962 it was a fact that he had played a positively heroic part in seeking to steer Africa, and the

9. 'Bumsters are back after "World Record" coup', GN34229.

Commonwealth, towards a better respect for human rights. At his urging, following the disgrace of Amin, the Organization of African Unity had adopted the African Charter of Human and People's Rights and its Commission was based in Banjul. He had tried to get the Commonwealth to create a Human Rights Commission, and his Minister of Justice, Hassan Jallow, had chaired a review group which reported in 1990 on the Secretariat's Human Rights Unit.

It will be apparent that Gemini's relationship with the Commonwealth Secretariat, in particular, had been a personal relationship of Ingram with successive Secretaries-General and their colleagues. Indeed, although the Secretariat subscribed to Gemini from the outset, it was often quite difficult for staff there to see Gemini as separate from its editor. No other working journalist, over such a long period, had such privileged access to the Secretariat.

Shridath Ramphal, the Guyanese who was Secretary-General from 1975 to 1990 recalled:[10]

> I knew him best as Derek, not as Gemini. And quite honestly there was no more stalwart friend of the Commonwealth through its years of growing up and standing up than Derek. He was absolutely the most reliable interpreter of the Commonwealth ... Certainly for me he provided an independent outreach which multiplied the impact of our information work tenfold. I came to regard him as a member of the extended family of the Secretariat, though he never lost his journalistic independence, or his ability to question

The Secretariat nevertheless valued Ingram differently from Gemini. Ingram was an unofficial press adviser to Secretaries-General and successive directors of information (he had a hand in the appointment of at least one of these). He could give an honest opinion on how to release material, whether to give a press conference, what the reaction of British and other papers might be.

He was privy to some of the news management ploys at heads' meetings, as for instance when Nicholas Harman at Kingston in 1975 started to brief the press ahead of Joe Haines' briefings for the British prime minister, Harold Wilson; during the 1980s, when Patsy Robertson was spokesman and director of information for the Secretariat, there were regular battles over timing and content with Bernard Ingham, who was Mrs Thatcher's press secretary. (The British delegation could be relied on to say that, whoever was prime minister, he or she was not only right but a star; other governments were not always so vigorous in their propaganda.)

Ingram could be given information by the Secretariat on a confidential basis with absolute trust. He was also sometimes a route by which information, which the Secretariat was happy to see passed on, reached other press persons. This occurred naturally at heads' meetings where many journalists, unfamiliar with proceedings which were not always easy to report, came to him for advice.

10. Interview, Sir Shridath Ramphal.

Some directors of information were worried that his closeness to the Secretariat might hamper Ingram or Gemini, on the grounds that journalists from newspapers which could take Gemini might think he was no longer independent. On the whole, however, they were extremely grateful to have someone who was read in so many developing countries interested, and on their side.

It was not only or even specially at heads' meetings that Gemini was seen as important. Patsy Robertson, who started at the Secretariat in November 1965 soon after it opened, and who retired as director of information in early 1994, was a good friend of Ingram's. She felt that it was Gemini's steady coverage – of the Commonwealth, and of issues of concern to developing countries such as the damaging effect of structural adjustment programmes – which mattered most.[11] Such continuous, sympathetic but not uncritical reporting was worth far more than any one story. Indeed Secretariat personnel, quite aware of Gemini and regularly seeing its output, often had difficulty in recalling a story of special significance.

The knock-on effect of Gemini on other journalists and on governments was recognized as substantial. Harman, a well-known BBC television journalist who was director of information for three years in the 1970s, stressed:

> Gemini (in the person of Derek Ingram) was the pillar of information about the Commonwealth. Journalists (and, even more, their editors) in the rich four Commonwealth countries tended to think the whole thing a pious charade. Journalists and editors in most other countries tended to regard the Commonwealth as in some way an imperialist ramp. Derek thought it was a force for good in the world. He knew everybody who counted, was always on the spot when things were going on, and was an excellent listener.

> Sometimes his example shamed first-world writers into taking the Commonwealth seriously. This was useful for rich governments engaged for their own purposes in Commonwealth activities, or seeking to stave off the critics who said it was all a waste of time and money. Much more often, Gemini articles, provided .... to third-world papers, put a favourable slant on things the Commonwealth was doing or trying to do. This was equally useful, for similar reasons, to poor-country governments.[12]

The Secretariat was delighted that Gemini consistently pushed a Commonwealth line rather than a British Government line in the successive issues of controversy. But it was a source of disappointment to some staff, particularly in the early years, that Gemini articles did not get into more British papers.

Ingram had good relations with all three of the Secretaries-General during his term as editor. But perhaps he was closest to Arnold Smith, the Canadian diplomat who set up the Secretariat. Smith was a gifted diplomat and administrator, imbued with that post-1945

---

11. Interview, Mrs Patsy Robertson.

12. Nicholas Harman, letter to author 22 March 1994.

Canadian internationalism associated with Lester Pearson. But he was not very good with journalists – waffly, and inclined to give them a lecture or a reminiscence when they just wanted a story.

Smith was delighted when Gemini came along and gave it every encouragement. His colleagues, like Chief Anyaoku and Patsy Robertson, did their best to persuade newspapers in Commonwealth countries to subscribe. And, when Gemini briefly ceased publishing in the 1980s, even in retirement he exerted himself to help it to restart.

During the Ramphal years Ingram relied heavily on Patsy Robertson, who was the trusted spokesperson for the Secretary-General. By the time Chief Anyaoku was elected in 1989 – he had been with the Secretariat almost since it began – Ingram had acquired a father-figure status in Commonwealth journalism. Chief Anyaoku felt that Gemini had always played an important part in explaining issues analytically, but that it had been most crucial at certain crisis points. He instanced two where Gemini had shown readers what was at stake – in 1971, when Edward Heath had tried to resume arms sales to South Africa, and in 1978–79 when there was a serious danger that the British Government might recognize the government of Bishop Muzorewa in Rhodesia-Zimbabwe.[13]

At a practical level, of course, Gemini also assisted the Secretariat. It bought Gemini graphics to illustrate its publications. It read the service, like others, to find out what was going on in Commonwealth countries. And its staff were more aware than most people in London, who did not see overseas papers regularly, that what Gemini was saying was getting projection around the world.

Ingram and Gemini also benefited from certain official requests. For example he was appointed media adviser to the Commonwealth observer team for the vital Zimbabwe elections of 1980. Around the same time the Commonwealth Foundation, the inter-governmental cultural body, invited him to go on a speaking tour of New Zealand. In 1993 and 1994 he was asked by the Commonwealth Secretariat to be an election observer in Pakistan and Malawi.

Like all good journalists Ingram was effectively on duty for 24 hours a day, seven days a week, and there was no clear demarcation between his personal interests and his work. As a bachelor he was also freer than other journalists to give his time and attention to what interested him. This was particularly relevant to his concern for the Commonwealth. As a result of his knowledge and his writing he became involved in a great variety of Commonwealth activities, which themselves gave him stories and contacts for Gemini. It is worth turning to some of these activities.

One of his longest commitments was to the Royal Commonwealth Society in London's Northumberland Avenue. Part club and part missionary for the Commonwealth it became better known as the Commonwealth Trust following an alliance with the Victoria League, a Commonwealth hospitality body.

Ingram was recruited to the RCS, as it then was, by an energetic woman named Betty Owen. He became involved before Gemini started and by 1973, when he and Peter Smith

---

13. Interview, Chief Emeka Anyaoku.

put up a reforming memorandum, he had already been on its central council for five years. His general attitude in the 1960s, as others remember it, was that the RCS was too stuffy, out of touch with the emerging Commonwealth, and contained too many sympathizers of apartheid South Africa. It was a favourite hang-out of retired colonial administrators and its classic Herbert Baker building was redolent of the late imperial era.

What is fascinating about the Ingram–Smith memorandum, though it relates specifically to the RCS, is that it encapsulates so many of Ingram's long-lasting views in his frustrating love affair with the Commonwealth. After commenting with flattery that 'there can rarely have been a time in the Society's long period when it has been so influential' and that 'the number of new ideas and thoughts that have percolated from this building to many parts of the world is truly remarkable' the paper goes for the jugular. The RCS image is out of date, and needs to be rejuvenated.

> It would be no exaggeration to say that tens of thousands of people must pass through our front hall every year, yet today its appearance is no less daunting and archaic than it was ten years ago.

> It still conveys no impression that it is the HQ of an organization that is promoting a young and dynamic Commonwealth whose members include something like 20 countries that are barely a decade old...

> The need is to convey the air of an international and not a national organization and one that is of the 1970s and not the 1870s. It is, for instance, little short of disastrous for members of Commonwelth countries to find themselves confronted with the words "Rhodes Room". Rhodes is a highly controversial figure in Commonwealth terms and one that is anathema to many who believe in today's Commonealth and not in yesterday's Empire...

Ingram and Smith pressed for more responsibility for young members, a student member-ship scheme, and dropping the use of the word 'Royal'.[14] Although this particular memo was sidetracked, some of Ingram's ideas reached fruition. A financial crisis engulfing the Society in the late 1980s led to plans for a major redevelopment in Northumberland Avenue in the 1990s which could complete the overdue modernization of its image.

In the meantime Ingram played an active role in putting up ideas for and chairing meetings at the RCS. One of the more controversial and effective was a series of meetings on South Africa in the middle 1980s which brought speakers from different political perspectives, including Oliver Tambo in 1986, then president of the African National Congress. Many Society members disapproved of the series and especially of Tambo – at a time when Mrs Thatcher freely anathematized the ANC as a 'terrorist organization.'

Ingram found himself chairing a press conference for Tambo that followed Tambo's public meeting (Thabo Mbeki had insisted that he stay in the chair). It was on this occasion that Tambo made the memorable remark, referring to black South Africans, that 'We never

14. Memorandum by Ingram and Smith for consideration by the RCS Central Council on Thursday 21 June 1973 (Ingram Archive).

left the Commonwealth.' He meant that Africans had never been asked their opinion when the white regime walked out. That day he was invited to meet Mrs Lynda Chalker, then a relatively junior member of the Conservative government in Britain. This was one of the first contacts of the Thatcher government with the ANC.

An important connection for Ingram was with the Commonwealth Institute, of which he was a governor from 1969 to 1988. The Institute was grant-aided by the Foreign and Commonwealth Office, which treated it then with benign neglect. James Porter, who had been heading an enterprising college at Bulmershe which had broadened out from the training of teachers, was appointed as director by David Owen, when he was Foreign and Commonwealth Secretary. Porter, who had acquired a national reputation as an educator, wanted to push the Institute into the visual and performing arts. Although the Institute's grant did not keep pace with inflation much was achieved through combined programming and exhibitions on major Commonwealth regions such as Africa, the Caribbean and the Pacific, backed up by sponsorship funding.

Ingram was delighted at the vitality shown by the Institute – which also provided a venue for national day parties for High Commissions – though he still worried that the task of educating children and adults in the nature of the modern Commonwealth was inadequately served. But for Gemini the Institute connection was most important at the time of the shutdown. The effort put in then by Porter, who was also helped on legal matters by Aubrey Rose, the Institute's legal adviser, was critical in putting together the board of NewsConcern and in providing credibility for funding bodies.

The Institute was perceived as semi-official, for in addition to its British Government funding all the Commonwealth High Commissioners in London sat beside Ingram as governors. But, through its editor, Gemini was also in touch with significant professional and non-governmental Commonwealth bodies. He was an office-holder in the Commonwealth Press Union, the organization for publishers founded by Sir Harry Brittain with the backing of Lord Northcliffe in imperial days. He helped start the Commonwealth Journalists Association, as an organization for working journalists. And he was a crucial supporter of the non-governmental Commonwealth Human Rights Initiative.

Ingram's relationship with the CPU, which gave him its annual award in 1978, was sometimes prickly. It was a conservative, establishment organization, Anglocentric in bias which had a significant budget for the training of journalists but otherwise was best known for its jolly conferences for proprietors, managers and their spouses. To Ingram, with his awareness of the newer Commonwealth members, it was the kind of organization which had to be modernized if the Commonwealth was to have a future. The newspapers it represented were not doing enough to tell readers about the contemporary Commonwealth. It was too out of touch with the realities of journalism, and with the journalists its members employed.

On the other hand the CPU had for long been one of the most potent bodies in the Commonwealth network. Furthermore the newspapers it included still contained many of the most powerful groups in the developed states, as well as some of the most successful in those that were developing. They were, in short, a prime target for the Gemini service.

It was ironic that it was in 1978, at a CPU conference when Ingram received his CPU award for services to Commonwealth journalism, that he and a group of working journalists set up the Commonwealth Journalists Association. For basically he and his colleagues – who included Bethel Njoku, then with the *Nigerian Daily Times* – recognized that the managerial and traditional approach of the CPU made it unrepresentative of the concerns of the journalists.

The CJA followed a conference on Commonwealth non-governmental organizations at Dalhousie, Nova Scotia, and its launch had considerable help from the Commonwealth Foundation and Shridath Ramphal, then Secretary-General. Ingram was the first president. Although funding was always difficult it ran scores of training events and held major conferences in Cyprus (1983), New Delhi (1987), Barbados (1990) and Namibia (1994).

From the viewpoint of Gemini, some of whose contributors joined a CJA which gradually set up branches around the Commonwealth, the association was perhaps a mixed blessing. On the one hand it put Ingram and Gemini in touch with new journalists and potential contributors, such as Kabral Blay-Amihere of Ghana. On the other it represented competition in the training field which, by the late 1980s, was essential to the agency's economic survival.

Involvement with the CJA and Commonwealth Institute from the late 1970s helped to broaden Ingram's perspective, a process buttressed by his daily experience in the news service and his voluntary work for the RCS Trust. There was a great deal more to the Commonwealth than its inter-governmental aspect, especially when governments were often so blinkered.

This growing sympathy for non-governmental organizations (NGOs) had a fruitful result in his active backing, with the CJA, for a coalition of Commonwealth NGOs called the Commonwealth Human Rights Initiative. This came into existence in 1987, after a conference attended by Ingram at Cumberland Lodge in Britain. It aimed to force the official Commonwealth to take human rights issues more seriously and was also backed by the Commonwealth Lawyers Association, the Commonwealth Trade Union Council, the Commonwealth Legal Education Association and the Commonwealth Medical Association. Three of these bodies – the CJA, CLA and CTUC – had found themselves regularly protesting to Commonwealth governments over the imprisonment and abuse of their members.

Appearing in the dying days of the Cold War and of South African apartheid the Initiative had considerable impact. It helped persuade Commonwealth heads at Harare (1991) and Limassol (1993) to give more attention to their own accountability, and to human rights in their own countries. The Initiative moved its office to India in 1993, following a decision to rotate it around Commonwealth capitals, and Ingram was nominated by the CJA to serve on the Initiative's Commonwealth Human Rights Advisory Commission.

Gemini itself, as has been seen in the chapter on journalists, was fully aware of the problems of government abuse and media unfreedom. The Initiative was a response to the imperfections of the Commonwealth and one of many reactions in the 1980s – including a revulsion against economic mismanagement – to the optimism of the 1960s which had been part of the initial prospectus of Gemini.

However Gemini, which reported the Initiative objectively, was nevertheless implying that there were organizations in the Commonwealth which felt that it was still an instrument that could be useful. Along with Gemini's remorseless reporting of Third World debt and sub-Saharan Africa's impoverishment – issues involving collusion between greedy incompetent Northern bankers and ditto Southern governments – the human rights question was an example of the maturity and independence of its approach.

How then does one sum up Gemini's ties with the Commonwealth? Even if Ingram had not been a particular enthusiast for the association they would, implicitly, have been important for a London-based English-speaking news feature service which commenced in 1967. The Commonwealth then was the English-speaking market, with the exception of the United States and a handful of countries including South Africa, Ireland and Liberia. Although in the early days Gemini tried to enter the US market it was always up against the great strength of the US agencies and syndicated columns, as well as a different world view among editors and readers.

But of course the editor of Gemini was not just interested in the Commonwealth as an English-speaking market for the service. His concern for its survival and rebirth was a major determinant in launching the service, and the long hours of work and worry that followed. And this too was important. Chief Anyaoku has stated flatly that 'Gemini managed to survive its crises because it was a Commonwealth-linked medium. My view is that you wouldn't have had a Gemini if it hadn't linked its fortunes to the Common-wealth'.[15]

Certainly the collapse of rivals such as Forum World Features and Compass suggests that without the Commonwealth networks it would have been impossible for an under-financed, commercially loss-making news agency to have stayed alive.

But there are broader as well as more particular questions concerning the Gemini–Commonwealth connection. The first is the reduced significance attaching to the Commonwealth in its member countries in 1994 as compared with 1967. Too few others had joined Ingram in his multi-faceted struggle to rejuvenate the Commonwealth, to make it matter more in the present and future, and not let it be stereotyped as a relic from the past. Was Gemini actually suffering from maintaining its Commonwealth coverage? Even some of the young Canadian IDRC fellows felt Ingram was obsessive about the Commonwealth, and Gemini should let it go.

It is helpful to distinguish here between the Commonwealth institutions and the stories and issues of concern to Commonwealth countries. If information about the former may have seemed less important – could perhaps have been a reason why penetration in countries like India and Australia remained disappointing – the stories and issues of concern in Commonwealth countries continued to command interest. Gemini was willing

---

15. Interview, Chief Anyaoku. This aspect, of course, strongly motivated James Porter, Arnold Smith and Clyde Sanger in 1982–83 when they helped to reconstruct Gemini.

to write head-on about topics like water, the condition of women and children, population and the environment. Good engrossing coverage of matters which were important to many countries remained an attractive part of the service.

The Commonwealth was helpful to Gemini for its first 20 years for another reason. This was because the association had not formally enlisted on either side in the Cold War. Although its developed members were clearly part of the West most of its developing states were non-aligned and many of them were following a path of state socialism. This fluidity allowed space for independent journalism which would not have existed if Gemini had followed a British orientation, nor would this have been so easy if its office had been in many non-aligned or socialist capitals. It created new opportunities after the Cold War was over, when many around the globe still had reservations about the victorious North American model.

Commonwealth official studies focused on the needs of developing countries, but could not entirely ignore the views of the developed ones which footed the Commonwealth bill. The approach was consensual; indeed Commonwealth meetings abhor voting, which is odd in an association which dedicated itself to democracy at Singapore in 1971. Nonetheless this environment was one in which Gemini material could be acceptable both to government-controlled papers in countries like Tanzania and Zambia, but also to fiercely independent papers from New Zealand to Nigeria.

Hence even if leader-writers ignored or disparaged the formal Commonwealth a kind of living Commonwealth, based on common interests and the English language, was still a bedrock of the Gemini operation. Although there were fluctuations, roughly 60 per cent of the output from 1967 to 1994 originated from Commonwealth countries. In a much more lucrative way that living Commonwealth had also been exploited by magnates like Rupert Murdoch, whose expansion from Australia had important stops en route in England, Hong Kong and India; similarly, coming from Canada, Conrad Black had made profitable media purchases in England and Australia.

For Gemini this bedrock was added to, from early in the history of the service, by some papers outside the Commonwealth which were interested in the content. Some were English-language papers; others, like the east European papers which subscribed after the Berlin Wall fell, were not. The English-language press in non-Commonwealth states – like the *Riyadh Daily*, *Kuwait Times* or *Bangkok Post* – tended to expand and become wealthier during Gemini's life. They served growing expatriate and English-speaking communities in countries whose economies were rising fast, but which were also hitting environmental and other problems.

But if some Commonwealth countries were disappointing as subscribers there was one category that was appreciative – the small island developing states. For most of Gemini's life over half of Commonwealth states have had populations of less than a million. Both geographically and psychologically they were insular. For longer than was true of bigger states the Commonwealth, and their historic connections with Britain, have loomed large in their sense of identity and in their view of the world. Yet they could never afford foreign correspondents as such.

Fig. 26. Derek Ingram in the Lodi Gardens, New Delhi in December 1994 while attending a meeting of the Advisory Commission of the Commonwealth Human Rights Initiative.

James Porter, who has travelled widely in the islands of the Caribbean, observing how Gemini material is used, is quite definite. 'I began to see that Gemini is ideal as a small countries' newspaper service,' he remarked. The articles and graphics seemed informative and thoughtful and had the rare quality of not diminishing the papers in which they appeared. Whereas material from Associated Press or Reuter stuck out like a foreign body, Gemini fitted well. Quite often a Gemini piece stimulated an editorial comment.[16]

Gemini knew that attitudes in the Pacific were similar, as it received glowing tributes from papers such as the *Cook Island News*. Papers of this size tended to be invisible to or incidentally exploited by the large media corporations. But they knew that Gemini took them seriously, recognizing that they had interests which were quite as valid to them as those dominant in London or Washington. When cyclone Namu devastated the Solomon Islands in May 1986, killing dozens and leaving around 150,000 islanders homeless it rated only a paragraph or two in many Northern papers: Gemini put out an immediate and full report.[17]

Finally it is appropriate to examine an issue which arose from time to time. Was Gemini anti-British in its general bias, and was this one cause of its failure to be more widely used in Britain? There is no doubt that some British government spokesmen and staff in the Foreign and Commonwealth Office felt that Gemini was hostile, especially in coverage related to Rhodesia and South Africa. There was no doubt too that the bulk of the British press, provincial as well as national, has a conservative tone.

The question is of course simplistic, for there were always many in Britain who thought, like Gemini correspondents, that the government was behaving foolishly. But it also goes to the heart of the post-imperial dilemmas faced by British editors and public opinion, and which tended to be answered by a shrugging off of the Commonwealth connection even when the development lobby was arguing strongly on the underlying issues.

---

16. Interview, James Porter.

17. Case quoted by McParland in 'Gemini and the Commonwealth', *The Round Table*, 1986.

In its first Ingram–Carruthers phase Gemini was probably more widely used by notable British papers than ever again. Yet this was a period when Rhodesian UDI was a hot story. So-called bias against the British government position did not deter newspapers which supported the Conservative Party, such as *The Sunday Times* and *Evening Standard*, from taking Gemini.

Later in the 1970s, when Gemini was a *Guardian* subsidiary, this fact was probably more important than issues of content in limiting access to other British national newspapers. And, as recounted earlier, Gemini was unlucky in 1985–86 in putting all its eggs into the *Today* basket when it had rebuilt something of a British provincial subscriber base.

By the 1980s, however, there were other factors apart from its attitude to the British government's policies which could have worked against Gemini. The switch to computerization in the British press left Gemini looking outdated. There was a squeeze on foreign news in many papers. Development issues were regarded by mainstream editors as a minority concern. The Commonwealth meant little to them. Europe and the East–West story occupied what interest they had in 'abroad.'

A cool view of Gemini's stance on Rhodesia in the 1970s was given by Nicholas Harman:

> My view of the Rhodesia business was that it kept the Commonwealth together by providing a serious issue for its governments to talk about. Gemini was right about it all along. That infuriated British diplomats. I was once nearly struck at a party for suggesting that the British were foolishly acting against their own interest in refusing to act; that was just before they decided to be sensible, and British diplomats will forgive anything except being right when their masters are being silly.[18]

There is little doubt that Gemini's firmness in regarding the Commonwealth as something different from Britain was hard to take for an older generation, who had equated the two. In taking the Commonwealth seriously it challenged, and risked being ignored by, those who did not wish to do the same. Its interest in any international organization was deeply unfashionable in the Thatcherite Britain of the 1980s, whose Prime Minister promulgated the belief that only national interest counted and international bodies represented compromise, unaccountability, inefficiency and possibly corruption.

To some extent the agency had reduced its interest in the official Commonwealth by the time Ingram handed over the editorial reins to Nelson: inter-governmental programmes like the Commonwealth Youth Programme and Commonwealth Fund for Technical Cooperation, which seemed new and newsworthy in the early 1970s, had been starved of funds and looked less exciting by the 1990s.

But at a deeper level there was still a connection. Interestingly the Commonwealth itself had survived into a genuinely post-imperial phase, where the issues were no longer those of race and decolonization, where heads of government did not share a British-style

18. Harman letter, *ibid.*

education, where the traumas of independence and the Cold War were of the past. If the Commonwealth could show a use for itself in this new world, and generate a fresh commitment, Gemini's long crusade might actually pay off.

8 Pioneering

In a sense the agency had always prided itself on being distinctive, both in scope and approach. As it evolved some of what it had been doing was taken up by others. Larger international agencies were recruiting indigenous journalists. Regional and other agencies had a remit to report events of importance to developing countries. Specialist services, including the Panos Institute, were supplying environmental articles. Other bodies were involved in training journalists (an activity which had the benefit of putting Gemini in touch with fresh correspondents).

In a highly competitive market it was always hard, therefore, to stay ahead as a pioneer. However, along with its bread-and-butter role in reporting development and Commonwealth issues, global trends and events in developing countries, Gemini was seen as a pioneer in certain types of journalism. Among these fields were science and health (including space, in which Gemini had a lasting interest both from developed and developing world perspectives); in rural reporting (for which it raised funds and invested considerable effort); and in the environment (where it was prepared to consider some of the awkward conflicts between development and the environment, and correspondents brought fresh perspectives to bear).

The fourth selection of articles put out by the service, reproduced in this book, aims to represent this kind of journalism. It would be too much to say that Gemini was always first even here. Its significance was that it opened up and persisted with types of coverage that might have seemed incidental to a bigger agency. Where only 12-14 items were going out each week, priorities and commitments were highly obvious. As in previous chapters, these items are republished unabridged in their original form.

The mosquito bites its way back in India

by K K Duggal
New Delhi

Malaria is a severe and debilitating disease, widespread in tropical and developing countries. Already by the 1970s there were environmental concerns about the unlimited use of DDT to kill its carrier, the mosquito. This alarming report from India was bad news for many Gemini subscribers. (15 October 1973 – GAS 145)

The mosquito is waging a hit and run guerilla-type war against man in India, outwitting and outmanoeuvring him and frustrating a two-year effort to exterminate it. The mosquito just continues to multiply.

As a result malaria, which it was claimed had been eradicated a few years ago, has reappeared in many states. The authorities do not know what to do next.

The Indian Government declared all-out war on the mosquito in the early Fifties with the aid of the World Health Organization and the US Government which furnished the latest weapons and money and experts. The mosquito changed its strategy.

Although India still spends over 200 million rupees annually on the war, the mosquito is increasing everywhere again. For one thing, it has become immune to DDT. For another, it has changed its habits. In New Delhi, *culex fatigans* (carrier of the disease filariasis) is breeding in wells it never inhabited before.

In the southern state of Kerala mosquitoes are laying eggs in salt water. Until recently this was unheard of. Salt used to be added to water to prevent mosquito breeding. *Anopheles stephensi*, the malaria carrier, has learned to live in clean water. Hitherto it dwelled in dirty pools, stagnant lakes and drains.

In the eastern state of Assam, bordering Burma, where scores of people have died of malaria in the past few months, *anopheles* are employing a new trick: they do not stay on the walls of the room after biting the sleeping victim, they just fly out. DDT spraying inside the room has become a futile exercise.

Even the new technique of sterilization has failed. In villages around New Delhi entomologists released large numbers of sterilized male *culex fatigans* in the hope that they would compete with the natural male population in mating with females.

Such mating yields eggs which do not hatch. Scientists supposed the technique would drastically reduce the mosquito population.

Two elaborate experiments have been undertaken in the past twelve months, but the scientists found to their chagrin that the mosquitoes had migrated to more friendly towns. The mass migration upset Government plans to wipe out the mosquitoes in confined areas.

Indian mosquitoes are 'quite different' in behaviour from their cousins in other parts of the world, according to a WHO expert aiding the Indian Government. *Culex fatigans* in the US, for instance, fly a maximum of 500 metres, but their Delhi cousins make a seven-kilometre non-stop flight.

Field workers in villages on the outskirts of New Delhi say mosquitoes are whizzing round 'like sand in a dust storm'. Madras, the capital of Tamil Nadu, is faced with one of the worst mosquito attacks in its history.

In Bombay the Mayor, Sudhir Joshi, suggested the other day that grass cultivation be banned by law to curb the mosquito nuisance. And in the north-western border states of Haryana and Punjab the mosquitoes belong to a well-fed family. They are king-sized. Chandigarh is perhaps the only city in India relatively free of mosquitoes. The city invests a lot of money spraying lawns, houses and drains.

Not long ago malaria was the No 1 killer in India. At its peak there were 75 million malaria cases in a year. In 1953, when Government embarked on the national malaria control programme, the count was 63 million. It came down to 21 million in 1958.

At one stage the Government claimed malaria had been banished. But now it is causing over 100,000 cases a year, creating an unprecedented demand for repellants.

Cheaper beef – from a new sugar cane feed

by Tony Cozier
Bridgetown, Barbados

Finding new products of value in developing countries was an unending battle, requiring scientific expertise, capital investment and marketing skills. Reports like this, from a writer who became better known as a cricket correspondent and broadcaster, were a regular part of the information service. (9 November 1973 – GG 5425)

Beef cattle on government farms here are thriving on a new, relatively cheap feed mixture which will increase food production.

The new feed – Comfith – has as its base sugarcane which, for 300 years, has formed the principal crop of this 166-square-mile Caribbean island. In trials over the past three years, agricultural experts have been very pleased with the results.

Beef production per acre per year using Comfith has worked out at between 1,695 and 2,180 pounds deadweight, carrying five animals to the acre. Compared, for instance, with the best Canadian yields of around 1,000 pounds an acre this is very high.

In addition, the cost of production has been low, 25 to 30 cents (US) a pound liveweight or 52 cents a pound deadweight. This compares with a price in Canada of between 35 and 40 cents (US) a pound liveweight, a price that is steadily rising.

It means, among other things, that the new discovery offers Barbados and other tropical underdeveloped countries a chance to cut beef imports. In addition, it could well make tropical beef highly competitive in the North American market where prices have risen considerably.

The Barbados government, in conjuction with the sugar industry, is now moving from the pilot plant stage to full-scale implementation of the new development. One of the standard sugar factories at Uplands in the parish of St John has been converted to a plant for the manufacture of Comfith and further cattle feedlots are to be established. Already, the Barbados government and those engaged in the experiments have been flooded with inquiries from all over the world.

What is Comfith and how was it discovered?

It is the result of an invention by two Canadians, of a machine to split the sugarcane and remove the soft, central pith that contains most of the sugar. Robert Miller, a businessman from Calgary, and Ted Tilby, a mechanical engineer from Edmonton, spent a holiday in the Caribbean in 1964 and were surprised to find that the milling process for extracting juice from the cane had not changed in more than a century. It was still being squeezed between massive rollers, leaving the potentially productive rind and wax comparatively useless.

Their machine, the Miller-Tilby Cane Separator, as it is called, was seen as doing little more than separating the hard fibrous rind from the pitch of the cane so that the rind could be used for the manufacture of wallboard and other construction materials.

It was, however, the Comfith, the soft pith of high sucrose content, that was to prove the most important derivative.

It has always been known that sugarcane far outyields other crops grown in the tropics in terms of energy per acre. The fact that the rind had never been removed from the cane ruled it out as a potential food for animals. Miller and Tilby deduced that the fluffy pith left after sugar extraction in their separator might be used as feed.

Scientific tests, carried out by Dr W.J. Pigden of the Canadian Department of Agriculture, proved that it did, indeed, have potential – but before the extraction of the sugar.

Here, however, the process met with another problem. While Comfith is high in its content of readily available carbohydrate as sugars (60 per cent), it is low in protein (only 2 per cent). So a way had to be found of providing the livestock with protein as well.

Again, this was overcome. Ruminants (cattle, sheep and goats) are capable of utilizing cheap, non-protein-nitrogen sources, such as urea, and manu-facturing much of their own protein requirements. The balance was reached by using Comith and urea.

It was found, in fact, that is possible to reduce the intake of the animal by less than half without in any way affecting its growth – another breakthrough in the cost of production.

During the experimental period of a joint project by the Barbados govern-ment, the Canadian International Development Agency (CIDA) and Cana-dian Cane Consultants, much of the beef raised on Comfith was tested in hotels.

Barbados attracts thousands of tourists a year, most of them North Ameri-cans accustomed to high quality beef. The response of hotel chefs and guests to the local beef was, according to Keith Laurie, manager of Canadian Cane Consultants, 'extremely encouraging'.

So was that of the retailers. Former Minister of Agriculture, daCosta Edwards, in opening a seminar on the Comfith project, quoted a letter he had received from one of the island's major beef importers and suppliers.

Referring to 1,840 pounds of beef he had bought from the government, he wrote: 'It was cut into steaks and joints for roasting and displayed among similar cuts of hard frozen New Zealand meat. It was remarkable that several customers noted the difference and remarked on the improved quality after eating this locally-grown meat'.

Economists involved in the experiment have scotched any fears that cane growers would be losing by turning their crop over to livestock feed rather than sugar production. Far from it, the gross profit on an acre of cane used for sugar seldom exceeds $4 (East Caribbean) a ton; for that used for beef production, the profit would be approximately $800 (EC) a ton.

Even so, sugar production should hardly be affected since it will require only two per cent of cane grown and milled annually in Barbados to produce 6,000 head of beef cattle.

The scheme still has a few stages through which to pass before it can be labelled an unconditional success. It is a highly sophisticated process needing proper management and expertise at each stage of the operation – qualities often lacking in developing countries. Also a variety of sugarcane needs to be developed which would allow for year-round harvesting and planting so that material for Comfith will be continuously available. These are problems which can be overcome.

Getting away from 'man bites dog' news values

By Brij Khandelwal
New Delhi

Gemini followed with sympathy the attempts to establish an international news agency answerable to the needs of the South, but this report prior to a Non-Aligned Movement summit in Colombo in 1976 was perhaps too optimistic about the possibilities. Ironically, if the efforts had been more successful, Gemini might have found it harder to survive. (8 June 1976 – GAS 211)

Efforts are being made to set up a news agency of the Third World aimed at providing objective news coverage which, it is increasingly felt, is denied to the developing countries by Western news media.

Delegates from leading non-aligned countries agreed at their conference last August in Lima, Peru that such an effort is necessary if they are to be freed from their dependence on major world news agencies and distributors which monopolize the collection and dissemination of news.

Many Third World nations have, over the years, expressed their dissatisfaction with the style and content of news put out by these agencies. It is felt they have been catering almost exclusively to western and neo-colonial interests despite the decolonization process that began after World War Two.

A resolution adopted at Lima called for co-operation in the reorganization of communication channels inherited from the colonialists. The conference had warned that news agencies run by some former colonial powers were working against the interests of the developing nations, presenting a false and perverse picture according to their likes and dislikes.

But the transition from abstract to the concrete has been long and arduous. Leaders from developing countries have often felt irritated, and even humiliated, at the news coverage by Western news agencies, but hardly any efforts were made to build a parallel organization.

The gap is now sought to be bridged. India's Minister for Information and Broadcasting recently told Parliament that the conference of the Non-

Aligned Nations' ministers to be held in New Delhi in July preparatory to the August 9 Colombo summit would finalize details of the new organization which would project happenings in the developing nations and prevent 'insidious exploitation of the situation by certain news agencies of the capitalist world'.

If these efforts bear fruit, the non-aligned news agency will not be a distant dream. As a start the developing nations will form a pool of news agencies which would provide extensive coverage to developmental and success stories in the Third World countries.

As a first step the Indian government has promoted the merger of the country's four national news agencies into a single organization called Samachar (News). The board of Samachar consists of working journalists, editors and other public men.

The four dissolved agencies are the United News of India, the Press Trust of India, the Hindustan Samachar and the Samachar Bharti. The UNI was formed in 1961 at the recommendation of the press commission to provide healthy competition to existing news agencies. In 15 years it emerged as the third largest news agency in Asia.

However, the Indian government felt that competition for its own sake was wasteful and that, in view of the limited resources a single agency would have a better chance of expanding and preventing duplication of effort.

While the idea and philosophy behind the creation of a Third World news agency are laudable, it is doubtful if, the new organization can replace the established news agencies of the West.

First, the developing countries lack financial and manpower resources. Second, the readers in these countries have got so used to a particular style of reporting and selection of news that all coverage of the new agency may not be in tune with long-established reading habits.

Besides, the press in many developing countries is still in the hands of the elite who have their roots in the colonial era and so find themselves in tune with everything Western.

The formation of a news agency with a distinct feel for the Third World will have to encounter several problems before it can achieve success. Although most Third World countries are economically backward, their political systems range from dictatorship to democracies.

Some countries have a free press, in others governments cannot tolerate any criticism or dissent. The only common point seems to be their urge to be heard and understood by the outside world.

And in the changed circumstances, when the poor nations are struggling hard to liberate themselves from a neo-colonial stranglehold, it is natural for them to resent the 'Dog bites man' approach of most Western journalists.

Mass communication, it is recognized everywhere, has a leading role to play in a society's socioeconomic transformation. Therefore it is only proper for the leadership of the country concerned that it should devise ways of using various channels of communication for the welfare of the people.

For the last two decades, the accent has primarily been on developmental journalism, which largely keeps politicians and politics out of its scope. In the words of the Indian Prime Minister, journalism of this type is a 'nation-building activity'.

The press in a developing country must explain government policies and strengthen the foundations of the nation. This necessitates identification of concepts and techniques of mass communication to aid development programmes.

How a uniform style or technique can be evolved is not yet clear because the Third World includes countries with conflicting ideologies – from Algeria and Tanzania, which follow a leftist path, to others which believe in free enterprise or a mixed economy.

In the formation of the Third World news agency India is bound to play a pioneering role. The press in India is well developed and the country has an army of journalists and media experts.

In 1965 the government of India founded the Indian Institute of Mass Communication in New Delhi with Unesco and Commonwealth assistance. The Institute trains scores of Third World journalists in developmental journalism every year.

A similar institute is being set up by the Association of South East Asia Nations (ASEAN) to provide journalistic training and research for the region. An ASEAN press seminar held in Jakarta last February called for the establishment of an ASEAN news agency.

Participants felt that the 'proposed agency could be realized through the closest possible co-operation among national news agencies in the region' which could start with a regular exchange of ASEAN features followed by an intensive exchange of news.

The determination that characteristics the recent moves of the Third World countries gives hope that the new agency will be a viable venture reducing to a large extent the reliance on Western communication channels, and helping to forge lasting ties among the have-nots of the world.

Who-pays-what? storm at the UN

by Ted Morello
United Nations, New York

In the front rank when it came to demystifying the West's role in the international debt debate, Gemini was also unwilling to let the Soviet bloc get away with inflated claims for its overseas aid. Its articles were regularly published in the UN journal Development Forum *and one of these brought an angry response from Soviet and East German spokesmen. (28 July 1987 – GN 32765)*

A bitter debate has erupted between the Soviet bloc and a group of industrialized democracies over their relative generosity in the voluntary funding of the United Nations' multi-billion-dollar humanitarian assistance programme.

A new study submitted by eight Western nations and Japan asserts that the Eastern European alliance gave only one per cent of all voluntary funds funnelled through the UN for Third World activities in 1985, the most recent year for which statistics are available.

Release of the report by the nine – all members of the Organization for Economic Cooperation and Development (OECD) – coincided with Soviet and East German protests over publication in an official UN periodical of similar assertions based on an earlier OECD study.

In a long letter to the Editor of *Development Forum*, a monthly publication oriented towards social and humanitarian activities, Counsellor Guenter Schumann, the East German UN mission's third-ranking diplomat, branded the article 'a completely unbalanced picture of the voluntary contributions made by socialist states'. It was, he added, 'tendentious' and 'misleading'.

In a similar letter, also carried in the publication's July-August issue, Deputy Permanent Representative Victor A. Zvezdin, the Soviet delegation's No. 3 official, cited a UN document to substantiate his claim that in the 12-month period ending in April 1984, 'the volume of assistance extended by the USSR for these (humanitarian) purposes exceeded the volume of corresponding assistance rendered by many Western countries'.

Both letters were reactions to a Gemini News Service article written nearly a year ago but published in *Development Forum* only last May. The article was based on statistics submitted last year to the UN General Assembly by Secretary-General Javier Perez de Cuellar and covering 1984 contributions and on the nine-nation study analysing that report.

The letters were apparently written before the authors had seen the new OECD study, which is based on this year's updated report of the Secretary-General and contains final data for 1985.

The new study, not significantly different from last year's, was released in July as a General Assembly document. It was signed by representatives of the United States, Britain, Japan, Canada, Australia, West Germany, Spain, Belgium and Iceland – all leading voluntary contributors to UN development programmes.

The study says: 'The Soviet Union and the countries of Eastern Europe provide only one per cent of the voluntary contributions made by all countries to the United Nations multilateral assistance efforts.

'The Western developed countries provided approximately 87 per cent of the voluntary contributions in 1985 (and) developing countries provided 12 per cent'.

The most striking contrast occurs in the Secretary-General's report under the heading 'Contributions to refugees, humanitarian, special economic and disaster-relief activities' from governments in 1985.

The grand total from all governments was roughly $500 million. The largest amount – $216 million – came from the United States, followed in order by Japan, $62.7 million; West Germany, $34.1 million; Britain, $26 million; Sweden, $21.1 million; Canada, $20.5 million; Norway, $20.1 million; Denmark, $15.8 million, and Italy, $15 million.

Even some of the most financially depressed countries made token contributions. Mexico, for example, gave $63,000, Argentina $30,000 and the Philippines $7,000. War-racked Lebanon contributed $19,000, and among the least-developed countries, Mali and Niger provided $13,000 and $1,000 respectively.

In that same category, according to the Secretary-General's report, contributions by the Eastern European grouping – the Soviet Union, East Germany, Bulgaria, Byelorussia, Czechoslovakia, Hungary, Poland Romania and Ukraine – added up to zero.

In his rebuttal, Zvezdin conceded: 'It is true that the level of the USSR voluntary contributions to UN operational activities is not very high'. But he added:

*The Soviet Union increased its voluntary contributions to the UN Development Programme (UNDP) by 35 per cent and to the UN Children's Fund (UNICEF) by 28 per cent at last November's pledging conference. (The Secretary-General's report for 1985 shows that the Soviets contributed $1,724,000 to UNDP's main programme and $751,000 to UNICEF. Figures for the US were $135,495,000 and $70,836,000 respectively.)

*The USSR is prepared to increase its UNDP contribution further if the agency will make use of millions of unspent roubles given by Moscow. UNDP has made no effort to spend the roubles, 'though many developing countries are interested in utilizing these contributions'. (UNDP has long contended that because the roubles are noncovertible, they are virtually unspendable.)

*The Soviet Union 'is one of the major bilateral donors aiding the developing countries'. (The Secretary-General's reports for 1984 and 1985 deal only with multilateral funding through the UN system. They do not include bilateral assistance. If they did, they would have also to include the multi-billion-dollar aid packages given to developing countries through the US Agency for International Development (USAID), the Canadian International Development Agency (CIDA) and other Western government bilateral programmes.)

Western and UN development officials contend that the Soviet bloc pads and distorts statistics on its Third World assistance by misrepresenting bilateral aid as contributions made to UN programmes. As they explain it, the tactic typically works like this:

Moscow prepares a report that purports to show how much each Eastern European country gave in development aid. It is then submitted to the Secretary-General with a request that it be published and distributed as a General Assembly document.

Such requests are granted routinely without any review of the contents. The unverified statistics, now bearing the imprimatur of the Secretary-General, then can be cited as 'an official UN document', usually with no mention of its origin or the fact that the funds never passed through the UN's accounting system.

Schumann's letter, for example, cited a UN document as proving that in 1985 East Germany contributed over two billion marks 'to support developing countries and liberation movements'.

Actually, the UN document was simply a reproduction of a communication received from the East German Foreign Ministry.

Sputnik plus 30 years – what happens in the next 30?

by Geoffrey Hugh Lindop

Fascination with space was an enduring feature of the service, and Geoffrey Hugh Lindop was a regular contributor. Gemini pioneered here by seeking to explain what was happening in terms that were meaningful to developing countries, and regularly looked for implications and applications affecting the South. (22 September 1987 – GSC 222)

Just 30 years ago, on the night of October 4 1957, the Russians launched the world's first artificial satellite. They called it *Sputnik* – Fellow Traveller.

Today Cosmonaut Yuri Romanenko is about to break the endurance record for manned flight – 236 days achieved by Kizim, Solovyov and Atkov in 1984. Progress in space in three decades has been phenomenal. Much of

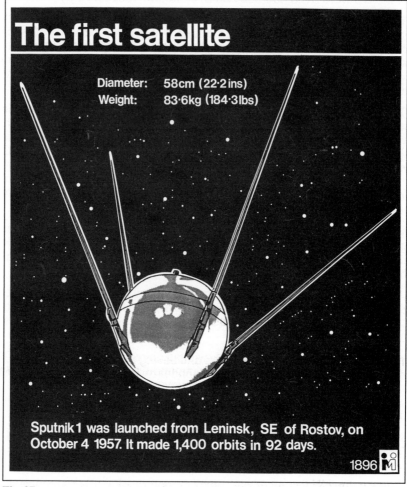

Fig. 27.

what has happened was foreseen but much was not even imagined.

Arthur C Clarke, writing before Sputnik-1 was launched, suggested the feasibility of communication satellites. His theory proved correct, but none of his contemporaries foresaw the remote sensing satellite.

Using such satellites experts are now able to look at Earth and determine not only what crops are growing, but whether those crops are healthy or diseased.

Even when the first Earth Resources Test Satellite, ERTS-1, was launched geologist could not see that it was relevant to their field of study. Now satellites locate potential oil wells and search for water-bearing rocks in the deserts.

Nobody expected the dramatic advance of computer technology. Space probes of the sophistication of Voyager and Viking, which can use onboard computers to enable the probe to think for itself, were beyond comprehension.

Paradoxically, robots were featured in pre-Sputnik science fiction. These were built in the image of Man and although thought of as being superhuman in terms of strength and brain-power, they were restricted to the human form.

Even so in the late Fifties and early Sixties, robots were still science fiction whilst manned spaceflight was reality. The drive to put men on the Moon demanded more powerful and more compact computers for operation on spacecraft.

In the Fifties as men dreamt of colonizing space, the future seemed a re-run of how the West was won, with spacemen taking the place of cowboys and bug-eyed monsters being the space age equivalent of the Indians.

The space frontier was to be won with Man at the forefront, possibly assisted by robots under the direct control of the explorers. Now the advance in technology has been so dramatic many people question whether manned spaceflight is necessary.

Robotic devices might explore space more efficiently, with Man directing operations from the comfort of his Earth-based laboratory.

Such a concept lacks the romance of the Fifties dream, but in the wake of the Challenger disaster, may prove more realistic. It is claimed, however, that a manned presence in space is needed to correct unforeseen problems and to react faster to changing circumstances.

Advocates of this idea point to the success of manned flight on Skylab, the Shuttle, Salyut and Mir in fixing faults and saving missions. But if computer science develops over the next three decades as fast as it has since Sputnik 1, robots may take the place of Man at the frontiers of space.

Yet Man is essentially an explorer. He will not be content to watch television pictures sent back by robots. He will want to be physically at the frontier.

So what can we expect in the next 30 years? Naturally, we will build on what we have achieved. Communication satellites will become more powerful so that smaller ground terminals will be needed. In the not-too-distant future lorry drivers will be able to speak by telephone with their headquarters through a satellite link.

Remote-sensing satellites will become more sensitive and sophisticated enabling archaeologists to use them to detect the sites of ancient cities.

As Man increases his stay in space on orbital stations, we can expect a greater commercial participation, bringing drugs of very high purity on to chemists' shelves. Materials made in space, such as exotic alloys, will become commonplace.

It will be possible to harness the power from the Sun and beam it down to Earth to form a continuous non-polluting form of energy to supplement and eventually replace coal, oil and nuclear energy.

As we use up our natural resources on Earth, we will be able to tap cosmic minerals. It will be possible within the next 30 years to capture asteroids, kilometre-sized chunks of rock, and mine their wealth. As a spin-off, only the core of the asteroid will be used leaving the shell as the basis of a spacecraft.

It is cheaper to bring things down to Earth than launch them into space. Industry is likely to move to the source of raw materials, namely the captured asteroids. With the added bonus of plenty of solar power only the finished products may be shipped down to Earth, taking industry with all its problems of pollution away from the face of the Earth.

Who will operate the machines – Man or robot? How will this affect employment on Earth? Will the poorer countries in the Third World become yet poorer?

The 21st Century will present a unique set of problems, but none greater than any of those set in the past as Man has developed his life on Earth.

Bango celebrates its 'dance with a difference'

by Dupe Motojehi
Bango Village, Nigeria

Some of the most creative and far-sighted journalism produced since Gemini's restart emerged from its rural reporting initiative. Dupe Motojehi spent two months in this village and her report, readable in itself, throws a fascinating light on population and family issues in northern Nigeria. (29 April 1988 – GS 4342)

The sound of the gong started early in the spring evening, the first crash of it carrying across the village about 7 pm, before we had sat down for supper.

It was followed by the shouts of the village children, clamouring excitedly. Halima Hassan, wife of Raymond Hassan, the missionary in the small Nigerian village of Bango, said the noise was in preparation for 'the dance'.

'Dance'? I asked.

She replied: 'Yes, a dance with a difference'.

Nearby the hut people were already gathering, hundreds of children and adults who had collected on bicycles and wooden stools around a group of drummers. At the centre of attention were dozens of young boys and girls, the girls' features specially painted, both groups eager with anticipation, clutching the flashlights that would feature in the night's event.

Tonight, as every year at this time, there was to be an engagement dance. Not the general *biki* celebration, the Hausa word for a marriage engagement that is typified by much cooking, feasting and dancing.

This was a Bango-style engagement, and by dawn many of the growing crowd of children, most of them aged 7–14, would have selected a spouse. Although the ceremony itself might be several years off – the male of the pair is expected to be almost self-supporting before the deal is closed – tonight dozens of boys and girls would pledge themselves to a partner for life.

About 500 people live in the group of five settlements recognized as Bango, but an open invitation had been sent to villages throughout the region, where similar dances had been going on for weeks. Many of the children at Bango's dance had already been to a number of others but had failed to find the right mate, and the crowd was a considerable size.

Bango's dance, in fact, is near the end of the season, and those who fail to make a match tonight would have little choice but to wait until next year when the round of public courting begins again.

At the dance site 100 yards from the hut where Mrs Hassan prepared *tumo* the guineacorn evening meal, a group of drummers had formed a semi-circle with their drums arranged according to size. The crowd that surrounded them had separated into groups, parents at the back, where they could keep a wary eye on proceedings, children in front, facing each other across the way.

Bayi, a village woman whose daughter Rakiya was in the ring, confided that she and her husband already had an idea who Rakiya should marry.

'The father is very hard-working, wise and has a good character. Besides, there is a chance of educating our children through his close connection to the missionary who works among us'.

The missionary was Raymond Hassan, who was teaching the village children to read and write. The villagers are very suspicious of education, considering it an intrusion from the unfamiliar world of the city, but without the ability to read they likewise feel unable to join local agricultural organizations that might help their work in the surrounding fields. The boy Bayi had her eye on was Hassan's best student.

Within the circle, the master-of-ceremonies appeared, a farmer named Malam Maidawa Asabe. He ordered the crowd to make the circle larger, then danced a few steps in the ring, followed by a group of small children. The would-be brides appeared under the dim lantern light, their short hair plaited and braided, their faces, palms and feet painted, parallel lines bracketing their features and a red circle in the centre of each forehead.

The boys were on the other side. Suddenly flashlight beams began to shoot across the rings, as one side surveyed the other, searching for prospective partners as they danced. The beams jumped from face to face, searching. When the beam returned repeatedly to the same person, a contact was made: the chosen partner followed the beam back to its source and the negotiations began.

Though the point is to find a spouse, the dance means more than that alone.

177

A family's prospects can rise or fall on the choice of a partner, and – as with Rakiya – some planning goes on in advance.

It is traditional that a boy who chooses a wife should be able to support her. He must be strong enough to farm, and is expected to provide a home. His parents may build him a hut in their compound, or he may seek help from friends.

Most boys are ten or 12 before they reach this stage – the ages are approximate, as the villagers estimate age by seasons. Rakiya's choice, like her, was about seven. Though he was in the crowd, it would be several years before he could fulfil Rakiya's parents' hopes – and by then their daughter might have found someone else.

Each dancer makes up to four choices. The deal is sealed with a small down payment, rejected suitors receiving a refund when the list is later pared down. Parents eliminate partners too young or insolvent, while the children themselves may have a change of heart. A boy without prospects, or who takes too long to produce the required home, can quickly be eliminated from the shortlist.

Villagers say the early marriages combat promiscuity. Single mothers are unheard-of in Bango other than through widowhood, and most men are counting their children by age 16. Intermarriages between villages are common, and help cement regional bonds.

As the night approached the small hours of morning, Bango's dance was just warming up. It would last until just before dawn, then reconvene again that night, and the night after that.

By the end of the third night, most prospects of marriageable age will have been chosen. The unlucky ones, and children dropped later from the lists, will be back again next year.

How TV brought dissatisfaction to Balana

by Jennifer Henricus
Balana, Sri Lanka

A second example of an article in the Village Reports series, but also another comment in the media debate. Most people in the developing world still live in the countryside, but the ambiguous impact of TV has encouraged a flight to the towns in search of a better life. (20 January 1989 – GS 439)

It is 5.00 pm and the children of Balana village temporarily forget the aches in their bellies as they jostle for space on the mud floors of their huts in front of a 12 inch box. It is television time.

Run off a used car battery, the television not only brings the world to these illiterate villagers but even quells, albeit momentarily, their gnawing hunger.

For the next six hours Balana's children and most of its adults will join the fantasy world that prevails on the flashing screen.

Popular American 'soaps' like *Dynasty* and *Dallas*, Britain's *Mind Your Language* and *Crown Court*, and Australia's *Return to Eden* flash before their eyes, interspersed by government propaganda, a few good Sinhala teledramas and not so good romantic songs from the Sinhala cinema. Plus sophisticated commercials.

It is of little consequence that most programmes are in English and the villagers can barely understand a word. They are mesmerized by the drama and lifestyles that none of them has ever known. Most villagers have not been to a city; some have never left the precincts of the village.

Albert Pahalege, a railway worker, brought the first set to the village – a gift from his labourer brother in Saudi Arabia. It was love at first sight for the villagers.

Each evening over 100 enthusiasts would crowd into Pahalege's small yard to watch the box. An enterprising young man, he charged a fee and sold sweets and cigarettes to the viewers. Most had never seen a film or been inside a cinema hall. Owning a television soon became a status symbol.

Parents urged their children to work even longer hours in the nearby spice plantations to collect enough money to buy a television. Indra Premawathie sold her old sewing machine, a gift from her grandmother and her only valuable possession, in order to buy the television.

Now about 100 families own televisions and enterprising Pahalege is still making money, re-charging the used car batteries on which the sets work.

But the initial passion for television is quietly eroding, at least among the adults. A love–hate relationship for the box is slowly replacing it. The children's feelings, however, remain unchanged.

The adults love television for its ability to take their minds and those of the children off their hunger: they hate it for arousing material desires and new wants.

For along with the mesmeric songs and soaps that come into their ram-shackle huts every night come a host of attractive consumer products, most of which they did not even know existed.

Plump children in pretty dresses, well-heeled yuppies, and rich middle-aged executives preen and prattle about the virtues of Japanese electronic gadgetry, Swiss chocolates, New Zealand dairy products, Australian meat and local fabrics.

Now Balana's children want Swiss chocolate, New Zealand milk and beverages such as Coca Cola and Pepsi. The adults are not immune, either. The women crave for 'energy saving, wonderful and marvellous' Japanese electric rice cookers (complete with 'electronic timer switches'), fashionable clothes and make-up. The men hanker after hi-fi stereos, expensive trousers instead of their traditional sarong and, God willing, a car.

The irony is that most villagers cannot afford to have one square meal a day and lack the basic facilities taken for granted in the towns. The average monthly income of a family of five or six is $20.

The village has no electricity, a kerosene oil lamp being the only source of light. It has no pipe-borne water, but a few wells in the valley, hundreds of precarious metres down from the houses, which dry up at the first sign of drought, forcing residents to go to neighbouring villages in search of water.

A common sight in Balana is that of women balancing huge clay pots of water on their slim hips and treading the treacherous path from well to hut and back.

The village has no sanitation either – a hole in the ground surrounded by thatched coconut leaves serves as a toilet. It has no medical facilities; no doctor or even a midwife.

But they did not know the exent of their deprivation and poverty until television revealed it to them. Sighs Nanda Premawathie, a mother of four malnourished children: 'We have suddenly woken up to the extent of our poverty. We see those nice, well-fed children on television and then look at our thin, malnourished ones and feel anger and desperation'.

Her wood-cutter husband, Sarath, earns about Rs 20 whenever he can find work – a wage barely sufficient to give their children one meal a day. Laments Nanda: 'Most often we have to make do with a loaf of bread and unsweetened tea or a few yams I pick in the nearby jungle. I cry myself to sleep, when little Menika or Chuti pester me for imported milk or chocolate. They say they want to have the same things that the children on television have – nice clothes, good food, and fancy toys. Being a mother I want to give them all these things and get quite desperate when I can't'.

She says she has tried to explain to the children the extent of their poverty, that city children are rich. But it does not help: 'So I skip meals and have started working in the nearby spice plantation to earn a few more rupees to buy Chuti her favourite butter, or Menika her chocolates. Last month I managed to buy them two very expensive dresses from the town'. (Each dress cost Rs 150 – a fortune for Nanda). But the children want more.

She says she does not blame them, because she, too, has new cravings. 'I want to give up cooking on that old, smoky wood fire and have a clean gas or electric cooker. Of course I know we don't have electricity and gas is not available even in the nearest town, but I still want to have it'.

Television advertising has caused so much anguish and desperation in these poverty-stricken villages that recently a group of village parents marched to Colombo asking the government to do something to quell the demands of their children.

In response, the minister in charge of television requested advertising agencies to refrain from using children in their campaigns, especially in milk food commercials. The request was not heeded. The pretty, plump children are still on TV singing the praises of at least a dozen brands of milk.

There are other problems. Balana's children spend more time in front of the television than with their schoolbooks. Only a handful of Balana's youth have passed the government's general certificate of education even at ordinary level.

Premawathie says that her son Chandana was doing well at the village school and she had great dreams for him. But since the television came to the village, he has lost all interest in his studies:

'He is now mooning around, chasing after the village girls when he is not in front of the TV'.

Village boys and girls used to be reserved. They had respect for their elders and for each other. The rule was that they should wait till their parents found suitable marriage partners for them. 'Now they want to court and date from their early teens and say they want to choose their spouse', Premawathie fumes. 'Soon we parents will have no say in whom our children marry. This is nonsense. They are taking after those modern city people'. But she confesses that she has no control over the changes, short of getting rid of every single television in the village.

Yet not all programmes aired on Sri Lanka's two television channels are consumer-oriented or glamorous. The fledgling Rupavahini Corporation also has an educational service aired in the mornings. It taps highly qualified and competent teachers attached to top schools in Colombo (120 kilometres from Balana), and other professionals to take 'TV classes', through which their expertise is beamed to even the most remote classroom.

The government has set up solar-operated sets in most remote and underprivileged schools throughout the country but Balana's school has yet to receive a television. When the educational programmes are aired, most of Balana's children are either working in the spice plantation or picking firewood. The few who actually get to school play or chatter because more often than not the class teacher is absent.

The limited number of Sinhala language teledramas produced by Rupavahini (which means 'Television') are of good quality, but have been accused of 'over-moralizing'.

Says Albert Pahalege: 'We like to watch *Kopi-Kade* (a serial woven around a village tea-shop) because we see ourselves there. Most of the things that happen to villagers in *Kopi-Kade* happen to us'.

The villagers possess the ability to laugh at themselves, a gift shared by many Sri Lankans. By rolling in mirth whenever *Kopi-Kade*'s village villain is caught by the police downing the illicit *kassipu* brew, the villagers actually see their own husbands, brothers and sometimes themselves caught in the same situation.

'But there are only a few programmes like *Kopi-Kade*', Pahalege says. 'All other programmes are imported. We see a lot of big cities like New York and London, but they don't show us Colombo and Kandy'.

So Balana, and hundreds of other remote villages in Sri Lanka, sink deeper into poverty and deprivation, with little or no hope of escape. Television has struck a hard blow – it has dispelled their contentment, and replaced it with angry dissatisfaction.

In the south, the environment is a big yawn

by Mark Richardson
Kampala

Sometimes you don't find what you expect, and it is pioneering to report the discrepancy. Gemini had run a workshop on environmental coverage in Uganda and Mark Richardson, a Canadian IDRC fellow, wrote a sharp piece on mixed metaphors and muddled thinking. 'This was the grassroots, but we couldn't see the trees for the charcoal', he lamented. (10 April 1992 – GV 108)

At the source of the River Nile, deep in the pearl of Africa, is a tiny heap of rusting bottletops.

It was left there in March by a group of journalists concerned for the African environment, too busy thinking about invisible holes in the ozone layer to notice what was gathering at their feet.

We had stopped beside the river for a drink, about 30 of us, and popped open bottles of Fanta and Pepsi. The tops fell on the ground and lay among the grass roots, where they were ignored and left to rust.

No one will pick them up, those bottletops, even though they can slice a fatal tetanus infection into any bare foot that stumbles along. It's an environmental story in its own small way, but few people anywhere in the world would think it important enough to consider.

It's a small example, though, of how environmental reporting in the Third World is suffering from mixed priorities, apathy and ignorance.

The drive to Uganda's source of the Nile came on the third day of a four-day workshop organized in Uganda by Gemini News Service. It was intended to encourage and improve environmental reporting in Africa, and was attended by curious journalists from across the continent.

Such reporting, according to Wafula Oguttu, editor of Kampala's influential *Weekly Topic* newspaper, is often considered 'an unnecessary fuss or, at best, merely as a western-inspired and boring intellectual exercise'.

Femi Ajayi, science and agriculture editor for the *Daily Times* of Nigeria, was more blunt. 'Nobody wants to be an environmental reporter in Africa', he said. 'They want a more important beat so they can change their cars

SELLING THE FOREST
Bags of charcoal, protected by banana leaves

Fig. 28.

SOURCE OF THE NILE
Now just some rusty girders

Fig. 29.

every three years'.

Unlike the North, where grassroots organizations pressure their govern-ments to change policies toward the environment, the governments of the South must take responsibility for educating a generally ignorant public.

In Uganda, 12 officers travel to villages throughout the country, attempting to teach the 17 million people about the dangers of cutting trees for clearance or charcoal, as well as over-cultivating land and draining wetland areas for crops.

Such a massive task needs the help of the media, but readers are not interested in seemingly endless stories of deforestation, toxic waste and invisible ozone holes. 'Environment is still the most boring topic in the *Weekly Topic*', said Oguttu.

The disappearance of the forests, for example, is one of the biggest stories in Africa, with repercussions around the world. Few Africans want to know. Millions of trees are taken to fuel cooking fires, but there is little point in producing articles that warn of global climate changes when the only alternative fuel, kerosene, is scarce and expensive.

It is difficult for people to relate to the big stories they see on television, read in the newspaper or – most common in the Third World – hear on the radio. And while 'getting down to the grassroots' was the most stressed catch-phrase of the workshop, few journalists know what the grassroots are.

Certainly none of the reporters who took the drive to the Nile's source gave a second thought to buying goat kebabs and roasted bananas from the stalls we visited along the way.

We tut-tutted at the charcoal vendor and took his photograph beside the sacks of charcoal, quaintly (and practically) covered with banana leaves, but we were happy to buy food cooked over that charcoal. And we bought bananas from the stalls set up illegally in the forest to cater to tourists.

This was the grassroots, but we couldn't see the trees for the charcoal.

Journalists have the potential to be among the most influential people in society, yet many are so preoccupied with looking for corruption and large-scale abuse that the smaller abuses, including their own, are ignored.

In the Third World, they are given little encouragement or initiative to become environmentally aware. The responsibility for their training, says Oguttu, lies with the industrialized Northern countries.

'Forests in the Third World are estimated to consume about 50 per cent of the carbon dioxide produced in the North. Without these forests in the South, the North would be heavily polluted by their numerous vehicles and factories', he says.

'It is therefore logical that the North comes in and pays for the preservation of these forests. Such funds should then be used to meet the costs of training journalists and other communicators in the skills of reporting the environment, and for preparation and dissemination of all types of environ-mental education material'.

There are many more environmental stories than just deforestation, of course. Northern journalists consider the environment to be perhaps the biggest story on the planet, yet few Third World press agencies can afford the luxury of an environmental specialist. When such an assignment occurs, such as at the source of the River Nile, much of the story is missed.

At the river, it was possible to wander out onto some rusty girders poking into the water and place a hand in the Nile and another hand in Lake Victoria. The waterfall that John Speke saw when he explored the lake in 1860 was flooded away when the Nile was dammed.

The Owen Falls dam provides barely enough electricity for the district and power cuts in Kampala are frequent. The obvious big story is that a beautiful and historic site has been sacrificed for an inefficient government project, but few would care.

Most Ugandans do not have the luxury of an electrical supply, and nor do they care for the explorations of a foreign adventurer. What they do understand, though, is that people will starve to death when they cannot open their mouths to eat after catching lockjaw, or tetanus, from a rusty wound.

The story – our bottletops – was gathering at our feet, but we were too busy peering across the river to notice.

9 An educational enterprise

Built into Gemini from the start had been a number of educational ideas. Although the educational nature of the operation changed, and it acquired a highly specific orientation after the relaunch in the 1980s, it is worth emphasising that the communication purpose with which it began in 1967 had educational aspects.

The first of these was that Commonwealth countries did and should have a curiosity about one another. It had been a concern of Ingram's in the 1960s that there was a high degree of mutual ignorance about the new Commonwealth that was emerging, an ignorance that neither governments, media nor formal education systems were combating. He thought, correctly as it turned out, that there was a common interest in English-speaking countries facing similar problems of political and economic development. He also believed that they ought to be interested in each other, if the Commonwealth was to have a future.

Hence, in supplying news features about a wide range of topics, Gemini was not merely filling space in papers or operating what was hoped to be a commercially viable service. It was actively educating readers in many countries about ideas, events and issues of concern to them. It was contributing to their own countries' development after the transition to independence. And it was making real the Commonwealth as a living, growing association, not just a fag-end of the British Empire.

The second idea of educational significance was Gemini's insistence on using resident, indigenous journalists in Third World countries. This had two implications. One was that they would be reporting from inside a society, with their own national assumptions, effectively over a longer timescale than was used by a British or western foreign correspondent. Items which might appear strange to the outsider would not be worth reporting; items which could seem invisible to the visiting fireman journalist – for instance the adverse effects of foreign company activity or a World Bank stabilization plan – would be covered as life-and-death matters to a resident population. This was not only a fresh approach to news-gathering, it was a contribution to international education.

The other implication of this policy was that Gemini would find itself drawn into the education of journalists. To begin with this was relatively informal. By the mid-1980s it was a significant commitment for the office, organizing a series of workshops around the world; it was also a main purpose for NewsConcern International Foundation.

It might seem contradictory that a commitment to using local journalists, which assumed that their material deserved a wider audience, should actually lead to efforts to raise professional standards. But in truth the situation was complicated. The press in some developing countries was and is small, with restricted chances for training and peer group emulation. Political and other controls could lead to blandness, lack of balance and a want of investigative effort. Even able journalists lacked confidence in striving for international exposure, and needed help in meeting the requirements of a world-wide market.

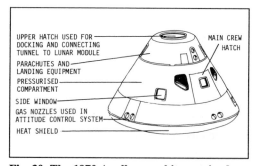

Fig. 30. The 1970 Apollo spacekit contained ten items, sold as a spacecraft commander's briefing, exact scientific data supplied by NASA. Apollo Command Module.

In pointing out educational elements in Gemini from the start – which helped explain why one of its first subscribers was the Commonwealth Institute, Scotland – a further factor should be mentioned. The quite extraordinary tenacity of Ingram, and of those who helped him keep the service alive, had a kind of missionary quality. Gemini was not just any old news agency or features service which would be allowed to stand or fall on purely commercial grounds.

In the 1970s it could be said that aid agencies and the world of education caught up with Gemini. The concept of development education – education about the needs of developing countries and the interrelated nature of North and South in what was dubbed Spaceship Earth – became current in developed countries. It was financially supported by Britain's 1974–79 Labour government through the Ministry of Overseas Development. However, due to conservatism in school curricula, its impact was less than its protagonists hoped and in Britain official support was abruptly cut off by the incoming Conservative government in 1979.

Development education through the media was what Gemini had been doing. When it restarted in 1983 this was the main rationale for the financial support of international agencies, along with the professional advancement of journalists in developing countries. These were prime purposes of NewsConcern International Foundation whose foundation deed object was, in English legalese, 'the advancement of education by commissioning, promoting and publishing through newspapers and other media anywhere in the world of reliable objective and balanced articles on subjects not normally available to such newspapers and ... in particular ... structures and issues of developing countries ... and the significance for such countries of developments talking place elsewhere'.[1]

In its first phase a different type of educational product had been important – these were the GeminiScan kits and *Orbit*, the magazine published for the Zambian government. The kits were part of a vogue in Britain initiated by the Jackdaw folders; they were bought by

1. Excerpt from deed attached to report by Aubrey Rose, 23 September 1987, to the Governors of NewsConcern Inernational Foundation. Rose, who was legal adviser to the Commonwealth Institute, investigated the possibility of charitable status under British law for NewsConcern.

parents for children and were expected to provide educational information in an entertaining way. When they were distributed in the United States by the Lark Publishing Company of New York they were said to be for 7 to 12 year olds. But in retrospect many of the participants felt that the kits, which were carefully produced and well-illustrated, should have been a much bigger success. The Apollo space kit, timed to coincide with man's first footprint on the Moon, was outstanding.

Fig. 31. Interior, Command Module.

However the kits were badly promoted, and Gemini suffered from disadvantageous deals with distributors who only paid a modest royalty. Their impact was reduced because of the lack of business skills in the office. At the same time the artists and graphics illustrators were getting enmeshed in frustrating executive functions. Peter Clarke, for instance, had become managing director of Gemini-Scan, responsible for the kits and *Orbit*.

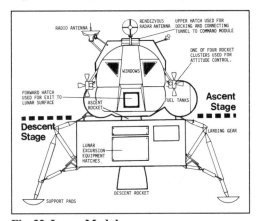

Fig. 32. Lunar Module.

In a memo of 1 January 1971 he complained with forgivable exaggeration that 99 per cent of his time had become occupied with administrative and executive functions. He intended to take three months' holiday, and then to reduce his schedule from 60–70 hours a week to 40. 'None of this represents a diminution of my professional or emotional commitment to GeminiScan. It is simply a self-imposed timetable which recognizes a conviction that my total involvement in a corporate effort ultimately leads to the occlusion of my most valuable talent – which is to invent, to initiate, to inspire those entrepreneurial activities on which Scan's fortune is based.'[2]

The idea of 'Scan's fortune' was unhappily an aspiration, not a reality. By 1970, after two years of Scan's activity on kits and only one year into a three year agreement with IPC, IPC started to cut back on its commissions. IPC never set up the special marketing unit which had been the subject of discussions with Scan. Although with the help of the late Labour MP Guy Barnett, the Commonwealth Institute sold 200 educational kits on the Common Market and the Commonwealth to British schools in 1972, the steam was going

---

2. Peter Clarke memo, Ingram Archive.

out of this venture. By May 1972, when the *Orbit* experiment was also coming to an end, Clarke had given up the title of managing director and moved to Norfolk.

There was always a danger that the kits, more ephemeral than books, might not be a long-term market. But *Orbit*, a product of Gemini's close association with the Zambian government – Richard Hall, in particular, was a friend of President Kaunda – looked set for a long run. Its title reflected the fashionable interest in space exploration. It was heavily backed by the Zambian Ministry of Technical Education. Its sale rose from 50,000 to 75,000 after just two issues and it had an attractive comic strip style.

It is still remembered fondly in Zambia by adults who knew it at school. A teacher, Judith Mulenga, recalled in 1994 how important it had been and 'how void since the late 70s secondary school pupils' lives have been without a national magazine.' Another former reader, Alfred Nalube, loved a character called Fwanya, 'a very funny fellow' but was disappointed that his questions to the editor were never answered. Reading the cartoon strip, *Space Safari*, had given him dreams of becoming an astronaut: 'maybe in the next life I will be at NASA,' he wrote 20 years' later.[3]

Orbit's full-time editor, Wendy Bond, was based in Zambia, design was done in Britain and production involved a skilled Anglo-Zambian collaboration. The stories were not only about an imaginary Zambian in space and a real Zambian air hostess, but also contained scientific and technical information in digestible form. There was an *Orbit* calendar. It was a very exciting educational product, and the people at Gemini had hopes that variants could have been produced for Ghana, Singapore and elsewhere.

However it depended wholly on the deteriorating public finances of Zambia, still basically reliant on copper exports and not well managed even prior to the Yom Kippur war and the oil price hike of 1973. Good as it was, Zambia could not afford to go on subsidizing *Orbit*. (Much later, a Zambian delegate to the 1994 Commonwealth Education Ministers' conference in Islamabad stated that an attenuated version of *Orbit* had managed to survive, though its publication had been interrupted.)

Nonetheless Ingram, though his first love was the news service, was alive to the specific educational possibilities it gave rise to. In a memo of 1972 he wrote, 'Education. Here everything points to opportunities, especially because of our strong graphics side. The concept of a topical newsletter, comprising mostly material already used for the news service and lying on our shelves, needs exploiting. The recent experimental exercise with the Common Market kit through the Commonwealth Institute was an eye-opener to all...'[4]

There were always a handful of educational subscribers to Gemini and during its period as a *Guardian* subsidiary there was a further attempt to sell a special service to schools in Britain. But the trouble was that, although the service contained material which was useful for sixth form current affairs, parts of the geography syllabus and so on, there was neither enough of curricular relevance, nor was it obviously within the budget or subject interest

---

3. Letters from Judith Mulenga, 20 July 1994 and Alfred Nalube, 29 July 1994 obtained by courtesy of Cedric Pulford, who requested memories of *Orbit* in the Zambian press.

4. Ingram Archive.

of one teacher. It was a service conceived for the media which would have needed more educational input and staff time than Gemini could afford to make it effective in schools. School budgets for books and materials in Britain were anyhow going through a thin time at this period.

In the 1980s, after the restart, Gemini acquired a different type of educational reputation. Its function as a North–South news feature bridge became an explicit commitment to the education of journalists – of Canadian journalists on the one hand, and of developing country journalists through specialist activities on the other. This was a process particularly nurtured by Elizabeth Pritchard and Bethel Njoku. Without the financial support this work brought, and the subsidies for subscriptions from newspapers which otherwise could not have afforded to pay, Gemini would not have survived.

It is worth describing the experience of the Canadians first. As mentioned in chapter 1 the story started by chance when Jane Taber, from the *Ottawa Citizen*, came to Gemini in August 1983 with a CAN$20,000 grant from the International Development Research Centre to study a Third World country. Much as she enjoyed her time, in London and Zimbabwe, it was not an easy ride:

> I spent the first few months of my Gemini life fighting to get a telephone, a desk – some space of my own. I spent the other part trying to get disciplined and figure out what I really wanted to do.

> So there was much angst, conflict and worry. Derek and the Gemini people were not completely satisfied with the arrangement; neither was I.

It was only when she went to a UNESCO conference in Paris, a couple of months later, that she felt she got some focus. The letters and reports she sent back to IDRC reflected her increasing confidence and she remains proud that it was on the basis of her reports that the Centre thought it would be useful to send other young Canadian journalists to Gemini.[5]

IDRC is a research organization, not an aid agency. Although Clyde Sanger had seen the annual award as a way of producing an extra staffer and greater Canadian support for Gemini, for IDRC it was an initiative on behalf of a Canadian journalist designed to enhance his or her professional experience. The longer-term aim was to strengthen the capacity of Canadian institutions to work in cooperation with developing countries and, ideally, to build a critical mass of Canadian journalists which could improve the country's coverage of the developing world. More recently the Communications Division at IDRC has seen the award also as a way of obtaining good public relations for the Centre's work.

Margaret Owens, who had been a programme officer for IDRC from 1989 to 1992 subsequently became a governor of NewsConcern. Although the Gemini fellowship formed only a tiny part of her CAN $1M annual portfolio of responsibilities she became interested in its role. In 1991 IDRC held an evaluation at Ottawa attended by a number of the awardees. This was not only an opportunity to air criticisms and suggestions for

5. Taber letter, *ibid.*

improvement in the scheme, it also aimed to create a network among former fellows. This process was carried further a year later, in a conference at Regina, Saskatchewan, where IDRC fellows and Gemini scholars from the Regina School of Journalism met journalists from the South to debate the coverage of the developing world after the end of the Cold War.

The IDRC scheme, as it evolved, broke the fellow's year into three equal four month parts. The first was spent editing in London; the second on a journalistic project at a location in the South of the fellow's choice; the third back in London in the Gemini office. It became usual for the Canadian journalist to be a graduate with at least three years' experience, ideally unattached because the stipend was not excessively generous. (The award for the year was raised from CAN $20,000 to CAN $25,000 and then to CAN $30,000; however holders still felt the need to freelance to raise extra funds, a process which could bring them into conflict with Gemini.) It was desirable for the journalist concerned to be adaptable and self-motivated.

Curiously, a scheme which might have seemed attractive to ambitious journalists in their mid to late 20s who wanted to travel, never had that many applicants. Each year there were eight to ten, sometimes as few as six. Among the reasons seem to have been anxiety that the IDRC award might take one out of Canadian journalism at a crucial stage for career promotion (though an employer had to agree to the fellowship, and guarantee reemployment at the end of the year); the fact that the scheme was never designed for couples, although in some cases partners of an award-holder made a satisfying year of it; the fact that the field experience and the London editing were not equally alluring; and a suspicion that IDRC may not have advertised the fellowship as hard as it might to avoid the administrative effort in sifting more applications for what was only a single award.

There were various culture shocks in bringing energetic Canadian journalists into the Gemini office, and in two or three cases the personal chemistry did not work out in what was a very small establishment. In the early years, before the office was computerized, the Canadians looked aghast at the antiquity of typewriters and a service reliant on the post. At the same time it forced them to examine some of their own assumptions.

Kelly McParland writes, 'You could get a letter to Lesotho or Uganda in record time, but Canada took longer thanks to the wonderful Canadian postal service and its unions. It was very quaint, and it looked fairly rinky-dink to anyone who didn't appreciate its finer qualities, but the point was that for a huge proportion of the outlets it served, Gemini was one of the best sources they had. It carried news about countries nobody else bothered with. Its viewpoint was international rather than Western-oriented. It was written by people who lived in the countries they wrote about, rather than journalists who had stopped by for a brief visit. It treated the interests of small countries as equally important as big ones. It assumed poor countries had as much right to achieve their goals as wealthy ones did. And it was available'.[6]

For McParland, who was so influenced by his fellowship that he stayed three years longer,

6. McParland letter, *ibid*

the key lesson was his escape from the US-led news agenda of North America into recognizing that all countries have their own national interests. He learned, for example, that people in Zimbabwe do not care how events in South Africa affect North America, but only how they affect Zimbabwe. He saw the world as more complex, and the North American media as more parochial.

But there could also be difficulties for the IDRC journalists. For Sue Montgomery, who came from the Canadian Press in 1989–90, this began at London's Heathrow Airport when she was detained by the immigration authorities who took her passport. There had been confusion over whether she needed a visa for entry to Britain and she felt she had no support from either IDRC or Gemini.[7]

Several felt that they were dropped in at the deep end, either at Gemini or in the field, but in retrospect that had not necessarily been bad. Allan Thompson from the *Toronto Star* told IDRC in his final 1991 report, 'The experience of being dropped in at the deep end at Gemini – copy editing a news service with no copy editing experience, and at the end of the year, running the news service for one month unsupervised – was beneficial.' He thought he might apply for a copy editor's position on his return, and subsequently worked part-time as a copy editor in addition to his reporting.[8]

However those who had applied for the award because they wanted to report from a developing country could resent the editing time spent in London, and were critical of the quality of the raw copy that came in. Mike Urlocker from the *Financial Post* in Toronto, the 1993 fellow, was one of these. He spent most of his time out of London in India, with visits to Vietnam, Cambodia and Russia and for him the Indian time was less productive than he hoped.

In India he wrote stories about the nuclear industry and India's space programme but had little contact with Gemini's Indian correspondents. 'I used to be in love with India, but I'm not any more. India has a really brutal society, and they were inept in their dealings with western correspondents,' he said in London later. He found the practicalities unexpectedly complicated – making phone calls, or getting copies of official reports. His criticisms were no different from those of other western correspondents assigned to New Delhi for a short stay: what was unusual was that a Canadian attached to Gemini should see himself as a western/Northern correspondent, and echo them.[9]

The IDRC fellows provided an element of challenge in the Gemini machine – they did not necessarily share its founder's interest in the Commonwealth, for example – but they were also challenged themselves. One of the most educational, if depressing lessons, was to find out how it felt to be on the wrong side of the North–South news agenda.

Allan Thompson, with an Arab-speaking wife, had special opportunities to learn about the North African countries of the Maghreb and was able to provide Gemini with unique copy

---

7. Interview, Sue Montgomery. Daniel Girard, 1993–94 IDRC fellow, also had unexpected but serious problems arriving at Heathrow in November 1993.

8. Allan Thompson, final report to IDRC, Gemini Archive, quoted by permission.

9. Interview, Mike Urlocker.

during the Iraq–Kuwait Gulf war. But he wrote to IDRC, 'Perhaps the greatest single disappointment of this year was the near total lack of interest on the part of the *Toronto Star* in what I was doing.'

He went on to describe the difficulty he experienced in convincing his newspaper to publish articles from North Africa. Only interviews with PLO chairman Yasser Arafat and a story about the shrine at the Libyan leader Moammar Gadaffi's bombed-out house in Tripoli made the *Star*. A piece on life in Gadaffi's Libya, another on Canada's peacekeeping role in the Western Sahara and a firsthand report from Algiers in the midst of martial law were apparently not of interest.[10]

However Daniel Girard, the 1993–94 IDRC fellow who went to Thailand and Malaysia, was able to freelance a bit more successfully for the *Toronto Star*, for which he had been working for the previous five years. Even so it took less than half the pieces he offered. Like the majority of IDRC fellows he described his time, both in the office and field, as 'an absolutely tremendous experience'. He was struck by the lack of environmental controls in Thailand which had led to fires, poison emissions and dry river beds. But he was also impressed that economic development in Malaysia was not accompanied by crime on the streets – illustrating a model of development different from North America's.

He managed to spend a week with rebels against the military dictatorship in Myanmar (Burma) and paid a quick visit to Vietnam after the United States had lifted its trade embargo and the communist authorities had opted for *doi moi* (openness). He realized that an ability to buy Pepsi Cola did not put an end to people bathing in mud pools, and met fathers, emerging from re-education camps, who were trying to keep a family of six people on CAN $100 a month.

Girard's particular interest was the environment, and he had been wise enough to tear up all his preconceived story ideas before he reached Thailand, to start afresh.

> Working in Thailand was much tougher than expected. I knew language would be a problem but naïvely I hadn't anticipated the difficulty I encountered in regularly coming up with the tools of the trade: a reliable phone and phone book. It made for some frustrating – and in retrospect, funny – times. The whole humbling experience made me realize I will never again take my desk and phone at Gemini or One Yonge Street [the *Toronto Star* office] for granted.

> The Thai bureaucracy was also a nightmare. All roads lead to Bangkok and with a highly-centralized political system, official comments for most stories led me there as well.

Only Vietnam, of the countries he visited, matched his visual expectations. He felt he successfully fought off the danger of letdown on return to London, although money was tighter there. Like other Canadians, he found that London was expensive.[11]

One IDRC fellow who felt that the rather timeless quality of some Gemini journalism had

---

10. Allan Thompson, *ibid*.

11. Interview, Daniel Girard and report to IDRC.

its advantages was Mark Richardson. Like others he wrote regularly to the London office to keep it in touch with a changing itinerary. His trip involved Togo, Ghana, Nigeria, Cameroon and Kenya. From Togo he wrote in August, 1992:

> As far as stories are concerned, I hope to send something from what I learn in Ghana in two weeks' time, certainly within three weeks, then probably every couple of weeks after. I may, though, ask you to hold back publication until a certain date, so that I can leave the country. I don't think that the Nigerian government, for example, will be very impressed with some of the results of my visit and I might want to return to the country in November. The stories will be timeless enough to hold until then.[12]

Richardson's fellowship had a lasting impact. In 1994 he was given leave of absence by his paper, the *Ottawa Citizen*, to be press officer for CARE Canada in Rwanda at the time of its civil war, massacres and humanitarian crisis. He subsequently joined CARE full time.

Few Canadians were fully prepared for the mind-blowing aspects of the IDRC fellowship. Some found it hard to adjust to the need to generate their own stories, having been used to following up stories given to them by news editors, and they would have liked more guidance and feedback from Gemini, particularly in their first months in London. Most were basically reporters. They had to be persuaded that editing in London was not cheap labour for Gemini, but part of a rounded educational experience without which their field trip would be less valuable. Coming from compartmentalized, sophisticated organizations they started out feeling insecure in a small service which some felt suffered from a lack of focus.

There were risks of all sorts in taking up a fellowship, and there might be personal danger. The most upsetting experience, ironically, occurred in London in the late 1980s when Gavin Wilson's Canadian girlfriend was found murdered in her flat. Wilson was an IDRC fellow who went on to be an information officer at the University of British Columbia. He and his friend Scott Simmie, who was a Regina awardee in the same year and later a CBC Moscow correspondent, were subjected to prolonged police questioning before a tramp was arrested and charged with the offence.

Three years after the IDRC scheme had begun Gemini linked with another Canadian institution, the University of Regina, in a different kind of collaboration. From 1986 onwards an outstanding student from the graduate School of Journalism there came over every summer to spend three months with Gemini. Ingram and others would introduce them to British and Commonwealth institutions and take them to press conferences; they also had opportunities to write and edit copy. However they did not get the exposure in the South which was the most treasured aspect of the IDRC fellowship until 1993, when CIDA funded a further three months in a developing country.

The Regina fellows were younger than the IDRC fellows, valuing the visit to London itself as their reward, and they generally lacked the experience as working journalists which

12. Mark Richardson, letter from Lomé, Togo to Gemini, 27 August 1992, Ingram Archive.

could stimulate criticism. Although their attachment was so much shorter, however, it too could be dramatic in its effect.

Jill Forrester was full of praise. Her three months' Regina fellowship spread into two years in London and she commented:

> Gemini was for me an experience that changed the course of my life and I know will influence everything I do in the future.

> Although I had an aunt and uncle who worked for CIDA and lived in various places in Africa, and although I was concerned about learning in general and gave good attention at school, I grew up with almost no sense of what differences in culture existed in the world. Living with hundreds of miles of flat prairie in all directions always made me feel the rest of the world was unreachable and too huge to comprehend. You'd think having North America's indigenous people all around would give us an idea of what a different culture really is ...

> I took advantage of government cross-cultural programs and lived in Quebec for a few months, and spent a summer working on an Indian reserve not far from my home, but still, going to London and working for Gemini was like the world opening up before me. I grew up believing things like democracy and paved roads and fridges full of food were natural. Until I started editing Gemini copy that came to us typed on ratty old typewriters or written by hand, I hadn't realized what turmoil the world was really in. I knew of the world's 'poor' but didn't know that there were many man-made reasons for their poverty, and I hadn't realized how interconnected their lives are with mine. And I would not say my naïveté was uncommon.

> Not only has Gemini made the rest of the world real to me, but I see Canada's strengths and weaknesses more clearly and I recognize the issues – such as indigenous people's rights, environmental practices, global trading blocks and NAFTA – that tie us to the rest of the world. The Gemini experience is like a gift that Derek and his contemporaries have given to Canada, helping a few of us every year to see ourselves and the world in a new way. Lack of perspective is one of Canada's biggest handicaps.[13]

Forrester also enjoyed being taken to events, press conferences and places. She appreciated the touches of humanity, the envelope-stuffing, the fact that on Gemini's 25th birthday in 1992 Ingram insisted that the staff take a day to prepare the food, drink and decorations for the party. 'Allan Thompson and I laughed when we were out with Derek once that we felt like cousins out with "grandpa" [Derek Ingram].' But she recognized too that not everyone had been happy at Gemini.[14]

Gemini's ability to affect people, even if they were working there for only a short time, was illustrated by the Regina fellows. Nearly all took part in the October 1992 conference

---

13. Jill Forrester, letter to author, 20 January 1994.

14. Forrester letter, *ibid.*

in Regina on post-Cold War reporting. Elaine Shein was a Regina fellow who rose rapidly to the post of managing editor of the *Western Producer*. She commented, 'There are so many good things about Gemini, and it has an attraction for many of us over the years that seems almost like an umbilical cord – the ties never seem to totally sever.'[15]

Summing up these two fellowship schemes, therefore, it is clear that on the whole they brought considerable benefits to the individual journalists and to Gemini itself. Their success encouraged CIDA to support a slightly similar arrangement for Canadian journalists attached to a French-based agency concerned with environmental and development issues, particularly in the Francophone countries. But in the wider context of Canadian media it was obviously only a small contribution to changing perceptions on news desks, or building a constituency of voters, taxpayers and consumers with a greater understanding of North–South issues.

It was also ironic that it was easier to get funding for a Northern journalist to join Gemini than for someone from the South whose other opportunities might be more limited. One of the few cases of a journalist coming to Gemini in London from a developing country was Ogen Keven John Aliro of Uganda. He came to Britain on a three month UNESCO award in 1990. Better known as John Ogen he had first become aware of Gemini as a second year university student in 1985, when he realized that a number of features in his favourite weekly magazine, *Weekly Topic*, had a Gemini tag. 'These guys are not sensational. They always get to the bottom of things', a roommate said to him after reading a Gemini analysis of the Falklands War.

On graduating he joined *Weekly Topic* as a journalist and saw the postal packages arriving from Gemini in London. He recalled that, during a crisis over the abortive Gemini–Panos tie-up, the deputy editor of the *Topic* warned that Gemini might have to close down. When at a later editorial meeting it was announced that Gemini was continuing, everyone cheered.

He was consequently delighted to get the UNESCO fellowship but, like many in developing countries who had come to rely on the service, had a massively exaggerated view of its size. When he paid his first visit to its office in Islington he could not believe that its space was so small, its permanent staff so tiny. The agency seemed a lot smaller than his own *Weekly Topic* with its staff of ten. It owned neither car nor bicycle, and staff borrowed each other's travel cards to get around in London. There were few clear divisions of labour and everyone did what needed to be done.

Nonetheless he greatly improved his sub-editing, was impressed with the frugality with which Gemini was managed in order to keep down the costs to subscribers, and by the hard work done. 'We worked every day for as long as there was something to do. Bethel Njoku always came in at 6 am, and we sometimes worked up to 10 pm'. On his return to Uganda he was rapidly promoted to be Senior Assistant Editor, the equivalent of a chief sub-editor.[16]

---

15. Elaine Shein, letter to author, 31 March 1994.

16. John Ogen recollection, Ingram Archive.

Gemini's structured educational and training work in developing countries has been threepronged. It has consisted of special programmes designed to enhance journalists' skills; these also produce articles for the service. It has involved workshops, typically reaching 20–25 journalists at a time. And it has resulted in three publications – training manuals on rural reporting and environmental reporting and the book of the 1992 Regina conference – *Whose Story? – Reporting the Developing World after the Cold War.*

It was with IDRC support that Gemini began its three year health and science reporting project in the mid 1980s. Journalists were paid more for this copy and special efforts were made to edit and promote it. It was generally felt that the programme had enhanced the skills of the participating journalists, and increased awareness in developing country media of the importance of health and science.

The rural reporting initiative, which has already been described, was funded by SIDA and CIDA and is still continuing. The handbook *Views from the Village*, written by Kelly McParland and designed and illustrated by Paddy Allen and Jenny Ridley, is one of the most practical and useful instructional manuals for it is filled with examples and explains why one type of story is more likely to interest a reader than another. All the time it stresses vitality and humanity over press release jargon, clichés or vagueness. The examples included were all real examples of Gemini editing.

For instance instead of an introduction to a story from Malaysia which reads 'The question of pesticide control is becoming an issue again' it prefers, 'On the day she was born, Abida was already poisoned. The crops surrounding the village were already poisoned. The ground beneath the crops was poisoned. Yet the authorities had assured Abida's parents that pesticides were safe.'[17]

It illustrated the need for brevity in the way it cut the following story from Roseau, Dominica: 'Sun-worshipping visitors to most of the Caribbeans's Windward Islands can be counted annually in the hundreds of thousands, but fewer than 40,000 of them will have holidayed this year on Dominica, the largest in the Windward chain and arguably the most beautiful island in the West Indies.'

The sub-edited version read, 'Dominica, population 80,000, is arguably the most beautiful island in the West Indies, but fewer than 40,000 people holidayed there last year.'[18]

The rural reporting exercise was backed up by a seminar in New Delhi in 1988. There were also a series of environmental reporting seminars from 1989 onwards which resulted in a special handbook, published in 1992 to coincide with the UNCED Earth Summit in Rio de Janeiro. Environmental reporting workshops were held in Harare in 1989 (with European Commission funding), in Kuala Lumpur in 1990 (supported by the Hong Kong Bank Foundation), in Accra in 1991 (European Commission), in Kampala in 1992 (UNICEF), and in Bangkok in 1993 (UNICEF again).

The manual was enlivened by nine rules for environmental reporting chosen by Khaba

17. *Views from the Village*, p. 9.

18. *Ibid*, p. 32.

Mkhize, editor of the *Natal Witness Echo* in South Africa. These are: (1) Be on the side of the environment; (2) Understand what is sustainable and what is unsustainable development; (3) Don't be sentimental; (4) Knowledge is the best form of defence; (5) Expose, but do not victimize; (6) Do not depend on familiar stories; (7) Adhere to the facts; (8) Invest stories with fun and excitement; and (9) Give many sides to a story.

Mkhize backed this up by a notably unsentimental analysis of a mining debate on the South African coast at St Lucia Bay, where environmentalists were opposing a plan to mine titanium. After spending six days there, talking to local people in squatter camps who were benefiting from the schools and employment provided by the mining company, he asked:

> Can't the conflict of interests be resolved by way of compromise? In other words, can't conservation exist side by side with development of social lifestyles for the disadvantaged residents? Let the quality of life of the dunes residents be rehabilitated and conserved first before the natural joys of the St Lucia ecosystems flow for international consumption.[19]

SIDA funded Gemini to run four workshops in Africa from 1993–95 to strengthen the skills of senior journalists for development journalism. These are for news editors and above. They are designed to help them in the reporting of sustainable development in a newsy and non-biased way, using investigative techniques and presenting material in ways their public will understand.

Plainly this series reflects a fall-out from the Earth Summit. The switch to multi-party systems has also had enormous significance for journalists and in Malawi, where Dr Banda's presidency for life was terminated in 1993–94, Gemini was contracted by two European bodies to run basic and follow-up training workshops.

Bethel Njoku, who as managing director of Gemini has been active in stimulating training projects, sees them as a logical development for the agency. In the 1960s there was little formal training for journalists in the South; information was mainly western-oriented, negative and concerned with wars and disasters; at the same time, the writing from within developing countries dwelt more on the injustices of colonialism and repression by the ruling authorities. He commented:

> Today, news and information, especially those flowing from and among the South need to address the concerns of the rural areas, local environment and sustainable development. And, more importantly, they require to be written with proper journalistic skills and integrity.[20]

Partly because Gemini's survival had been so hazardous it always made much of its anniversaries; this was particularly true after the restart, and there were considerable celebrations of its 20th birthday (1987) and its 25th (1992). With funding support from CIDA, the agency and the Regina School of Journalism joined forces in October 1992, to

---

19. *Environmental Reporting Handbook*, pp. 26–27.

20. Bethel Njoku, 1994 memo to author, which included a list of workshops.

mount a special conference in Regina to mark the 25th anniversary in a relevant and thoughtful way.

The collapse of east European communism and the emergence of a single superpower had created anxieties in the South. There seemed to be one dominant world model, of the market economy and multiparty democracy. Yet the North's obsession with eastern Europe was threatening to reduce still further its interest in the developing countries and there were significant cross-currents – of Islamic fundamentalism, of aspirations to the settlement of regional quarrels, of attempts to strengthen the UN and human rights and, by China and southeast Asia, of claims for an economic model of an authoritarian kind.

Gemini, Regina and CIDA agreed that the time was ripe for a full-scale conference to address the consequences, and around 80 people gathered in the prairie city in hot late fall weather. It brought together many who had been associated with Gemini – including NewsConcern governors like Professor Rex Nettleford, and Daniel Nelson, who at that stage was a managing editor with the Panos Institute, as well as contributors and former Gemini fellows. There was also strong representation from the developing world (including the managing editor of *The Sowetan* and the deputy editor of *China Daily* in Beijing) and a good scattering of persons from the Canadian press.

The conference was important because the participants were frank and they came from major regions of the world – Africa, the Caribbean and Latin America, Asia and the Pacific, China. They dealt with the problems of the western media as well as the problems of developing countries. They were quick to see through headline words and phrases. Nelson blamed journalists for allowing themselves to believe that there was a 'New World Order' because it had been mouthed by politicians and it fitted headlines. Nelson stated:

> It seems to me that the nearest thing we have to a world government is the World Bank. It is not the United Nations. And that's why I get personally terribly angry when journalists take the phrase, which is completely manufactured, 'New World Order' – it's absolutely meaningless. Personally, I don't think there is a New World Order. I think we have the same world order, but without the Soviet Union which was never a major part of the world economy. And if you live in Katmandu or Kampala, there is no change.[21]

Nettleford pointed out that an expression like 'sustainable development' does not get one far on its own. 'I do think it's very important, with these new words which come into the vocabulary, that we ourselves be very watchful about them. I mean, sustainable development has hit us like anybody's business. We are grappling with that in the Caribbean. Does it mean preserving the trees or does it mean cutting them down and putting up marvellous high-rises as in Hong Kong, so that you can be economically prosperous?'[22]

Other speakers rubbed other sore spots. Ngozi Anyaegbunam of the *Daily Times* in Lagos referred to the sense of powerlessness in much of the South: they were observers of the Cold War, and their economy was being dictated by outsiders who really didn't care. Sue

---

21. Quoted in *Whose Story?*, pp. 10–11.

22. *Ibid.*, p. 12.

Montgomery, former Gemini IDRC fellow, described the frustrations of a Northern feminist reporter in Africa – keen to shake women out of patterns of abuse, yet sensitive to accusations of meddling undemocratically in a local culture. Allan Thompson, another such fellow, explained how the North had completely misunderstood and misrepresented Islam. Gerald Knight, *Guardian* NewsConcern governor, warned against expecting too much of the Northern media: space was limited for overseas stories, interest likewise. But Clyde Sanger, another governor, spoke of a growing maturity in the Canadian media as journalists with overseas experience acquired more senior posts and were willing to take a broader view.

Issues of culture, trying to bring home the oneness of humanity, the relative performance of TV and the press in explaining global stories, and the supine nature of journalists faced with various types of news management – all got a good airing in Regina. Like many of the best conferences it was a series of exchanges rather than a drafting committee for neat prescriptions. The book of the conference – *Whose Story? – Reporting the Developing World after the Cold War* – was edited by Jill Spelliscy and Gerald Sperling of the University of Regina.

It was appropriate that the 25th birthday of Gemini should be celebrated with a major educational event because what had originated as a news service, pure and simple, had come to occupy an educational niche. The mixture of people who attended was testimony to the recognition it had won. The quality and authenticity of the debate was not only worthwhile for those who attended. It showed that Gemini is one of the few players in the English-speaking world which can bring together relevant practising journalists, thinking realistically about how to report life for the majority on this planet.

10 Conclusion

At a low point in Gemini's fortunes in April 1972, when the two original partners were quarrelling and Ingram was threatening to resign as a director, he wrote, 'The business has no prospect of moving into a profitable situation, or a near-profitable situation, in the manner in which it is being handled at the moment:

> I do not intend to go on living on the edge of this precipice. Working up the news service on a shoestring is tough enough on its own, but when it is accompanied, after five years, by almost day-to-day anxiety about the business side it becomes impossible. There is no light at the end of the tunnel ...[1]

Gemini was then moving into the first of at least three serious crises in its existence, and staff never lost the sense of living on the edge of a precipice. Even when individuals moved on to safer, better-paid jobs they retained a memory of that insecurity. A note to the office in 1994 from Kelly McParland, turning down a cheque for an article, added a throwaway line – 'Everyone knows the streets in America are paved with gold – when I want cash, I just hack off another piece of the sidewalk.'

The truth was that to maintain a regular news feature service of reasonable quality, oriented to the developing world, was always a struggle. Much bigger, better-known news organizations – such as Reuters, before it struck riches from computerized economic and stockmarket information – have only been marginally profitable. The Compass feature service, financially supported by the Aga Khan's fortune, was unable to survive.

That Gemini has not only kept alive but made a valued contribution in its own field is a remarkable achievement. It never had a strong home base, in the sense of a large body of affluent subscribers in Britain; indeed Britain itself was economically in the doldrums for most of Gemini's life, one reason for a reduction in the significance of the Commonwealth for Britain. Its most devoted users were, as has been seen, newspapers in the poorer parts of the world.

What kept the service going, and enabled it to reemerge from suspension in 1983, was the power of certain ideas. The key idea, perhaps, was the promotion of development in countries which had just gained their independence. The collapse of the old colonial empires had made more obvious the enormous difference in standards of living between

---

1. Memo to Carruthers, 18 April 1972, Ingram Archive.

the dependent and the metropolitan centres. To provide for economic and social growth which reflected autonomous traditions in the South was the main aim of the politicians and the educated elites which had acquired power.

'Development' was a vogue word in the early 1960s, as much in Latin America as in Africa and Asia. It concealed many tensions. There was a statist, socialist approach, designed to promote growth by government action, public enterprise and the rationing of resources. Early Five Year Plans in India, reflecting Soviet experience and Fabian programmes in Britain, followed this line, as did President Nyerere's programme of *Ujamaa* (self-reliance) for Tanzania.

At the same time there were many, amongst those who had tasted life abroad and who were politically opposed to socialist or communist models, who saw development merely as the transfer of western capitalism to their own countries. Cross-cutting this conflict were the interests of donor agencies, big companies, the United States, Europe and the Soviet bloc.

By the 1970s more questions were being asked about the real effectiveness of development projects, their impact on the environment, and the inequitable distribution of power and resources within the so-called 'developing countries'. At the same time it was becoming obvious that some formerly poor states had made great strides: by 1980 Japan, Taiwan and Singapore were major economic forces, while Saudi Arabia and the Gulf states were rich thanks to oil.

What was indisputable was that development was a matter of endless controversy. The simplistic days of the 1960s, when development was in danger of becoming a kind of religion in countries like Brazil under President Kubitschek, or among the followers of some campaigning charities in the North, slipped into the past as more asked 'Development for whom?' 'Is development merely economic, or is it human and social?' 'What are the costs of development, now and for future generations?' 'Is the North thwarting the development of the South?' Or, alternatively, 'Is much of development really a form of neocolonialism?'

If development was not a single panacea then development journalism could not be one-dimensional either. A few government ministers in the South may have imagined, in pushing for a New World Information Order, that this would require journalists to become government propagandists, promoting only the good news about progress in their countries. Where there was a controlled press this was the reality at home, and governments were tempted to export it.

But Gemini, in trying to make sense of development journalism, remained open-minded. It reported small-scale and community efforts, as well as the big international issues of trade and debt. It preserved a sense of actuality and of critical objectivity, and a sense of humour. It was interested in the bread-and-butter events and trends – stories which had meaning for other states in the South, even if they lay outside the often narrow focus of the North.

Its minnow-like and unbureaucratic structure gave it flexibility, and an empathy with

202

countries and papers which lacked resources. It was at an opposite pole to the committee-ridden and hierarchical efforts of governments which tried to run media, and it was critical too of the commercialism which drove the big business media empires. Its refusal to be boxed in to too tight a remit paid off as, by the end of the 1980s, the categories of East *vs* West and North *vs* South began to fray. It was basically a journalistic enterprise, obeying journalistic values. If these values, of fairness, objectivity and reader interest were ones which had originated in the North they were also widely accepted by journalists and subscribers in the South. The failure of governments or entrepreneurs to establish any lasting, world-wide Southern news agency left space for Gemini.

If development itself was problematic, the experience of Gemini demonstrated that reporting developing countries by relying heavily on indigenous resident journalists also raised difficulties. Their own situation was sometimes quite different from that of users elsewhere, and so were their standards of investigation and impartiality. In tightly controlled or authoritarian regimes it was genuinely hard for a resident to report certain stories and a kind of 'parachute journalism', to which Gemini was normally opposed, was the only way to get them out. Min Thu in Burma/Myanmar was arrested for what he wrote: Abby Tan, a visitor, was able to get in and out and provide a balanced piece which did not conceal either the economic progress or the human rights violations. The editorial role in London, both in selecting contributions and editing what came in, was crucial to safe-guarding standards for subscribers.

But there was no getting away from the fact that, although it was a central service for many users, it was going in a different direction from that being followed by most of the publishers and editors in Britain, Canada and Australia. In spite of periodic panics over famines, AIDS and the like, and in spite of the devoted lobbying of internationalists, it was hard in the 1980s for Gemini and the stories of the developing world to break into the mainstream. Yuppie values were in the ascendant, fraternity was held in contempt, and conventional wisdom was that there was little money to be made from the poor (even if, in appalling reality, there were net resource transfers from poor to rich countries during this decade).

In the old Commonwealth countries there was little sustained interest: Gemini was seen as a marginal player serving a marginal constituency. In important ways an unrestrained tabloid press was setting the agenda in Britain and Australia, and the quality papers there rarely looked to Gemini when they scanned the developing world. Even in Canada, economic forces in the media threatened overseas coverage. The competition from TV and broadcasting was forcing quality papers into a more features-oriented direction, but this did not strengthen the Gemini market. It was striking that *The Guardian*, for example, which had owned Gemini for a vital period, was in the 1990s taking news features about developing countries from the US correspondents of papers like the *Washington Post* and *Los Angeles Times* rather than from Gemini.

Nonetheless the conundrums of development, and the real problems and successes of developing countries, added up to a genuine journalistic market. Its robustness and potential were further illustrated after 1989 when the Soviet bloc broke up. By 1994 there were 15 papers in the former Soviet Union and eastern Europe which were paying for the service. It turned out that there was a hunger for interpretation in eastern Europe, if not always a recognition that the region shared some problems with developing countries, and a welcome for an agency which was not promoting a western or Northern line.

Development, then, was a key and creative concept for Gemini. But a second, perhaps more important in the agency's first 15 years, was the Commonwealth. Ingram's belief in the Commonwealth fuelled the launch of the service, and the faith and backing of Commonwealth supporters were crucial to its restart in 1983. As interpreted by Gemini the Commonwealth was not only a continuing force for good, actually doing things which should concern its citizens, but it also represented a sum of common interests and affections which lay below and outside politics.

No other press agency showed such a steady curiosity about the facts and movements of Commonwealth activity. Gemini persisted in treating it as if it counted. Although this might seem incurably sentimental to sophisticates in larger member states who had their own reasons for consigning the Commonwealth to history it was actually a rational service to provide, even by the 1990s. Over half the Commonwealth states had a population of under a million, with needs peculiar to them. Gemini had regular subscribers among the small island states in the Caribbean and Pacific. For them, and other small states, the Commonwealth offered a user-friendly club and a privileged balcony on the world stage.

Nor, in spite of its editor's well-known enthusiasm, could the Gemini service be described as uncritical in its reporting. While good Commonwealth news was treated as good news there were periodic admissions that Commonwealth news was bad – as after the Singapore Heads' meeting in 1971 – and quite often that it could have been better. It was not by chance that Ingram's two books of 1960 and 1962, *Partners in Adventure* and *The Commonwealth Challenge* were followed in 1977 by his more critical and tentative title, *The Imperfect Commonwealth.*[2]

Ingram had refused to accept that British entry into the European Community spelled the end of the Commonwealth, and he was often relaxed as the ties binding Commonwealth members appeared to loosen. There was no paranoia in Gemini's coverage. However there was a danger that subscribers might think the association was getting more attention than was its due, given the reduction in concern shown by its main political leaders, and the modest budgets at its disposal.

There was, of course, an issue surrounding British membership of the Commonwealth on which Gemini periodically dwelled. Could the association really outlast a long period of

---

2. *The Commonwealth Challenge*, George Allen & Unwin, 1962, was an expanded and rewritten version of the 1960 Pan book, *Partners in Adventure*. *The Imperfect Commonwealth*, Rex Collings, 1977, drew heavily on Ingram's regular commentaries at Heads of Governments meetings. In his Foreword, Shridath Ramphal wrote of Ingram, 'His knowledge of the Commonwealth has tended to confirm him in the view that it matters, and that its place in the world, while very different from what it was only ten years ago, is secure.

'I am sure he is right. I only regret that so many commentators do not take the trouble to ascertain the persuasive facts that so strongly support his view.'

British disinterest? Was it really more dependent on the British connection than the theory of an association of equals might imply?

There was in fact an element of ambiguity in Gemini's reporting. On the one hand it supported the notion that the Commonwealth was a post-colonial partnership of volunteers, each with their own interest in belonging. On the other, both in criticizing Britain and – especially in its early years, in providing a lot of material from and about Britain – it testified to an underlying curiosity elsewhere in what was happening in the erstwhile mother country. Some of the most amusing and effective pieces in the late 1960s, written by non-British London-based staff like Gamini Seneviratne and Fred Mpanga, reflected an outsider's reaction to life in Britain.

This ambiguity reflected a central issue about the post-colonial Commonwealth. In spite of the ideology of equality it was still importantly dependent on British attitudes and official policy. Barbados, for example, was not in size or economic and political weight an equal to Britain – in fact its population was the size of a London borough's. Britain had a firm grip on the finances of the Commonwealth Secretariat by paying 30 per cent of the budget (the point at which, in a British public company with many smaller shareholdings, it is normal to recognise one investor as having control.) With its inter-governmental headquarters in London it was impossible to insulate its servants from the negative or amnesiac views around them. If British governments and public opinion discounted the Commonwealth, preferring local regional cooperation and other priorities, it was natural for other Commonwealth countries to follow this example.

The Commonwealth networks had given Gemini a start, but the service was never limited in its coverage or subscribers to the Commonwealth. The *China Daily* in Beijing, for example, was taking the service in the 1980s and Gemini ran a training workshop in Bangkok in the 1990s. Potentially the Commonwealth may return the favours which Gemini has done for it. The moves to economic liberalization, multiparty democracy and greater freedom of the media will, if maintained, all be helpful to Gemini. South Africa's remarkable transition out of apartheid opens up enormous possibilities for the journalistic market in southern Africa. Any moves which make the Commonwealth seem less marginal to media in its bigger and more affluent members may increase their appetite for information.

But there are many ifs here. All the time both sceptics and friends have asked about Gemini's future. Is it really possible for such a small news feature service to survive in an era of wealthy media conglomerates, and rapid and punishing changes in media technology?

History shows how fragile Gemini has been, and how unlikely its survival. But fragile plants often demonstrate the greatest tenacity and longevity. In fact Gemini has shown considerable adaptability, especially since its restart in 1983: it has pioneered new types of journalism, such as its rural reporting; it has grown an important educational arm, in arranging specialist training for journalists; it has strengthened its subscriber base, through English-language papers outside the Commonwealth and with its east European clients; and it has not been afraid to raise subscriptions regularly while keeping its own costs down.

In talking about the future, therefore, it is worth looking harder at journalistic quality, specialization, technology and marketing. There is little doubt that, in a highly competitive business, journalistic quality is paramount. Inaccuracies, misspellings, the outdated or the merely ordinary will perilously handicap a news feature agency which has to fight to be used. In the past the arrival of correspondents and copy into the Gemini network has sometimes been too haphazard. Finding and keeping good correspondents, and losing poorer ones without too much heartbreak, are of the essence.

There are different types of specialization which matter. In the past Gemini has experimented with specialization of content – a science series or economic material, for instance, as well as Africa, Asia and London columns. Is an output of 12–14 items a week sufficient, given the great weight of material from other sources, or does this preselection enhance their utility? There is always a danger that some articles are completely wasted for some subscribers, while they would have liked more on other topics. What is valued in Bulgaria may be looked at askance in Vanuatu. Only a marketing effort which can explore the needs of different users would cast more light.

There is clearly a continuing scope for pioneer journalism as illustrated in Chapter 8, and the Gemini graphics should have a long future. There is also potential for continued specialization in training workshops, in bringing journalists from the South to Gemini's London office, and in encouraging the creative process by which journalists from one developing country report on events elsewhere. Is it possible to imagine a rather larger Gemini, putting out more material, with two or three regional bureaux away from London?

The technological problems faced by a small agency are serious, but ought to become more soluble as information highways broaden for the media. Essentially the electronic transmission of articles and graphics together, in small quantities, was expensive and not entirely efficient into the 1990s. Many users were still quite happy then to get their postal deliveries – in the 1960s and 1970s Gemini had given joy to stamp collectors round the world. Gemini was receiving articles by fax, but faxing them out to subscribers was too time-consuming and costly.

Before long this difficulty will be overcome. But in providing a more instant and topical service there is a danger that Gemini's more considered, lateral and critical style of journalism may be eroded. The discipline imposed by having to write in the knowledge that your article may not be published for four weeks has its uses. You are engaged in a kind of contemporary history, and required to focus on what really matters. Nevertheless, without a more immediate distribution of the service, it will be hard to get it taken seriously in more affluent newsrooms.

Not since the earliest years of Gemini has it been possible to afford any sustained and systematic marketing. Much of what selling of the service has happened since has been through the friendships of and meetings attended by Ingram, Nelson, Pritchard and Njoku. Yet plainly the news feature service needs a full-time marketing manager, as does the educational side. The bank of graphics alone, built up over the years, could yield a tidy income. The office has just been too short-handed to run to a full-time marketing operation, and has not had the capital to invest. The feedback from a systematic promotion would also yield other editorial and commercial ideas. It could point to new possibilities as developing countries increasingly become self-sufficient in types of training which Gemini supplied in the 1980s.

Much will depend on the changing communications environment, and especially the future of print media and the future of the English language. Hitherto, with one or two exceptions, Gemini has been unsuccessful in supplying radio and TV stations: its basic service has been to supply articles for print. Assuming that remains its chief thrust it will have to accommodate a worldwide trend for people in more and more nations to get their news from TV and radio. In the North this has already forced quality newspapers to become more like magazines, and popular tabloids to become parasitic on TV. Even though more papers in the South may find themselves running features there is no law which says that they must take more from Gemini.

The issue of English is also interesting. The onward march of English as a universal language in the second half of the twentieth century is a remarkable story, and one in which the Commonwealth figures strongly. English is the working language of the Commonwealth and one or two member countries which sought to downplay it after independence, such as Malaysia and India, have tended to reverse their position more recently.

For Gemini, putting out its packets in this one language only, use of English was one of the hidden assumptions on which its launch and continued existence rested. But there was always a fallacy with regard to the Commonwealth. Only a minority of the citizens of this association could or can speak English with ease: for large numbers, in Africa and the Indian sub-continent especially, English is a second or third language where it is spoken at all.

Unless this situation changes, therefore, the Gemini material can only reach the English-reading, educated elites. Yet in India, for example, where the agency has always had difficulty in winning subscribers, the circulations of English language papers have been stagnant in the 1990s. It has been the sale of the Hindi press, and papers published in regional languages, which have benefited from the rise in Indian prosperity.

No-one could say that the future of Gemini is assured. Indeed it is possible that the sense of always living on the edge of a precipice, always being not quite sure that the books will balance at the end of each month, is part of the secret of its survival. It prevents complacency and enforces adaptability. But in the light of its history there is no reason why the agency may not have many successful years ahead. Daniel Nelson, in accepting the challenge of becoming the second editor at the end of 1993, was certainly looking to a long-term future rather than a rapid requiem.

Indeed Gemini's unwillingness to be stereotyped may stand it in increasingly good stead as distinctions between 'developed' and 'developing' change their shape, and there is a continuing need to make sense of global trends in a world with only one superpower and no Cold War. When Gemini started it would have been difficult to imagine that income per head in Singapore would, by the 1990s, have exceeded that in Britain; or that the Indian Prime Minister could, by then, quite plausibly state that 250 million of his fellow citizens enjoyed a middle class standard of living. Some of the social problems in apparently affluent countries were acquiring a Third World air: while there was an increase in beggars on the streets of London there were none to be seen in Nicosia.

Just as the interest in development grew naturally from a concern for the Commonwealth, so may a perspective that has emerged from outside the Cold War and its American and Soviet news agenda be helpful in future. Although London is physically on the edge of Europe, and exposed to American cultural and commercial influences, it remains open to wider international breezes. It still provides a good journalistic listening-post. Yet Gemini, in both personnel and the content of its service, has become decreasingly British.

So what, in conclusion, has been the impact of Gemini? This is hard to assess, and has varied over time and in different parts of the world. There are obvious pointers. Its service has been hugely valued by major international bodies, like the Commonwealth Secretariat and UNICEF, for its sustained and sympathetic coverage of their concerns. The sharp reaction of subscribing papers, during the closure crisis of 1982-3, testified to their sense of its uniqueness.

Ordinary readers would always be less conscious of it than the editors and other agencies, but some individual correspondents, and the graphics accompanying Gemini articles were known world-wide. Indeed, although articles gave the flavour of the town or country from which they originated, the output as a whole reflected a global agenda, and a particular concern for the poor majority of the world's citizens. This was and remains an unusual perspective in an international media service.

Far more than is usually realized what is described as 'world news' reflects what a particular audience – national, regional, defined by wealth or other characteristics – wants to hear. The joke about the 1930s headline in the London *Times* – 'Small earthquake in Chile, not many dead' – was not a joke to the people in Chile at the time. What is of marginal interest in one place can be of driving importance to another readership. The overseas reporting of French or British papers, for example, reflects a subtle amalgam of cultural, political and economic assumptions of which the writers and sub-editors are often themselves unaware.

In most countries international news of any kind is followed only by an educated elite. But it may be argued that in countries where such an educated class is small, a steady service of reporting and explanation is particularly influential. The huge reputation of Gemini in such diverse countries as Zambia or the Cook Islands is a product of this phenomenon. Its features belonged to newspapers and readers there in a way in which the backgrounders of the major international agencies never could.

But of course the future of Gemini depends above all on the intelligence of its correspondents and editors. By definition it is not a spot news service, or a 'Minister said' propaganda agency. Its value lies in detecting trends, covering parts of the world overlooked by others, offering a different angle, and in providing interesting, readable copy which is accessible everywhere. It is judged on its output in each week. The media business is incredibly competitive. New journals, programmes and media products are being launched every day and many have only a brief life. No agency's survival is guaranteed.

Gemini has been around for nearly 30 years. It has a portfolio of interests – feature supply, training, graphics – and a bank of goodwill among correspondents, users and funding agencies. All of these can be built on. It has proved tough and resilient. Its foundation guarantees its independence. It will inevitably alter over the next quarter century. But in a world of changing patterns, where too much information is unequally distributed and there is an absolute dearth of explanation, its greatest contributions may lie ahead.

List of figures

Bibliographical Note

In a book of wide compass, which has relied heavily on non- documentary sources, a conventional bibliography is not easy to compile. However readers may wish to have some pointers, given that the debates in which Gemini is involved remain current and unresolved. This is likely to be particularly true of academics and students with specialist interests. The following brief reading list, prepared with the help of Professor Hugh Stephenson and Daya Kishan Thussu, is offered in that spirit.

Article XIX. *Press Law and Practice: A Comparative Study of Press Freedom in European and Other Democracies*. UNESCO, 1993.

Benthall, Jonathan. *Disasters, Relief and the Media*. IB Taurus, 1993.

Bourne, Richard. *Lords of Fleet Street – The Harmsworth Dynasty*. Unwin Hyman, 1990.

Boyd-Barrett, Oliver & Thussu, D.K. *Contra-Flow in Global News*. London: John Libbey/UNESCO, 1992.

Cameron, James. *Point of Departure*. Granada Publishing, 1980.

Chomsky, Noam & Herman, Edward S. *Manufacturing Consent: The Political Economy of the Mass Media*. New York: Pantheon, 1988.

Dunnett, Peter. *The World Newspaper Industry*. Routledge, 1987.

Dunnett, Peter, *The World Television Industry*. Routledge, 1990.

Fisher, Glen. *American Communication in a Global Society*. New Jersey: Ablex, 1979.

Graham-Yooll, Andrew. *Committed Observer – Memoirs of a Journalist*. London: John Libbey, 1995.

Hamelink, Cees J. *Trends in World Communication*. Penang: Third World Network, 1994.

Harrison, Paul & Palmer, Robin. *News out of Africa: Biafra to Band Aid*. Hilary Shipman, 1986.

Ingram, Derek. *Partners in Adventure*. Pan, 1960.

Ingram, Derek. *The Commonwealth Challenge*. Allen & Unwin, 1962.

Ingram, Derek. *Commonwealth for a Colour-Blind World*. Allen & Unwin, 1965.

Ingram, Derek. *The Imperfect Commonwealth*. Rex Collings, 1977.

Ingram, Derek (ed.) *Environmental Reporting Handbook*. Gemini, 1992.

Joseph, Ammu & Sharma, Kalpana (eds.) *Whose News? The Media and Women's Issues*. Sage, 1994.

Knightley, Philip. *The First Casualty*. Quartet, 1980.

Leapman, Michael. *Treacherous Estate*. Hodder & Stoughton, 1992.

McBride, Sean. *Many Voices, One World: International Commission for the Study of Communication Problems*. UNESCO, 1980.

McParland, Kelly. *Views from the Village*. Gemini, 1988.

McPhail, Thomas. *Electronic Colonialism: The Future of International Broadcasting and Communication*. Sage, 1987.

Nordenstreng, Kaarle & Schiller, Herbert I. (eds) *Beyond National Sovereignty: International Communication in the 1990s*. New Jersey: Ablex, 1993.

Pilger, John. *Heroes*. Pan, 1987.

Read, Donald. *The Power of News: The History of Reuters*. Oxford, 1993.

Sebra, Anne. *Battling for News – The Rise of the Woman Reporter*. Hodder & Stoughton, 1994.

Seymour-Ure, Colin. *British Press and Broadcasting since 1945*. Blackwell, 1991.

Smith, Anthony. *The Geopolitics of Information*. Faber, 1980.

Snoddy, Raymond. *The Good, the Bad and the Unacceptable*. Faber, 1993.

Spelliscey, Jill & Sperling, Gerald B. *Whose Story? Reporting the Developing World after the Cold War*. Calgary: Detselig, 1993.

Tunstall, Jeremy. *The Media are American*. Constable, 1977.

Tunstall, Jeremy & Palmer, Michael. *Media Moguls*. Routledge, 1991.

Index